Punitive Damages

Punitive Damages
How Juries Decide

Cass R. Sunstein, Reid Hastie,

John W. Payne, David A. Schkade,

and W. Kip Viscusi

With an Introduction by George L. Priest

The University of Chicago Press

Chicago & London

The University of Chicago Press, Chicago 60637
The University of Chicago Press, Ltd., London
© 2002 by The University of Chicago
All rights reserved. Published 2002
Printed in the United States of America

11 10 09 08 07 06 05 04 03 02   1 2 3 4 5
ISBN: 0-226-78014-7

Library of Congress Cataloging-in-Publication Data

Punitive damages : how juries decide / Cass R. Sunstein . . . [et al.];
with an introduction by George L. Priest.
    p.   cm.
Includes bibliographical references and index.
    ISBN 0-226-78014-7 (cloth : alk. paper)
    1. Exemplary damages—United States.   2. Jury—United States.
I. Sunstein, Cass R.
    KF1249 .P86 2002
    347.73′77—dc21

                                                            2001005835

Contents

Preface and Acknowledgments   vii

Introduction

    The Problem and Efforts to Understand It

    George L. Priest   1

1   Overview: What We Did and What We Found

    Reid Hastie   17

Part I: How Juries Think

A From Outrage to Dollars

    Introduction

    Cass R. Sunstein   29

2   Shared Outrage, Erratic Awards

    Daniel Kahneman, David A. Schkade, Cass R. Sunstein   31

3   Deliberating about Dollars: The Severity Shift

    David A. Schkade, Cass R. Sunstein, Daniel Kahneman   43

4   Do Plaintiffs' Requests and Plaintiffs' Identities Matter?

    Reid Hastie, David A. Schkade, John W. Payne   62

B To Punish or Not?

    Introduction

    Cass R. Sunstein   75

5   Judging Corporate Recklessness

    Reid Hastie, David A. Schkade, John W. Payne   77

6 Looking Backward in Punitive Judgments: 20-20 Vision?
Reid Hastie, David A. Schkade, John W. Payne 96

C Jurors and Judges as Risk Managers
Introduction
Cass R. Sunstein 109

7 Corporate Risk Analysis: A Reckless Act?
W. Kip Viscusi 112

8 Do People Want Optimal Deterrence?
Cass R. Sunstein, David A. Schkade, Daniel Kahneman 132

9 Deterrence Instructions: What Jurors Won't Do
W. Kip Viscusi 142

10 Judging Risk and Recklessness
W. Kip Viscusi 171

11 Do Judges Do Better?
W. Kip Viscusi 186

Part II: Conclusions

12 Putting It All Together
Reid Hastie 211

13 What Should Be Done?
Cass R. Sunstein 242

Appendix: Judge's Instructions 259
Glossary 261
Bibliography 267
List of Contributors 277
Index 279

Preface and Acknowledgments

This is a book at the intersection of law and social science. Our principal goal is descriptive. We seek to understand why juries do what they do when faced with punitive damages cases. With that understanding, we hope to provide a better sense of how people think about both dollars and punishment—and in the process to contribute to the continuing social reevaluation of juries, punitive damages, and risk regulation in general.

Lawyers and social scientists know very little about how juries set damages awards, for punishment or for anything else. With a series of interdisciplinary collaborations, we attempt to take a close look at what juries think and care about, what they do well, and where they run into difficulty. We intend, above all, to present the results of that close look, in order to understand what juries do and why they do it. These findings have large implications for law and legal reform, and we will present those implications in some detail. But the overriding goal is to describe jury behavior, not to propose legislative or judicial change. Our plea is that any changes should be based on an accurate, rather than fanciful, understanding of jury behavior.

In the course of our projects, we have gained great respect for the virtues of jurors—and also a better understanding of their limitations in this particular context. Jurors are astonishingly conscientious. Even in the experimental setting, they work hard, attempt to do their best, interact well with one another, and almost never engage in selfish or strategic behavior. We have seen tapes of many (experimental) jury deliberations about punitive damages; no observer could fail to be impressed with the seriousness, decency, and common sense with which jurors from diverse walks of life approach their task. Equally striking, perhaps, is the moral seriousness of jurors and their determination to do what they think is right.

At the same time, jurors suffer from the same limitations that all human beings face—together with several limitations that are distinctive to the setting of damages judgments. Like almost everyone else, jurors show *hindsight bias:* They believe that what did happen was bound to happen. They have a difficult time in following complex instructions. With respect to dollar punishments, they are often making a stab in the dark. Hence they are susceptible to manipulation. And for this reason, different juries are likely to reach different conclusions about similar cases, not necessarily because they evaluate the plaintiff and the defendant differently, but only because they do not know how to use the scale of dollars—and end up making very different guesses. For this and other reasons, juries are not always able to operate as effective managers of social risks.

If all this is right, we will be able to predict, with a high degree of confidence, that whatever your theory of punitive damages, some awards are far too high and some awards are far too low—not because jurors are not conscientious or smart, but because of certain identifiable features of human cognition. The basis for this conclusion is the principal topic of this book. As we shall see, the findings here bear on many questions at the intersection of law and social science and are hardly limited to the problem of punitive damages. The problems that we identify are highly likely to play a role in many domains in which juries, or ordinary people, are asked to assess liability, generate dollar amounts, or impose punishments. It is for this reason that we hope to make a general contribution to social understanding of the legal regulation of risks, with particular attention to the role of jurors.

*

THE ORIGINS OF THIS BOOK lie in three independent lines of research. For many years W. Kip Viscusi has worked on empirical issues relating to risk reduction. With the prominent use of punitive damages awards to control social risks, Viscusi produced a series of papers, both empirical and theoretical, on the causes and consequences of such awards. Reid Hastie, John W. Payne, and David A. Schkade have written a large number of papers at the intersection of psychology and public policy; some of their collaborations have attempted to understand the ingredients of liability judgments and also to see what makes a punitive award high or low. Daniel Kahneman, David A. Schkade, and Cass R. Sunstein have been engaged, to some extent on their own but mostly in collaboration, in a program of research focused on the determinants of dollar valuations in connection with punitive damages, contingent valuation, and administrative penalties.

After much of this research was completed (some of it remains in progress), it occurred to us that selections from these independent lines of work might fruitfully be combined. Insofar as all of us had been working, to some extent, on the award of punitive damages by jurors, there were important common themes among the resulting papers. We thought that it would be valuable to collect our findings in a single place and also to rethink them in a larger collaboration. By restricting ourselves to empirical work dealing with punitive damages, we hoped that we could give the book a sharp focus. We also hoped, and continue to hope, that the whole is more than the sum of its parts.

As for the nature of the collaboration: As indicated throughout, particular chapters are the responsibility of particular authors. We stress this point because different authors have different emphases and different concerns. Nonetheless, we met a number of times and we worked together closely, in order to integrate the book and achieve coherence. If there are some internal differences, they are dwarfed by the commonalities and, above all, by our interest in obtaining an accurate understanding of jury behavior in this important domain.

We are grateful to many people for their help. Thanks go first to Daniel Kahneman, a coauthor on the original versions of chapters 2, 3, and 8. Kahneman did not participate in the production of this book and should not be held responsible for any errors in its content or exposition. But he deserves credit, and thanks, for his role in developing many of the central ideas.

Many colleagues and friends generously commented on one or more of the papers. For particular thanks, we single out Richard Berk, John Hakes, Louis Kaplow, DeYett Law, Robert MacCoun, Martha Nussbaum, Eric Posner, Richard Posner, Jeffrey Rachlinski, Michael Saks, and Steven Shavell, and also participants in countless workshops, including those at Cornell University, Harvard University, the University of Chicago, and Yale University.

For financial support, we are grateful to ExxonMobil Corporation, the National Science Foundation, the Law and Economics Program at the University of Chicago, and the Olin Foundation. We are especially grateful to these institutions for the respect shown, at each and every stage, for the complete independence of the academic enterprise. The data here, as well as the opinions expressed, are the property of the authors, and those who helped fund the research exercised no control—explicit or implicit, direct or indirect—over any of its content and conclusions. We also thank our home institutions—Duke University, Harvard University, the University of Chicago, the University of Colorado, and the University of Texas—for support of many kinds.

The empirical chapters for this book, though substantially revised and rethought, grew out of the following publications, and we are most grateful for permission, from the respective journals, to draw on them here:

Daniel Kahneman, David A. Schkade, and Cass R. Sunstein, "Shared Outrage and Erratic Awards: The Psychology of Punitive Damages," 16 *Journal of Risk and Uncertainty* 47 (1998). Also, Cass R. Sunstein, Daniel Kahneman, and David A. Schkade, "Assessing Punitive Damage (with Notes on Cognition and Valuation in Law)," 107 *Yale Law Journal* 2071 (1998).

David A. Schkade, Cass R. Sunstein, and Daniel Kahneman, "Deliberating about Dollars: The Severity Shift," 100 (4) *Columbia Law Review* 101 (2000).

Reid Hastie, David A. Schkade, and John W. Payne, "Juror Judgments in Civil Cases: Effects of Plaintiff's Requests and Plaintiff's Identity on Punitive Damage Awards," 23(4) *Law and Human Behavior* 445 (1999).

Reid Hastie, David A. Schkade, and John W. Payne, "A Study of Juror and Jury Judgments in Civil Cases: Deciding Liability for Punitive Damages," 22 *Law and Human Behavior* 287 (1998).

Reid Hastie, David A. Schkade, and John W. Payne, "Juror Judgments in Civil Cases: Hindsight Effects on Judgments of Liability for Punitive Damages," 23(5) *Law and Human Behavior* 597 (1999).

W. Kip Viscusi, "Corporate Risk Analysis: A Reckless Act?" 52(3) *Stanford Law Review* 547 (2000).

Cass R. Sunstein, David A. Schkade, and Daniel Kahneman, "Do People Want Optimal Deterrence?" 29(1) *Journal of Legal Studies* 237 (2000).

W. Kip Viscusi, "The Challenge of Punitive Damages Mathematics," (30)2 *Journal of Legal Studies* 313 (2001).

W. Kip Viscusi, "How Do Judges Think about Risk?" 1(1, 2) *American Law & Economics Review* 26 (1999). Also, Reid Hastie and W. Kip Viscusi, "What Juries Can't Do Well: The Jury's Performance as a Risk Manager," 40(3) *Arizona Law Review* 901 (1998).

W. Kip Viscusi, "Jurors, Judges, and the Mistreatment of Risk by the Courts," 30(1) *Journal of Legal Studies* 107 (2001).

Introduction

The Problem and Efforts to Understand It

George L. Priest

I. The Punitive Damages Phenomenon Today

Over the past two decades, our country has experienced a dramatic increase in the incidence and magnitude of punitive damages verdicts rendered by juries in civil litigation. Perhaps the most extraordinary example is the July 2000 award of $144.8 billion in the Florida class action brought against cigarette manufacturers. But there are many other examples of huge verdicts beyond the tobacco litigation. For example, in July 1999 a California jury awarded a punitive damages verdict of $4.8 billion,[1] and in May of that same year an Alabama jury, in a case in which the economic damages were alleged to equal no more than $600, awarded a punitive damages verdict of $580 million.[2] Moreover, although the punitive damages determination is largely assigned to juries, judges, too, are awarding or affirming punitive damages verdicts of extraordinary dimension. Again, as further examples, an Illinois judge awarded a punitive damages verdict of $600 million (October 1999),[3] and a federal judge in South Carolina affirmed a jury's $250 million punitive damages verdict (December 1999).[4]

These verdicts are notable for several reasons. First, their magnitude alone is remarkable. The award in the tobacco case, for example, equals 2.4 times what our federal government spends each year on education, 52% of the amount spent on national defense, and a full 80% of the amount the federal government collects annually in corporate income taxes. The relatively smaller $580 million punitive damages verdict in the

---

1. *Anderson v. General Motors Corp.*, Los Angeles, Calif.
2. *Carlisle v. Whirlpool Financial National Bank et al.*, CV-97-068, Hale County, Ala.
3. *Avery et al. v. State Farm Insurance.* Under the Illinois Consumer Fraud Act, the determination of punitive damages is an issue to be determined by the judge in the case.
4. *Jimenez v. Chrysler Corporation*, Civil Action No. 2:96-1269-11, D. S.Car.

single $600 Alabama case equals over one and three-quarters times the total annual amount that the state of Alabama spends on police protection and correction, including funding for its prisons.[5] Even more extraordinary is the comparison to verdicts of earlier years. Two decades ago it was unusual to observe a punitive damages verdict greater than $1 million; verdicts in the tens of millions, not to mention hundreds of millions or billions, were completely unknown.

As might be expected, the punitive damages phenomenon has generated substantial controversy. Many scholars and policy makers have emphasized the relative *in*frequency of punitive damages verdicts across the wide range of civil litigation.[6] The claim that verdicts of this nature are relatively infrequent must surely be true given the hundreds of thousands of civil claims filed and litigated each year in the United States. Of more general concern, however, is the inability to explain these various punitive damages verdicts on a rational basis. Our country prides itself on its dedication to the rule of law. As a result, it is an appropriate subject of concern to observe any important legal outcome that appears unpredictable and that cannot clearly be explained by principle.

The magnitude of punitive damages verdicts appears to vary substantially across juries. But this judgment, too, is problematic. In some sense, no two cases are alike. Thus, there is an inherent difficulty in evaluating one verdict against another and, especially, in evaluating these verdicts from the standpoint of a jury or judge, since no outsider can exactly put himself or herself in a similar position.

There seems, however, to be substantial variability in verdicts even in closely similar cases. A prominent recent case appealed ultimately to the U.S. Supreme Court involved a claim against BMW, the auto manufacturer, that BMW had committed fraud by selling cars as new after painting over parts that had suffered corrosion from acid rain while in transit to America. In the case appealed to the Supreme Court, an Alabama jury had awarded the purchaser both compensatory damages and a punitive damages verdict of $4 million.[7] Yet in an exactly identical case brought against BMW by a different purchaser, a different Alabama jury in the same court and before the same judge awarded roughly similar compen-

---

5. *Economic Abstract of Alabama 2000,* 171 (Deborah Hamilton ed., 2000).

6. E.g., Michael L. Rustad, "Unraveling Punitive Damages: Current Data and Further Inquiry," *Wis. L. Rev.* 15 (1998).

7. The Alabama Supreme Court reduced the verdict to $2 million, which was later overturned by the U.S. Supreme Court. *BMW of North America, Inc. v. Gore,* 116 S. Ct. 1589 (1996).

satory damages, but no punitive damages whatsoever, concluding that BMW was innocent of the reprehensible behavior that justifies punitive awards. There are so few identical cases, however, that this example constitutes no more than an anecdote, leaving significant dispute over the extent of jury variability.

The problem here is not simply that different juries can have different views about issues. The problem, instead, is that these discrepant and varying punitive damages verdicts constitute one element of the range of punishments our society inflicts on what it believes to be wrongful behavior. Our society is deeply committed to employing the force of government with reason and consistency. Discrepant punishments for the same act (or punishment in some and no punishment in others) or punishments disproportionate to the wrongfulness of the act are inconsistent with that commitment.

As will be described in more detail, the instructions presented to juries for the determination of the appropriate punitive damages verdict are extremely vague and employ terms that are largely undefined. As a consequence, different juries appear to employ different metrics for setting specific punitive damages amounts. For example, interviews with the California jurors who awarded the $4.8 billion award above suggest that the number came from an estimate of the defendant's advertising budget for the year.[8] In another case, recently appealed to the U.S. Supreme Court, the jury appears to have set the punitive damages verdict by multiplying a figure against the number of products that the manufacturer sold worldwide.[9] Our courts have not announced a principled reason— and it is difficult to explain—why an appropriate punishment for some corporate decision is measured by the company's advertising budget or its worldwide sales or, for that matter, why its advertising budget is an appropriate metric in one case and worldwide sales appropriate in another.

In still other cases, however, the jury's punitive damages award is simply inexplicable. For example, in the $600 Alabama case leading to the $580 million punitive damages verdict, no one can determine how the jury came up with that amount. The attorney for the plaintiff had asked the jury to award only $6 million in punitive damages.[10] The jury came up with the additional $574 million purely on its own.

---

8. "Jury Orders G.M. Corp. to Pay $4.9 Billion," *Boulder (Colorado) Daily Camera,* July 10, 1999, at 1A, 5A.

9. *Ammerman v. Ford Motor Co.,* 705 N.E.2d 539 (Ind. 1999).

10. *Carlisle v. Whirlpool Financial National Bank et al.,* CV-97-068, Hale County, Ala.

That different juries can come to different decisions is a well-known feature of the institution of lay juries and, arguably, defensible in certain types of difficult cases.[11] In the context of a form of coerced payment that resembles criminal punishment, however, it is not so easy to defend variability. Since the middle of the last century, reform of our criminal justice system has consisted of making punishment increasingly more predictable and more rational, in the sense of defining a quantum of punishment for different crimes that is rationally related to the relative severity or heinousness of the respective crime. The introduction of sentencing guidelines in the federal courts over the last decade is the most prominent endeavor toward this end, reducing to a minimum the range of available *judicial* discretion with respect to punishment. Our punitive damages regime, in contrast, remains committed to allowing the jury unlimited discretion to award any amount, subject only to subsequent judicial review. At our current state of knowledge, we believe that there is substantial variability in punitive damages verdicts, but—prior to the studies presented in this book—we have had only the vaguest understanding of the sources of that variability.

II. The Ambition of This Book

The studies summarized and reported in this book seek to look behind and beneath juries' punitive damages determinations. The studies have been conducted by a diverse group of researchers, including behavioral psychologists, a legal scholar, and an economist, who, in aggregate, bring a wide range of skills and backgrounds to the task.

Each of the studies proceeds through the experimental method. For the jury-decision studies, lay citizens—all eligible to become jurors— were recruited as jurors; in some instances the researchers compared the jury outcomes by conducting identical experiments with actual sitting judges. In both cases the experimental decision makers were given scripts describing facts that closely resemble those of actual disputes. As will be described more fully below, the participants were asked to read the script carefully and in many cases to view a televised narrator reading it to them, and then to answer questions or render an individual ver-

---

11. Harry Kalven, for example, justified differences in contexts of disfigurement or defamation, where a jury was asked to determine a damages award for an injury that bore no clearly rational relation to any dollar figure. Harry Kalven Jr., "The Jury, the Law, and the Personal Injury Damage Award," 19 *Ohio St. L.J.* 158 (1958); Harry Kalven Jr., "The Dignity of the Civil Jury," 50 *Va. L. Rev.* 1055 (1964).

dict. In some instances they then deliberated to a verdict with others as a mock jury.

Admittedly, there are both limitations and virtues of the experimental method. Decisions by mock juries or by judges in experimental contexts are not the equivalent of decisions by real juries or judges in real cases. The jury participants (not the judges) were paid a small amount to engage in the studies and were conscientious and careful in their work. Nevertheless, the context is surely different in a jury experiment than in real cases, where the actual plaintiff and defendant are standing before them. However serious the mock juror or judge, deliberation may well be different where one's decision leads not merely to an interesting result, but is certain to affect the lives of real litigants.

As important as realism in litigation is, however, realism, as described above, is not easily amenable to research and evaluation. Thus it is that no clear conclusions have been derived from the current debate over punitive damages, and there is no prospect of future consensus.

In contrast, with mock juries, researchers are able to define the contours of the decision, making it possible both to assess jury outcomes by probing features affecting the jury's decision in ways that illuminate the actual determinants of the outcomes. Various techniques have been used. In some of the studies reported in this book, the facts or the context of the jury's decision were varied while everything else was held constant. In other studies, jurors were asked questions that revealed how they arrived at their decisions. In still other studies, juror and jury decisions were compared with those of judges regarding punitive damages in identical cases. And in every instance, sample sizes were made large enough to ensure that the results were reliable and reproducible. Through such experimental techniques, the researchers were able to uncover specific features of jury and judge decision making that have heretofore been largely speculative.

In my view, therefore, the important question in evaluating the significance of this experimental work is not whether juries or judges in experimental contexts make decisions that are exactly the same as in real-life contexts. More important is whether the experimental results of jury and judge decision making on punitive damages provide reliable insight into what we observe in the real world. Equally important is whether what has been uncovered in these studies helps us to identify and explain some of the key factors that influence the process of setting punitive damages.

III. How the Punitive Damages Process Operates

This section provides a short summary of how the question of punitive damages is presented to a jury, in order to set the stage for the experimental studies themselves.

A. *Qualification for Jury Service*

Although there are differences among states, virtually all U.S. residents are eligible to be selected for jury service. Most states choose randomly from voters' lists or driver's license and nondriver identification card lists to select individuals for jury service. Appearing for jury service, however, remains a long way from being chosen to sit on a jury and even further from sitting on a jury to determine punitive damages. Only a small fraction of those persons obliged to report for jury service ever ends up sitting on a jury in an actual trial.[12] An even smaller fraction ever serves on a jury determining punitive damages. Thus, it would be extremely unusual for any single person chosen for a jury to have had any experience whatsoever in determining an appropriate level of punitive damages.

B. *Becoming a Juror*

Although most Americans in recent years will have heard from the media alone something about punitive damages, the first mention of the subject in the context of actual jury service will typically occur when a person who has reported for jury service is then selected to be examined in a pool of potential jurors for an actual case.[13] When selected in a pool, the set of potential jurors will be asked questions by the attorneys for the plaintiff (the party claiming to be harmed) and the defendant (the party that the plaintiff claims caused the harm) that may involve punitive damages. Most states allow attorneys to present some facts of their case to the pool—without proof—before the trial begins, in order to investigate possible biases of a potential juror or to provide information about the juror so that the attorney may "challenge" (which is to say, dismiss) the

12. It has been estimated from a study of the Chicago courts over the period 1959–79 that the probability in any year of a Chicago citizen serving on a jury that is actually called to render a verdict (any verdict) was .0038, equal to service once every 260.2 years. G. L. Priest, "The Role of the Civil Jury in a System of Private Adjudication," *U. Chi. Legal Forum* 161, 188–89 (1990).

13. Most states have adopted a "one-case or one-day" limit for jury service, meaning that a person may sit all day in the courthouse and, though never called in an actual case, be released the same afternoon.

juror from the pool. Both attorneys are given a limited number of challenges that they use to try to choose a jury that is likely to be most sympathetic to their case.

During this process (called *voir dire*), the potential jurors might be asked, "Do you think that you could render a substantial punitive damages verdict against the defendant if we are successful in showing . . . ?" At this point in the process, however, the juror is generally given no instruction whatsoever as to what the standard for punitive damages is nor, surely, how a specific amount is to be determined.

In recent years because of the political controversy over punitive damages and other features of our civil litigation system, many courts have also allowed attorneys to ask potential jurors more general public policy questions, such as "Do you support tort reform?" or "Do you think that there is too much litigation in our society?" or, more directly, "Are you in favor of limitations on punitive damages?" Again, the purpose of these questions is not to determine that the potential juror has actually considered the punitive damages issue and has developed a thoughtful approach to it. Indeed, if a juror does have a developed view, he or she is almost certain to be dismissed by the one side or the other that disagrees with the view. Similarly, if the prospective juror has had any real experience with punitive damages—say, serving at some earlier time on a jury that awarded or declined to award punitive damages—he or she is equally sure of being dismissed. Instead, the purpose, again, is to provide information to the plaintiff's attorney so that he or she might challenge a juror who is suspected to be unsympathetic to the client's claim. (The defendant's attorney is allowed to ask a different set of questions toward the same end.) The inquiry serves only to provide information to the attorneys about potential juror attitudes. There is no effort to educate the juror about the standard for punitive damages, though such questions do serve to alert those persons ultimately selected for the jury that punitive damages may be involved.

C. Opening Statements

The jury may next hear about punitive damages in the opening statement of the plaintiff's attorney. In the opening statement, the plaintiff's attorney—again, without presenting any evidence—is allowed to summarize the facts of the case and to describe the plaintiff's claim against the defendant. The statement will typically be highly charged, consisting of a story placing blame for the harm suffered by the plaintiff squarely on the defendant. The defendant's attorney follows with a statement presenting a story typically exonerating the defendant from any responsibility. In the context of the plaintiff's opening statement, some further content—though not much—will be given concerning the standard for punitive damages. Thus, at the end of the plaintiff's statement, the attorney will say something of the nature, "We are going to be asking you [the jury] for a substantial compensatory damages award [explained below] to compensate the plaintiff for the harm he or she has suffered. We will be asking you for a substantial punitive damages award in addition." Since, as will be elaborated, it is the judge's responsibility to actually present the instructions to the jury as to the legal standard for punitive damages, the plaintiff's attorney will do little more here than state something to the effect, "The judge will be giving you the actual instructions regarding punitive damages, and you listen to what the judge tells you. For our purposes, punitive damages should be levied wherever the defendant has acted maliciously, with reckless disregard [egregiously, etc.]. We will show you that the defendant's actions here were so reckless that a substantial punitive damages verdict is necessary to punish and deter it from acting that way in the future."

Again, at this point the description of the punitive damages standard and the evidence supporting a punitive damages award are presented by the plaintiff's attorney both at a very general level and with some hypothetical cast, since the jury will have seen no evidence in the case whatsoever. Because the defendant's attorney's statement ends with exoneration, the defendant typically says nothing at this point about punitive damages.

D. Trial: Liability and Compensatory Damages

In conception, punitive damages are regarded as an extraordinary remedy—available and appropriately awarded in only a small number of cases. As a consequence, typically the jury will hear nothing more about punitive damages until the very end of the trial. Following the opening statements of the plaintiff's and defendant's attorneys, respectively, the trial will begin. The jury will be focused on hearing the evidence in the basic trial just as it would in a case in which punitive damages are not at issue.

For the trial itself, the jury must first determine what is called the *liability* of the defendant. The question here is whether the jury finds the defendant to be liable—legally responsible—for the harm suffered by the plaintiff. If the jury finds the defendant liable, the jury must secondly determine the level of damages that will compensate the plaintiff for the harm suffered by the actions of the defendant, called *compensatory damages*. The jury will reach the punitive damages issue only if it both finds the defendant liable and awards the plaintiff some level of compensatory damages.

To establish the defendant's liability, the plaintiff must present evidence showing (1) that the plaintiff has suffered some harm; (2) that the defendant caused the harm to the plaintiff; and (3) that, in causing the harm, the defendant violated some legal standard controlling conduct in the society. Legal standards controlling conduct differ according to the factual context of the case, though they all generally share the concept that there is some level of care toward preventing harms that a defendant must satisfy and that the defendant is alleged to have violated in the case at hand.

Although there is an infinite set of such contexts and specific standards, the chosen contexts for the studies in this book involved harm that resulted from some decision made by a corporation about the conduct of its business. (The specific experiments are described in more detail below.) For example, in one set of experiments, juries judged a case involving a train derailment with consequent toxic damage in which the question was whether the defendant railroad was sufficiently careful in maintaining the roadbed and assembling the train. A second set of experiments presented a context in which a child ingested pills notwithstanding a supposedly childproof bottle cap in which the question was whether the bottle manufacturer used an appropriate design for the cap. Contexts and issues of this nature are characteristic of a wide range of modern litigation.

The first evidence presented by the plaintiff will be directed toward establishing the responsibility of the defendant for the plaintiff's losses or injuries. After that evidence is presented, the plaintiff will introduce testimony about the extent of the plaintiff's losses for purposes of establishing compensatory damages. In conception, compensatory damages are designed to be set exactly equal to the plaintiff's loss. Thus, the plaintiff will introduce purely accounting information such as the extent of past medical bills or lost wages as a consequence of the injury. There are other elements of compensatory damages with less certain bases that will require substantial judgment by the jury. For example, the plaintiff may introduce expert testimony about future medical expenses, requiring what in essence is speculation about how soon the plaintiff will recover, what kind of care will be needed, and so on. If the case involves serious personal injury, the law allows the plaintiff to recover what are called *pain-and-suffering damages*. These are essentially unquantifiable —though the jury is compelled to put a dollar number on them. The plaintiff's attorney basically will describe how the injury has devastated the plaintiff's life and ask the jury for "compensation" for this loss.

After presentation of the evidence by the plaintiff attempting to establish liability and prove damages, the defendant presents its case. Most typically, the defendant will attempt exoneration by showing that it is not appropriately responsible for the harm, either because there were other causes or there were no practicable alternative actions available to the defendant that would have prevented the harm from occurring. Because it is thought to be churlish, the defendant seldom challenges the compensatory damages estimates of the plaintiff in personal injury cases, though where the loss is solely economic, the calculation of damages may be the central issue in the case.

E. Punitive Damages

Only after all the evidence on liability and compensatory damages is presented does the jury reach the issue of punitive damages. Procedures differ across the states in terms of the presentation of argument involving punitive damages. Some states allow the punitive damages question to be raised at the time of the basic liability and compensatory damages trial. Other states provide for what is called a *bifurcated procedure:* First, a trial on liability and compensatory damages; second, a separate trial on punitive damages. Still other states allow the parties to agree on whether they want a unified or bifurcated procedure.

Lawyers disagree as to which of these different procedural approaches most benefits plaintiffs versus defendants. That issue is not important to our purposes here, but a basic procedural similarity should be noted. Whatever the procedure, a jury is not allowed to reach the punitive damages question until it first has decided that the defendant is liable for the plaintiff's harm and, second, has determined the amount of damages that will fully compensate the plaintiff. In all contexts, therefore, the jury will be given instructions by the judge and a verdict form that follows asking the jury to determine question 1: Is the defendant liable or not—

for example, "Did the defendant violate the standard of due care when it failed to . . . ?" If the jury answers this question "no," the verdict form will tell it to skip to the bottom, answer nothing more, and return to the courtroom. If the jury, however, answers "yes," finding the defendant liable, then it is instructed to proceed to question 2: "Indicate the amount of damages that will compensate the plaintiff for its loss."

At this point the bifurcated versus unified procedures differ somewhat. Where there will be a separate, bifurcated hearing on punitive damages, the jury will typically be asked a third question: "Do you find that the defendant's actions were of a level of recklessness to justify punitive damages?" If the jury answers this question "yes," then a separate hearing will be convened at a later date to consider the quantum of punitive damages; if it answers "no," then the trial is over. I have skipped ahead somewhat here because, before this point is reached, the plaintiff's attorney will have been given some opportunity to claim in the closing argument that punitive damages are appropriate given the facts of the case (typically, the attorney will have said nothing about the amount of punitive damages), and the judge will have given brief instructions to the jury about the punitive damages standard.

In a unified procedure, matters are a little different. Again, to skip ahead, the verdict form given to the jury will have the same question 1: "Is the defendant liable?" and question 2: "Determine the amount of compensatory damages." But it will also have questions 3 and 4: "Did the defendant behave with reckless disregard . . . [etc., the standard for punitive damages]?" And, "Determine the punitive damages amount." For this purpose, the plaintiff's attorney will have made some argument, typically in its closing, about why punitive damages are needed to punish and deter the defendant and what the appropriate amount of punitive damages to achieve this end might be. In addition, and most importantly, the judge will have given the jury instructions describing the standard for the award of punitive damages. These instructions, which are described in more detail next, will be very similar to the instructions given to the jury at the conclusion of the bifurcated punitive damages hearing.

F. The Punitive Damages Instructions

After both the plaintiff and the defendant have completed the presentation of their evidence and concluded their closing arguments, the judge will speak at length to the jury, providing instructions concerning how the jury is to deliberate and reach a verdict. These instructions (which often take half a day or more to complete) will consist, first, of a general statement of how the jury is to evaluate evidence, then will describe how the jury is to decide whether the defendant is liable to the plaintiff, and then will tell the jury in general terms how it is to calculate compensatory damages.

Only after all of this does the judge instruct the jury about punitive damages. The punitive damages instructions are important because they constitute the only "training" or elucidation that the jury will receive concerning punitive damages. (Again, remember that no single juror is likely to have had any prior experience with punitive damages.) The jury's punitive damages instructions, thus, are the central element in framing the task of determining and calculating a punitive damages figure.

Although there are some differences in basic punitive damages instructions across states, they are generally closely similar. Here is a typical instruction in full:

Defendant's mental state — General instruction

If you find from the evidence that [the defendant] is guilty of wanton, willful, malicious or reckless conduct that shows an indifference to the rights of others, then you may make an award of punitive damages in this case.

Defendant's mental state — "Willful" and "wanton" defined

In order for the conduct of the defendant to constitute willfulness or wantonness, his/her acts must be done under circumstances which show that he/she was aware from his/her knowledge of existing conditions that it is probable that injury would result from his/her acts and omissions, and nevertheless proceeded with reckless indifference as to the consequences and without care for the rights of others. . . .

It is not necessary to find that the defendant deliberately intended to injure the plaintiff. It is sufficient if the plaintiff proves by the greater weight of the evidence that the defendant intentionally acted in such a way that the natural and probable consequence of his/her act was injury to the plaintiff.[14]

14. Ronald W. Eades, *Jury Instructions on Damages in Tort Actions* at §§ 2-6, 2-7, 2-8 (4th ed., 1998). Note that many courts require proof by "clear and convincing evidence," not simply "from the evidence" (which is called the *preponderance-of-evidence standard*). Although these different evidentiary standards are meaningful to attorneys, it is not evident that they importantly influence a jury's decision.

Often the instructions will make reference at some point to the proposition that the purpose of punitive damages is punishment and deterrence. In other cases (as in the example above), the jury is only given a suggestion of a connection between reckless behavior and punitive damages. Although there are some differences across states, the terms most commonly used as bases for a punitive damages award are "recklessness," "reckless disregard," "maliciousness," "oppression," "reprehensibility," "egregious or outrageous behavior," or similar such terms relating to the character of the defendant's actions. Also, in some form, the jury is told that it must find that the harm to the plaintiff was the "foreseeable and probable effect" of the defendant's behavior.

Once the jury has found that the defendant's actions can be characterized in one of these terms, then it is to set the dollar amount of punitive damages. Below is an example of the guidance toward this end provided to the jury in the California instructions:

> In arriving at any award of punitive damages, you are to consider the following:
> 1. The reprehensibility of the conduct of the defendant.
> 2. The amount of punitive damages which will have a deterrent effect on the defendant in the light of the defendant's financial condition.[15]

Typical instructions will also add:

> The law provides no fixed standards as to the amount of such punitive damages, but leaves the amount to the jury's sound discretion, exercised without passion or prejudice.

That is it. Those phrases constitute in the entirety the "training" of the jury with respect to the award of punitive damages. The judge tells the jury no more. In its closing argument, the plaintiff's attorney will typically have made some reference to the terms "reprehensibility" or "recklessness" or will have used some other adjective to describe the defendant's actions that relates to the punitive damages standard. It is also increasingly common for the plaintiff's attorney to make reference to the defendant's wealth, though often in only general terms. At either the closing argument at trial in the case of a unified procedure or at the separate punitive damages hearing, the plaintiff's attorney is also likely to

15. *California Jury Instructions, Civil; Book of Approved Jury Instructions* at 14.71, "Punitive Damages—Recovery of and Measure—Trial Not Bifurcated" (Paul G. Breckenridge ed., 8th ed., 1994).

suggest a specific number as the appropriate punitive amount. But that is all the jury will hear about punitive damages. The next step is for the jury to retire to the jury room and answer the questions relating to the defendant's liability and the amount of compensatory damages, then to address liability for and the appropriate magnitude of a punitive damages award.

IV. Determining a Punitive Damages Award: The Rationale of the Empirical Studies

As described above, the ambition of the experimental work described in this volume was to gain an understanding as to *how* jurors take these very general instructions regarding punitive damages and translate their evaluation of the character of a defendant's actions into a punitive damages dollar award that they believe is appropriate to the case. As hopefully is apparent from the description of the procedure, there is no obvious mechanism or process by which a juror is to execute this translation. The approach in this project was to conduct carefully controlled experiments in order to see how jurors who have been given a description of some event leading to harm translate the general terms of the typical punitive damages instruction into a specific dollar amount. In some of the studies, an essential element of the trial was varied, such as the dollar amount requested by the plaintiff's attorney or whether the defendant had performed a cost-benefit analysis before the accident. In other tests the context was varied: individual decisions compared to group deliberations; or a dangerous scenario judged with no knowledge of an accident (foresight) as compared with the same case judged after an accident (hindsight). In yet other experiments, mock jurors were asked questions to reveal their understanding of the judge's instructions or concepts of risk.

Greater detail about the studies and their findings will be presented in subsequent chapters, but here is a very brief overview of the research. First, a word about the legal context. Although on occasion a punitive damages verdict will be levied against a single individual (most typically in the context of an intentional harm, such as assault or rape), by a large measure, the most frequent and prominent punitive damages verdicts are levied against corporations for some form of corporate activity that is claimed to have resulted in harm to some plaintiff. As a consequence, in all of these experiments, the facts of the cases given to mock jurors and judges involved some form of corporate activity that had generated harm to some plaintiff or set of plaintiffs. The studies and findings of the researchers fall into three topics that serve to organize part 1 (chapters 2 through 11) and describe the experiments:

A. From Outrage to Dollars: What accounts for the apparent unpredictability of the punitive damages awards that are seen in actual cases? For a wide range of cases, these studies first probe jurors' reactions—the researchers describe them as *outrage*—at the defendants' behavior and their desire to impose punishment. Jurors were then asked to set a punitive damages award based on those reactions. In another study given the same contexts, individual awards are compared with those of deliberating juries. Yet another study looks at the sensitivity of jurors' awards to the amount requested by the plaintiff lawyer in the closing argument.

B. To Punish or Not?: The judge's instructions on liability for punitive damages require that jurors judge the defendant's mental process at some point prior to the accident that generated the litigation. These studies undertake to assess how well jurors comprehend and follow those instructions, compared with what is intended by the law. Another set of tests investigates how what is called *hindsight bias* affects jurors' abilities to put themselves in the place of defendants when the critical decision was being made.[16]

C. Jurors and Judges as Risk Managers: Our legal system has made punitive damages part of a set of legal commands aimed at optimal balancing of safety and cost—that is, deterring behavior that is too risky, but not discouraging valuable innovation and production. The first study investigates how jurors react to companies that have performed cost-benefit analyses prior to accidents that are being litigated. Additional tests in this section investigate jurors' and judges' understanding of risk concepts and the effect of hindsight on the assessment of risk. Still other studies probe jurors' attitudes toward the notion of optimal deterrence, which is often recommended as a basis for setting punitive damages awards.

---

16. Because the researchers focus on harms claimed to have been caused by corporations, they do not closely examine the jury's evaluation of the concept of malice. In all of the experiments, the fact situations presented to the mock juries comprise contexts in which the harm resulted from "normal" corporate behavior, not from the acts of deviant corporate employees or officers who might be acting out of personal malice, presumably in violation of the corporation's own guidelines.

Chapter 1 will describe the experimental method, the studies, and the empirical results in more detail. Then, chapters 2 through 11 will present the studies themselves and set forth the findings from the experimental data. I believe that the results of the experiments are highly interesting. They explicate—indeed, uncover—the extreme difficulty that jurors face in translating the very general characterizations of the behavior of a defendant as defined by the law—"egregious," "reckless"—into specific dollar amounts appropriate for punitive damages. As explained in more detail below, the studies demonstrate that the difficulties of translation are not the fault of the jurors. The individuals participating in the experiments were hardworking and conscientious. There is no doubt that real jurors deciding actual cases are more conscientious still.

The broader question raised by the results, however, is whether the task of determining a punitive damages verdict to achieve broad societal goals such as punishment and deterrence can be coherently achieved when charged only with the tools provided in the typical punitive damages jury instruction.[17] In part 2, Conclusions, chapter 12 joins the findings of the studies together and addresses the implications of these scientific findings from a broader behavioral perspective. Chapter 13 discusses the legal implications of the findings and proposes some possible judicial responses. To appreciate those discussions, however, it is helpful to look at the experiments and their findings themselves.

17. It should be remembered, of course, that a jury's award of punitive damages is not the end of the process of punitive damages review. Every state provides for appeal of the jury's verdict, first to the trial judge and then to different levels of appellate review within the state. Finally, a judgment of a state supreme court may be appealed to the U.S. Supreme Court to assure that the verdict complies with the due process requirements of the U.S. Constitution. See, for example, the discussion of *BMW of North America, Inc. v. Gore,* 116 S. Ct. 1589 (1996), in Rustad, *supra* note 6, at 15.

1

Overview: What We Did and What We Found

Reid Hastie

The overarching goal of the empirical research reported in this book is to investigate the cognitive, emotional, and social processes of jurors and juries making punitive damages decisions. The research comprises a collection of separate empirical studies, which, taken as whole, involved decisions by over eight thousand jury-eligible citizens and over six hundred mock juries, who made realistic punitive damages decisions under controlled, experimental conditions. Individually and collectively, these studies yield many new scientific insights into this controversial institution.

We started the research reported in this book because we were impressed with how little was known about the details of the cognitive and social processes involved in these civil jury decisions. Research on the punitive damages decision was especially scanty, and most available information seemed indirect or unscientific. When we initiated our studies, the primary sources of information about the behavior of juries deciding on punitive damages were derived from

- reports in popular news media, including journalistic commentaries on individual trials and post-trial interviews with jurors;
- observations from judges and attorneys—again, usually reports and commentaries on individual cases;
- post hoc statistical surveys of verdicts;
- applications of idealized models of the decision process (usually based on rational economic theories of behavior), to infer what jurors should be doing.

These sources offer many important insights, but they provide little direct or reliable information about the jury decision process. Perhaps most important of all, these approaches are limited in their ability to provide unconfounded tests of the causal effects of factors that produce awards. For example, scrutiny of journalistic reports or calculation of post hoc statistics on archival data sets can at best provide suggestive evidence about whether or not jurors or juries have been influenced by a specific procedure, instruction, piece of evidence, or attorney's argument. In contrast, experimental tests can be designed to answer specific questions about causality.

I. The Experimental Approach

The approach in the present volume relies on a venerable and widely used method of scientific investigation: systematic experimentation. This is the basic means by which causal laws are tested and established in the natural sciences and, for about a hundred years, in the behavioral sciences. If we want to know whether a particular factor has a causal impact on a decision, the most direct test is to hold everything else constant while manipulating that factor and observing the resulting behavior. An experiment can be conducted in which two test cases, identical except for a critical factor, are compared. If the experiment is well designed, a strong conclusion can be reached about the causal effects of that factor.

There is a major drawback of experiments: In order to achieve the control necessary to manipulate key factors, some elements of a corresponding naturally occurring situation must be simplified. Controlled experimental research usually involves making a trade-off between the ability to reach strong conclusions about causality and the ability to study directly a complex, naturally occurring situation that is often of primary interest. In the studies in this book, we attempted to design our experiments to ensure that the most essential elements of a real juror's task remained intact, without sacrificing the benefits of experimentation.

Experiments also provide some valuable opportunities beyond the manipulate-and-compare method: If we need a detailed view of some aspect of a process that is usually invisible, the experimenter can control and intrude to take a closer look at that process. In the present research, we often measured jurors' detailed "think-aloud" reports of their decision processes, from videotaped records of the jury deliberation process, jurors' memory for evidence and instructions, confidence ratings and justifications for verdicts, and many other indicators of the hidden details of the decision process. And if there is interest in the *variability or reliability* of reactions to an event, broad samples of respondents from many different backgrounds can be used to assess agreement and consensus in responses to that event or factor.

The present experiments are simulations of the jury decision task. The simulation research strategy—which is used routinely in engineering, medical, and behavioral research—involves creating a situation that is analogous to a real situation, and then studying the phenomena of interest in the controlled situation. In the present experiments, every effort was made to ensure that the simulation was as realistic as possible. Most of the experimental cases were based on real, decided cases; jury instructions were taken directly from actual trials; and only citizens eligible to serve on real juries were sampled as research participants.

The studies reported here use this method to examine the punitive damages decision in products liability and environmental damages torts (the studies, significantly revised and edited for this book, were originally published in peer-refereed scientific journals and in well-respected law reviews; see preface and acknowledgments for sources). In a typical experiment, jury-eligible citizens were contacted and assembled in a conference center. The locations in which the studies were conducted included urban and suburban venues in Colorado, Texas, Arizona, Illinois, and Nevada. These were chosen primarily for reasons of economy and ease of recruiting participants, although we deliberately excluded locations that have been sites for notorious punitive damages awards (e.g., Alabama). Participants were paid for taking part in a study of "public opinions." In most of the studies, they were shown a summary of the evidence, testimony, arguments, and instructions from an actual civil trial in which punitive damages were sought. After studying the trial summary, they were sometimes assigned to six-person mock juries and asked to deliberate to a unanimous verdict on the issue of liability for punitive damages. If the verdict was for the plaintiff, they were asked to continue deliberation to set a dollar punitive damages award. In other studies the focus was on individual juror decision processes, and the experimental procedure concluded with mock jurors rendering individual decisions, without group deliberation. (Sample case materials and instructions from some of the experimental studies are in chapters 2 through 11 and in the appendix to this volume.)

An obviously central question is whether our results are reflected in behavior in the real world. An initial reason to believe that they are is that many of the tasks were quite realistic. As compared with real jurors, our mock jurors' job was simplified, but it incorporated the basic responsibilities of the real-world juror. A second reason comes from the repeated replication of the research results across experimental tests within the research program, and from replications in independent research programs.

Of course, there is no pat answer to the question of whether the results from a well-crafted simulation study will project to an actual courtroom trial, and there are many differences between real jurors and the participants in our experiments. We did not use the full sequence of trial procedures. Most jurors asked to decide on punitive damages will have experienced a voir dire jury-selection procedure, have judged the defendant's liability for compensatory damages, and assessed a compensatory award, and these proceedings probably lasted for days or weeks. In addition, an actual courtroom trial includes many events that were not re-created in the experimental simulations. These include, most importantly, individual witnesses presenting testimony in a direct and cross-examination format, and attorneys asking questions, making objections, and presenting lengthy statements and arguments. An experiment cannot replicate the sense of gravity and importance of a courtroom decision.

A consideration of these differences may lead some readers to doubt some of the experimental findings reported here. In response, we would simply note that our simulation tasks captured the essence of the punitive damages decision, and that there is consistent convergence between the experimental findings and the results of every other form of investigation of punitive damages decisions. To our knowledge, there is not a single instance in which our results disagree with findings from other experiments conducted by independent groups of behavioral researchers or with any findings from the statistical analysis of actual trial verdicts (see chapter 12 for discussion).

One final note: Merely identifying a difference between the experiment and an actual trial is not sufficient to support the conclusion that the findings do not generalize. What is also necessary is that this difference provides a specific and valid reason to doubt generality. For example, in our experiments jurors were presented with instructions on punitive damages taken from actual cases and pattern instruction handbooks. We found that comprehension and memory for those instructions were remarkably poor. Should we project this finding to actual courtroom trials? We would argue, "Yes." If anything, comprehension and memory should be superior in the experimental presentation format, where both oral and written instructions are presented, where there is a low level of fatigue in the relatively brief experimental procedure, and where there is a short interval between the presentation of the instructions, the decision or deliberation, and the memory test. There is no reason to expect that the gravity of the actual trial would increase memory, especially in comparison with the relatively brief, intense experimental situation. But we do believe that any important finding needs to be evaluated by a careful review of the relevant similarities and differences between the experimental setting and the courtroom.

II. Questions Addressed in the Present Research

Table 1.1 is a list of some of the major questions, with brief answers, that were addressed by the present experiments. It is noteworthy that the findings do not project an image of a completely chaotic decision process. There are many systematic patterns in the conscientious efforts of jurors to solve the difficult problem posed by the punitive damages instructions and procedures. By way of introduction, we underline some of our key findings here.

The natural place to start an analysis of jury decision making is with the instructions given to jurors in the courtroom. The hypothesis of an ideally obedient juror is rarely confirmed, even though jurors are well intentioned and conscientious. For example, we were surprised by how rarely jurors mentioned judicial instructions when thinking about their individual decisions and even when deliberating as juries. And as mentioned above, jurors did not have accurate memories of the instructions, even when tested a few minutes after making their decisions.

In light of jurors' large-scale failure to heed instructions, it is striking that a substantial amount of consensus is apparent in individual judgments about the reprehensibility of the defendant's conduct and in punitive intent. Individual jurors' rankings of cases by blameworthiness showed high levels of agreement, with correlations between the average ratings and rankings of different demographic groups averaging over +.90 across cases judged (a perfect correlation is +1.00). We attribute this remarkable degree of consensus to shared cultural standards and habits for judging reprehensibility and responsibility in social conduct. Jurors apparently share a moral consensus on the initial ordering of defendants' conduct by blameworthiness. If the legal judgment task were concluded with a comparative evaluation of moral reprehensibility, the results would be consistent and predictable.

Table 1.1. Questions Addressed in Studies

Chap.	Question	Finding
		A. From Outrage to Dollars
2	Are jurors' outrage and their intent to punish predictable?	Judging cases of the same category and with fixed compensatory damages, jurors from different demographic groups using bounded scales (0–6) of outrage and intent to punish are quite consistent and predictable. They are about 80% consistent (correlations +.90 or more).
2	Are jurors' dollar awards predictable?	When asked to translate their intent to punish into a dollar award, jurors' judgments become erratic and unpredictable. They are only about 18% consistent.
3	Does deliberation by a group of jurors overcome individual biases and produce more just and more predictable verdicts?	Deliberating juries increased both the severity and unpredictability of awards compared with individual predeliberation assessments. When punitive damages were awarded, over 27% of juries awarded as much or more than any individual juror had awarded predeliberation, and 83% of the awards were above the median individual juror's award.
4	Are jurors influenced by the amount requested by the plaintiff?	All respondents were given the exact same case except for the amount of punitive damages requested by the plaintiff's lawyer. Half the respondents were given X and the other half, $3X$. Even though they were told that lawyers' arguments are not evidence and can be ignored, jurors who received the higher request awarded 2.5 times as much as those getting the lower request.
4	Do awards depend on whether or not the plaintiff is local?	Judging the same case, mock jurors awarded local plaintiffs 35% more than plaintiffs from out of state.

Table 1.1. *continued*

Chap.	Question	Finding
	B. To Punish or Not?	
5	Are jurors attentive to the judge's instructions?	Their recorded deliberations revealed that juries spent only a small fraction of their time discussing whether the defendant's behavior met the legal requirements for recklessness in the judge's instructions. After making an individual case judgment and then deliberating in a jury, individuals averaged 5% correct on a test of memory for and comprehension of the instructions.
5	Does it matter how much attention jurors pay to the judge's instructions?	The more discussion a jury devoted to the judge's instructions, the less likely they were to award punitive damages.
5	How do juries' verdicts on liability compare with judges'?	For four actual cases in which trial or appellate judges denied punitive damages, over $\frac{2}{3}$ of individuals and over $\frac{2}{3}$ of deliberating juries awarded punitive damages.
6	Can people judge defendants' pre-accident decisions objectively or is hindsight an overwhelming bias in jurors' judgments?	Two groups were told about a dangerous railroad track site. Both were asked to estimate the probability of a serious train accident. One group was told that an accident had occurred but their estimates should be made as if they didn't know about it. That group's accident probability estimates were 80% higher than the other group that was not told about the accident. In response to other questions, $\frac{2}{3}$ of those who knew about the accident favored punitive damages against the railroad while $\frac{2}{3}$ of the other group said fixing the track was too expensive and, therefore, unnecessary.

(continued)

Table 1.1. *continued*

Chap.	Question	Finding
	C. Jurors and Judges as Risk Managers	
7	How do jurors in an accident case react when told that the defendant company did a cost-benefit analysis?	A company that did cost-benefit analysis (CBA) before having an accident received a 50% higher punitive damages award than one that did not do CBA. If the company used a high government-recommended value of life in doing the CBA (leading them to spend more on safety measures), the awards went up an additional 20%.
8	Deterrence theory says that a punitive damages award should be raised when the defendant was unlikely to be prosecuted. Are punitive damages awards influenced by the defendants' probability of being punished?	Even though encouraged to notice the defendant's probability of being punished, individuals were not influenced by large variations in that probability.
8	What do jurors think of basing awards on the probability of the defendant's being punished?	Large awards against defendants because they were unlikely to be punished are viewed as unfair by ¾ of participating University of Chicago law students, all of whom were schooled in the theory of optimal deterrence.
9	Do jurors reliably use explicit instructions for setting punitive damages awards based on the probability of detection?	Less than 20% of jurors correctly calculated the award according to the instructions. When the plaintiff's lawyer suggested an award amount, the number of correct awards was cut to 10% as jurors ignored the instructions and focused on the lawyer's suggestion.
10	How well do jurors reason about the risk of accidents?	Subjects exhibited a variety of irrationalities regarding risk that would distort their judgment in assessing liability and awards in safety and environmental tort. Hindsight effects were particularly important.

Table 1.1. *continued*

Chap.	Question	Finding
	C. Jurors and Judges as Risk Managers	
11	Can judges overcome hindsight bias better than jurors?	Although their probability estimates were substantially lower than the jurors', judges' hindsight bias effect was identical—their accident probability estimates increased by 80%. Also, only 23% of the hindsight group favored punitive damages, and 85% of the foresight group said fixing the problem was too expensive and, therefore, unnecessary.
11	How well do judges reason about the risk of accidents?	Given the same tests as jurors, judges were less prone to risk biases and made more sensible legal judgments.

Note: All studies have been reported in published articles listed in the preface and acknowledgments.

However, when the first legally required decision is made—a yes-no absolute judgment of liability for punitive damages—consensus among jurors begins to disintegrate. Although jurors are in substantial agreement on the *relative* moral reprehensibility of the actions of another person or corporation, the present studies show that they do not agree on where to draw the *absolute* line between negligent and reckless conduct. Most jurors do not rely on the guidance that might be provided by their instructions on the law; to the extent that instructions might increase consensus, they are not given a chance to help. This theme of shared moral evaluations but lack of consensus on the legal threshold for liability, followed by erratic dollar awards, is the most general message of the present research.

Predictability is not the sole consideration in evaluating the quality of a legal institution. In behavioral science it is well-known that people tend to think that whatever happened was bound to happen—and hence people show *hindsight bias* in assessing probability of harm. The present tests find a large hindsight bias when jurors are assessing recklessness after an accident has occurred. We also find that jurors react in a harsh manner to evidence that a defendant has conducted a cost-benefit analysis of a product that was a factor in an accident.

When jurors conclude that the defendant is liable and move on to assess dollar awards, their judgments become more unpredictable and erratic. Jurors do not have a clear idea about the meaning of different "points" on the scale of dollars; they do not know whether $200,000, or $1 million, or $5 million is the right punishment for a particular instance of serious corporate misconduct. Hence we observe considerable variability when jurors translate their shared intention to punish into a dollar award. But some systematic trends can be identified: Jurors give consistently larger dollar awards to geographically local plaintiffs; they will punish wealthy defendants with higher awards; and they respond to plaintiffs' attorneys' requests for more money with larger awards.

Perhaps the most remarkable finding involves the effect of deliberation within juries. We find that a jury's award is systematically higher than the award of the median juror, predeliberation. We also find that the deliberation process acts to exaggerate the variability of dollar awards. This polarization and increased variability is contrary to most intuitions about the likely effects of deliberation on variability.

III. What Decisions Should We Ask the Jury to Make?

For the punitive damages decision, the most chaotic part of the process involves the translation of a moral evaluation, which we label *outrage,* into a dollar-award value. We have discovered no simple behavioral principles that allow us to predict the jurors' selection of the values for their dollar awards. Nor were jurors able to provide any insights into their theories of retribution and deterrence, or the manner in which they applied such principles to select an appropriate figure.

The overarching practical message from the present research is that the punitive damages decision is exceedingly difficult. Although jurors are well intentioned, they do not conscientiously heed their instructions on how to perform the task. Even when they try to reason about complex concepts like deterrence, they do not seem to be able to apply those understandings to translate their judgments into predictable dollar awards. The traditional punitive damages jury decision procedures violate the general principle of cognitive engineering that we should match human capabilities to the demands of the task. Present institutions and practices demand an enormously difficult performance from the jury, without providing much guidance or support.

Part I

How Juries Think

A. From Outrage to Dollars

Introduction

Cass R. Sunstein

In any particular case, it can be hard to predict the punitive damages award that will be chosen by the jury. In some cases, awards are in the many millions of dollars; in cases that do not appear much different, awards are in the hundreds of thousands; and in cases that are not so very different from those, awards are in the tens of thousands, or even less. What accounts for the variability?

This is the principal question that we investigate in this section. To make a long story short, we find that people have a hard time in arriving at consistent, predictable judgments *when using the scale of dollars*—even when their moral judgments are both consistent and predictable. We show that in personal injury cases, people's moral evaluations are shared, but their dollar judgments are erratic. We also show that a major source of this unpredictability comes from the fact that people do not know how to "translate" their moral judgments into dollar amounts.

Why is the task of translation so difficult? One reason is that the legal system does not provide a standard, or *modulus,* by which to make sense of various points along the dollar scale. Imagine, for example, that an individual or a company has committed some reckless act, perhaps by permitting an unsafe product to go on the market. Should the damages award be $50,000? Or $200,000? Or $500,000? Or $10 million? The legal system does not give people a sense of how to measure, in dollars, different moral evaluations of cases. Without a standard or modulus, different individuals, and different juries, will naturally come to very different conclusions about appropriate dollar awards, even when their moral judgments are entirely consistent.

Chapter 2 demonstrates this point by studying the reactions of individuals. But it is reasonable to wonder whether the process of deliberation makes things better, by "smoothing out" inconsistent reactions.

Chapter 3 shows that this does not happen—in fact, it shows that the very opposite happens. By studying individuals' judgments before deliberating and by comparing those individual judgments with (mock) jury verdicts, we show that deliberation systematically increases awards over the award of the median juror—so much so that in 27% of the cases, the jury's award was as high as or higher than that of the highest individual judgment, predeliberation. We also find that the pattern of actual jury awards shows less, not more, predictability than would come from taking the median predeliberation judgment of individual jurors. The simple conclusion is that the process of deliberation actually increases the variability of awards.

Thus far we know that the dollar scale helps produce unpredictability and that deliberation makes this problem worse; but we do not know what drives awards up or down. Attempting to explore this question, chapter 4 offers two conclusions. First, the plaintiff's demand makes a great deal of difference. Other things being equal, high requests produce high awards. A large part of the reason is that people lack standards by which to select any particular award, and the plaintiff's request provides a kind of *anchor* from which adjustments are made. The idea of anchoring is well established in the psychological literature, and anchors have been shown to affect jury judgments about dollars. What we add here is a demonstration of how this happens in the context of punitive awards, and a link between the phenomenon of anchoring and the general problem of *scaling* that we trace in chapter 2. Thus we find dramatic effects on the jury's judgments from the amount that the plaintiff seeks.

We also find that local plaintiffs receive more than geographically remote plaintiffs, apparently because of special sympathy on the part of jurors with people who live nearby. The lesson here is that plaintiffs seeking large punitive awards should sue locally—even though from the standpoint of the legal system, awards should not be affected by geography. The effect here is especially noteworthy in view of our finding that the location of the defendant does not have a significant effect on awards.

2

Shared Outrage, Erratic Awards

Daniel Kahneman, David A. Schkade,
and Cass R. Sunstein

I. Introduction

The goal of this chapter is to uncover some of the sources of unpredictability in punitive damages awards by juries. Our principal conclusion is that people have great difficulty in using the scale of dollars. Without guidance about what is meant by various "points" on the dollar scale, different juries choose different amounts, not necessarily because they disagree about anything of importance, but because the choice of one or another dollar award often amounts to a stab in the dark.

More specifically, we offer three central findings, based on a study of the judgments of 899 jury-eligible citizens.

1. In evaluating cases on a bounded numerical scale, people demonstrate a remarkably high level of moral agreement. At least in the personal injury cases we study, this moral consensus, on what might be called *outrage* and *punitive intent,* cuts across differences in gender, race, income, age, and education. For example, our study shows that all-white, all-female, all-Hispanic, all-male, all-poor, all-wealthy, all-black juries, all-old juries, and all-young juries are likely to come to similar conclusions about how to rank and rate a range of cases.

2. This consensus fractures when the legal system uses dollars as the vehicle to measure moral outrage. *Even when there is a consensus on punitive intent, there is no consensus about how much in the way of dollars is necessary to produce appropriate suffering in a defendant.* Under existing law, widely shared and reasonably predictable judgments about punitive intent are turned into highly erratic judgments about appropriate dollar punishments. A basic source of arbitrariness in the existing system of punitive damages (and a problem

not limited to the area of punitive damages) is the difficulty of expressing a moral judgment as a dollar amount.

3. The wealth of the defendant matters a great deal to dollar awards. *People will impose significantly higher punitive damages awards on significantly wealthier defendants*—even though people do not see misconduct by wealthy defendants as more outrageous than equivalent misconduct by less-wealthy defendants. The lesson—perhaps not surprising, but highly relevant to legal practice—is that jury awards will be greatly affected by knowledge of wealth of the defendant.

II. The Outrage Model

We propose a descriptive theory of the psychology of punitive awards, called the *outrage model* (fig. 2.1). The essential claim is that the moral transgressions of others evoke an attitude of outrage, which combines an emotional evaluation and a response tendency. In this chapter we do not address the rules that govern outrage and simply assume that outrage is determined largely by social norms. Judged by reference to these norms, a particular person's expression of indignation may be deemed too intense for its cause or not intense enough. Legal as well as social norms also regulate the mapping from transgressions to outrage.

An attitude is a mental state and is not directly observable. The various aspects of an attitude can, however, be "mapped" onto diverse responses, which might include facial expressions, verbal statements of opinion, gestures—even physical assault. Response "modes" might include judgments about outrageousness on a numerical scale. Under the outrage model, punitive damages are considered to be an expression of an angry or indignant attitude toward a transgressor. The evaluative as-

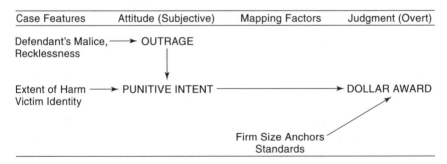

Fig. 2.1. The Outrage Model

pect of the attitude is labeled *outrage;* the response tendency is labeled *punitive intent.* Outrage is basic, and punitive intent is measured by outrage and additional factors, such as the degree of harm suffered by the plaintiff. Although punitive intent is affected by some factors that do not affect outrage, our general hypothesis is that most of the determinants of the two states are shared—and we therefore expect them to be highly correlated.

Both outrage and punitive intent are psychological states and must be expressed in some overt statement or action if they are to play a role in society or law. In some situations the expression of an attitude is restricted to a particular scale of responses. For example, in the situation that concerns us here, the responses of juries are restricted to a scale of dollars. Dollar amounts of punitive awards (like the length of prison sentences in criminal cases) are only one of a number of possible scales on which punitive intent might be expressed. These scales vary not only in their complexity, but also in the precision and consistency of the measurements that they provide: Some scales are less reliable than others, in the sense that they contain more random error. As we will shortly see, the dollar scale is an extremely unreliable expression of punitive intent.

III. Background and Hypotheses

Our two central hypotheses were that jurors would exhibit shared outrage, but that dollar awards would be erratic. The basis for the shared-outrage hypothesis is the belief that a bedrock of broadly shared social norms governs the outrage evoked by different scenarios of tortious behavior. With respect to *ratings* of outrage and punitive intent, we thus predicted that randomly selected juries are likely to be similar to one another. In addition, we predicted that *rankings* of different scenarios would be generally similar for different demographic groups, at least in the context of the personal injury cases given here. For the "erratic" dollar amounts, the hypothesis was that punitive awards denominated in dollars are susceptible to large and arbitrary individual differences, which could be a significant cause of the unpredictability of jury determinations. We tested this prediction by comparing the extent of variations in judgments about outrageousness and appropriate punishment with the extent of variations in judgments about appropriate dollar awards.

We also examined two additional hypotheses. First, we considered the *harm effect.* We hypothesized that punitive intent—as measured on a bounded numerical scale—is determined by the outrageousness of the defendant's behavior and by other factors, prominently including the harm suffered by the plaintiff. The prediction that harm affects punitive intent but not outrage was tested by presenting alternative versions of some scenarios in which the severity of the harm suffered by the plaintiff varied.

Second, we tested whether the defendant firm's size, or wealth, was relevant. We hypothesized that damages awards are determined by punitive intent and by other ascertainable factors, prominently including the size of the defendant firm. We tested this prediction by presenting each scenario in two versions, in which the size of the defendant varied, with "large" companies having profits of $100 to $200 million per year, and "medium-sized" companies having profits of $10 to $20 million per year.

IV. Study Design

A total of 899 respondents were randomly selected from the voter registration rolls of Travis County, Texas, and paid $35 to participate in the study. A set of ten short summaries of realistic personal injury cases was created in which a plaintiff (always an individual) sued a firm for compensatory and punitive damages. As noted, each case had versions that differed in the size of the defendant firm (medium or large). For four cases, there were additional versions that varied the harm that the plaintiff was said to have suffered, but not the description of the defendant's actions. In total, there were twenty-eight different variations of the ten cases. Each respondent evaluated ten cases, composed of one variation of each of the ten basic cases. In all cases the respondents were told to assume that compensatory damages had already been awarded in the amount of $200,000 and that punitive damages were to be considered. Three separate groups of respondents were asked to answer different questions about each scenario: (1) how outrageous was the defendant's behavior (on a scale of 0 = "not at all outrageous" to 6 = "absolutely outrageous"); (2) how much should the defendant be punished (on a scale of 0 = "no punishment" to 6 = "extremely severe punishment"); or (3) how much should the defendant be required to pay in punitive damages.

A. Shared Outrage

Our first question is whether the degree of outrage is consistent across individuals and across possible juries. A simple way to answer this question is to examine whether rankings of different scenarios are generally similar for different demographic groups. We therefore computed the means of the three responses (outrage, punitive intent, and dollar awards) separately for groups of respondents defined by demographic variables (men, women, white, Hispanics, African Americans, different levels of income and education). To measure the level of agreement across disjoint categories (e.g., men and women), we computed the correlation between their average responses over the set of cases.

The correlations were remarkably high for judgments both of outrage and of punitive intent. In particular, there was essentially perfect agreement among groups in the ranking of cases by punitive intent: the median correlation was .99. Men and women, Hispanics, African Americans, and whites, and respondents at very different levels of income and education produced almost identical orderings of the scenarios used in the study. Judgments of intent to punish in these scenarios of personal injury cases evidently rest on a bedrock of moral intuitions that are broadly shared in society. We also looked for differences among groups in the average severity of their judgments (i.e., the level of the average rating) and here, too, found no widespread disagreement.

Summary of Experiment

Description: Subjects read descriptions of personal injury cases and, for each, rated the outrageousness of the defendant's behavior and the appropriate level of punishment on bounded scales (0–6). They then selected a dollar value for punitive damages.

Number of subjects: 899 jury-eligible citizens.

Location: Austin, Texas.

Decisions: Individual.

Stimuli: Written case summaries and instructions.

Between individuals there is, of course, greater variation than between averages of groups. Not all members of even a given group (e.g., different women or different people from the same income category) rank the cases exactly the same. The average correlation between the rankings of a pair of individuals appears to be in the .50 to .60 range. What is remarkable is that when even a small group of people is assembled, such as in a jury, the correlation between two groups rapidly approaches the .90 level (see table 2.3). Thus, the disagreements at the level of individuals appear not to be sharp or systematic, but rather reflect random fluctuations that

Table 2.1. Correlations between Demographic Groups
on Intended Severity of Punishment

Gender		Men		
	Women	.97		

Ethnicity		Black	White	
	White	.98		
	Hispanic	.96	.99	

Household Income		< 30K	30–50K	
	30–50K	.99		
	> 50K	.99	.99	

Age		< 30	30–39	40–49
	30–39	.99		
	40–49	.99	.99	
	> 50	.99	.99	.99

Note: Entries are correlations between mean responses to scenarios by respondents in the indicated demographic categories.

result from the difficulty of making these moral judgments. These fluctuations are dampened or eliminated in even a small grouping of individual jurors.

This striking finding may not generalize to all domains of the law. For example, we might expect to find larger differences between communities and social categories in other areas of the law, perhaps including attitudes toward civil rights violations and environmental harms; at least it is possible that, for example, African Americans would *rate* civil rights cases more severely than whites do. We expect, however, that within the same category of cases, *rankings* may remain the same across different groups, so that different demographic groups would agree on which defendants have behaved least and most egregiously.

B. Unpredictable Dollar Awards

With respect to dollar awards, our central hypothesis was that such awards are erratic because of individual differences in the mapping of punitive intent onto the dollar scale. To test this hypothesis, we produced synthetic juries by randomly sampling, with replacement, groups of twelve responses to each case for each response scale. In this manner, we constructed a large number of three types of synthetic juries: *outrage juries, punishment juries,* and *dollar juries.* Of course, there is a large question about how a set of individual judgments will produce a jury verdict. We offer some data on that question in chapter 3, which suggests that our findings here actually understate the level of unpredictability that would come from deliberating juries. Without losing sight of the limitations of our estimation procedure, we apply the label *jury judgment* to these estimates for simplicity of exposition. Table 2.2 summarizes the synthetic-jury judgments for punishment and dollar awards.

Jury judgments can be considered shared and therefore predictable, in our use of that term, if there is high agreement between juries randomly selected from the population. In order to find a source of erratic judgments, we compared the predictability of the judgments made by simulated dollar juries, outrage juries, and punishment juries. First, we imagined that all of our case scenarios were tried on the same day by independent juries, analogous to how jury judgments for different cases are produced in practice. We then asked the question "If these same cases were tried again independently, how likely are we to get the same ratings and rankings as in this first set of trials?"

To answer this question, we conducted an analysis requiring four steps. (1) From our respondents we created a randomly selected jury for each of the 28 cases and computed the median judgment for each. (2) We then imagined that a time machine allowed us to replay each case again independently of the first trial, including the random selection of a new jury. We therefore created a second set of 28 randomly selected juries and corresponding median judgments. The correlation between the first and second sets of jury judgments is a measure of how erratic or consistent juries are in evaluating this set of 28 cases. (3) To get a more reliable indication of the typical correlation between juries, we performed step 1 sixty times for each of the three response modes, producing 180 sets of 28 jury judgments. (4) We then computed the correlations between every possible pair of these sets of synthetic-jury judgments. This computation was performed both within response mode (e.g., the correlation between two sets of 28 dollar awards) and across response modes (e.g., the correlation between a set of 28 dollar awards and a set of 28 punishment ratings). Table 2.3 shows the median correlations obtained for each response mode or response-mode combination.

As we had hypothesized, the individual differences in dollar awards produce severe unpredictability and highly erratic outcomes, even in the medians of twelve individual judgments (the results would be even more extreme with smaller samples, such as six-person juries). While there is strong agreement between independent sets of outrage or punishment juries (correlations of .87 and .89), agreement between independent sets

Table 2.2. Synthetic-Jury Response Distributions by Scenario

Scenario	Firm Size	Harm Level	Lower 95% Confidence Bound	Median	Upper 95% Confidence Bound	Mean Jury Punishment	Prediction Error Ratio ($/Punish)
Joan	Large	High	$500,000	$2,000,000	$15,000,000	5.14	3.36
Joan	Medium	High	200,000	900,000	3,000,000	5.03	2.27
Thomas	Medium	—	200,000	500,000	1,575,000	5.02	1.69
Martin	Medium	High	350,000	1,000,000	4,000,000	4.98	4.01
Thomas	Large	—	200,000	560,000	2,750,000	4.95	.50
Joan	Large	Low	175,000	1,000,000	12,500,000	4.93	13.57
Martin	Large	High	350,000	1,900,000	10,000,000	4.92	2.40
Frank	Medium	—	230,000	760,000	2,100,000	4.86	1.67
Frank	Large	—	225,000	1,000,000	4,000,000	4.82	2.62
Mary	Large	—	290,000	1,000,000	4,000,000	4.79	1.49
Joan	Medium	Low	150,000	750,000	5,500,000	4.71	9.90
Mary	Medium	—	250,000	710,000	2,100,000	4.70	2.51
Martin	Large	Low	350,000	1,000,000	5,000,000	4.47	3.63
Martin	Medium	Low	200,000	675,000	2,250,000	4.16	2.53
Susan	Large	—	100,000	300,000	1,000,000	3.27	1.78
Susan	Medium	—	50,000	225,000	800,000	3.03	.93
Janet	Medium	High	100,000	200,000	690,000	2.79	1.37
Carl	Medium	—	15,000	155,000	375,000	2.78	1.59
Carl	Large	—	50,000	200,000	750,000	2.64	1.59
Janet	Medium	Low	0	150,000	650,000	2.49	2.00
Janet	Large	High	0	287,500	1,500,000	2.39	4.41
Janet	Large	Low	12,500	200,000	1,000,000	2.38	1.30
Jack	Large	High	0	0	350,000	1.24	2.10
Jack	Medium	High	0	45,000	225,000	1.07	1.30
Jack	Medium	Low	0	0	112,500	1.03	0.89
Jack	Large	Low	0	2,550	500,000	0.95	2.91
Sarah	Large	—	0	0	1,000	0.51	1.12
Sarah	Medium	—	0	0	13,000	0.46	∞
						Median	2.18

Table 2.3. Median Correlations between Sets of Synthetic Juries

	Outrage	Punishment	$ Awards
Outrage	.87		
Punishment	.86	.89	
$ Awards	.47	.51	.42
Overall Median Award	.71	.77	.69

of dollar juries is quite weak (a correlation of .42). The variability of individual dollar judgments is so large that even the medians of twelve judgments are quite unstable. The problem could be reduced, of course, by drastically increasing the size of juries. For example, the correlation between sets of dollar juries rises to .80 when jury size is increased to thirty (correlations for thirty-person outrage and punishment juries rise to .95 and .97, respectively).

C. Severity of Harm

An action can be judged more or less outrageous without reference to its consequences. Consequences, however, are important to punishment in law, and we suspected that they would also be important to jurors' intuitions about the proper punishment for reprehensible actions. These predictions were tested by constructing alternative versions of four of the cases, which differed in the harm that the plaintiff had suffered. Note that the difference was manipulated qualitatively rather than in dollar terms; in all of the cases, the jury had awarded the same amount of $200,000 in compensatory damages, but in some of them, the description of the injury suggested less in the way of qualitative loss. For example, in the case in which a child playing with matches was burned when his pajamas caught on fire, the injuries were described as "He was severely burned over a significant portion of his body and required several weeks in the hospital and months of physical therapy" (higher harm) or "His hands and arms were badly burned and required regular professional medical treatment for several weeks" (lower harm).

As predicted, we found that the degree of outrage evoked by the defendant's behavior was not affected by the harm that occurred. In contrast, varying the harm had a small but statistically significant effect on punishment ratings, where defendants who had done more harm to the plaintiff were judged to deserve greater punishment. As predicted by the outrage model, the significant harm effect found for punishment ratings carried through to dollar awards. Thus, low harm produced an average award of $727,599 while high harm produced an average award of a substantially greater amount: $1,171,251.

D. Firm Size: Does the Defendant's Wealth Matter?

Within the academic community, opinion is sharply divided on the question whether the amount of punitive awards should depend on the size of the defendant firm.[1] Ordinary intuitions, in contrast, are quite clear. People naturally think in terms of retribution (see chapter 8 for more detail), and the intention to punish is an intention to inflict pain. Because larger firms are thought to suffer little when dollar punishments are low, this means that the size of the defendant matters a good deal. Our hypothesis was that firm size would affect neither outrage nor punitive intent, but that the same degree of punitive intent would be translated into a larger amount of damages when the firm is larger than when it is smaller.

As expected, we found no statistically significant effects of firm size on either outrage or punishment judgments. But large firms were punished with much larger dollar awards (an average of $1,009,994) than were medium firms ($526,398). This is substantial evidence that equivalent outrage and punitive intent are likely to produce significant higher dollar awards against wealthy defendants.

V. The Underlying Problem: Scaling without a Modulus

Why are dollar awards so variable? And how do these findings bear on the role of juries in setting punitive damages awards? As we have seen, a conventional understanding of such awards sees the jury as a sample from the community whose function is to provide an estimate of community sentiment. If jury judgments are erratic, this function is badly compromised, for any particular jury's judgment may not reflect community sentiment at all. The bottom row of table 2.3 presents the median correlations between sets of synthetic-jury judgments for the twenty-eight scenarios and the corresponding estimates of community sentiment, for which we used the overall median of dollar awards of all individuals for each scenario. *It is obvious that the judgment of any particular dollar jury*

---

1. See, e.g., A. Mitchell Polinsky and Steven Shavell, "Punitive Damages: An Economic Analysis," 111 *Harv. L. Rev.* 869 (1998) (arguing that wealth is irrelevant); and Dan Dobbs, "Ending Punishment in 'Punitive' Damages," 40 *Ala. L. Rev.* 831, 871–72 (1989) (arguing that wealth is sometimes relevant).

is likely to be a poor estimate of overall community sentiment. Indeed, the unreliability of dollar juries is so pronounced that the dollar awards that would be set by the larger community are predicted more accurately by punishment juries.

A key to our analysis is a distinction that psychologists draw between two types of scales. (1) *Category scales* are bounded and anchored in verbal descriptions at both ends; scales of this type are often used in public opinion surveys and were used here to measure outrage and punitive intent. (2) *Magnitude scales* are unbounded and are defined by a meaningful zero point; these scales are often used in the psychological laboratory, for example, to scale the brightness of lights or the loudness of sounds. Magnitude scales have occasionally been used to measure the intensity of response to socially relevant stimuli, such as the severity of crimes and the severity of punishments.[2] The dollar scale of punitive awards is obviously not a category scale; it satisfies the defining characteristics of a magnitude scale, for the zero point is meaningful and the scale is unbounded.

A common practice in laboratory uses of magnitude scaling is to define a *modulus:* respondents are instructed to assign a particular rating to a "standard" stimulus, defined as the modulus, and to assign ratings to other stimuli in relation to that modulus. Thus, for example, a modulus of 100 might be assigned to a noise of a certain volume, and other noises might be assessed in volume by comparison with the modulus. An experiment can, however, be conducted without specifying a modulus. In this situation of *magnitude scaling without a modulus,* different respondents spontaneously adopt different moduli, but their responses generally preserve the same *ratios* even when the moduli differ. For example, one observer may assign a judgment of 200 to one stimulus and 500 to another, while a different observer might assign the first stimulus a 40 and the second a 100. Even though these two observers are each rendering consistent judgments, in the sense that they both perceive the same ratio of the two objects, the absolute numerical judgments they produce would disagree sharply and create high variance.

Here, then, is the central point: Magnitude scaling without a modulus produces extremely large variability in judgments of any particular stimulus because of arbitrary individual differences in the selection of moduli. The assignment of punitive damages satisfies the definition of

2. Stanley S. Stevens, *Psychophysics,* 252–58 (Geraldine Stevens ed., 1975).

magnitude scaling without a modulus. This reasoning is what led to the central hypothesis of the present study, a hypothesis that we described and established above.

One note of caution is in order here. The fact that punitive damages share the known deficiencies of magnitude scaling is likely to be a significant cause of unpredictable punitive awards—but it is not the only one. Other factors include regional differences, plaintiff's demand, anchors of various sorts, differences in social norms over both time and space, and the quality of the lawyers on both sides. Of these, the plaintiff's demand is most important for present purposes. In chapter 4 we will see that a larger demand produces a higher award. This finding is closely related to the problem of scaling without a modulus. When jurors are at sea in choosing an appropriate number, the plaintiff's demand is likely to have special salience.

VI. Conclusion

A key cause of unpredictability in punitive damages awards is the difficulty faced by jurors in expressing their moral judgments on a scale of dollars. The erratic character of dollar awards obscures what is actually a bedrock of social consensus, shared by different demographic groups, on the relative egregiousness of various tortious acts by defendants. When juries produce unpredictable dollar awards, of the sort found in our experiment, a central reason is that jurors are asked to scale without a modulus—to come up with dollar figures for punishment without being given guidance about the meaning or consequence of different choices on the unbounded dollar scale. Punitive damages awards are unpredictable in large part because jurors lack an understanding of how to choose one or another point along that literally infinite scale.

3

Deliberating about Dollars: The Severity Shift

David A. Schkade, Cass R. Sunstein,
and Daniel Kahneman

I. Introduction

With respect to punitive damages, how does group discussion affect individual views? How, if at all, is the outcome of group deliberation different from a statistical aggregation of individual predeliberation judgments? How might jury deliberations depart from the median or mean of individual judgments made in advance of deliberation?

In this chapter we attempt to make some progress on answering these questions. We do so principally by reporting the results of a massive study of decisions by mock juries (over three thousand people and five hundred juries in total). Six-person juries were asked to deliberate about the appropriate punishment in civil cases involving personal injury. They answered this question in two ways: by setting punitive awards in dollars and by indicating, on a rating scale, the severity of the punishment they wished to inflict on the defendant.

Our most important and general finding is that with respect to dollar awards, deliberation produces a *severity shift:* The jury's dollar verdict is typically higher, and often far higher, than the median judgment of the same jury's individual members before deliberation began.

To compress a long story, our specific findings are these:

- Jurors followed a simple principle of majority rule in deciding whether to impose punitive damages at all; the decision to award damages was largely a function of the majority of individual predeliberation votes.
- As compared with the median of individual predeliberation judgments, dollar awards *increased* after group deliberation, often dramatically so: *Among juries that voted to award punitive damages,*

27% reached dollar verdicts that were as high as or higher than the
highest predeliberation judgment among their own jurors.
• With respect to dollar awards, jury verdicts were less consistent and
  predictable than the mean or median juror. *With respect to dollars,*
  jury deliberation substantially increases unpredictability.

The severity shift stems, we believe, from a systematic *rhetorical advan-*
tage held by those arguing for higher dollar awards, an advantage that op-
erates independently of the particular case at issue.

The study reported here has the advantage of being extremely close
to—in fact, part of the design is based on—the study reported in chapter 2. That study did not involve deliberating juries, and in the absence
of evidence about how deliberation would affect individual judgments,
we analyzed statistical juries by treating the median of a deliberating
group as a good predictor of the ultimate judgment of the deliberating
jury. In this chapter we investigate the received wisdom—and find overwhelming evidence that it is wrong. The dollar awards of deliberating
groups were not close to any measure of central tendency; they were
much higher. Moreover, dollar responses vary much more across juries
than do punitive intent ratings. Thus, we find shared moral judgments
but erratic dollar awards not only for individuals but for deliberating juries as well.

II. Deliberating Juries: An Experimental Inquiry
A. *Participants*

Jury-eligible citizens from Phoenix, Arizona, were recruited by a survey firm and paid $35 for their participation. Each juror was randomly
assigned to a six-person jury and to a response-mode order; half of the
juries judged dollar awards first and punishment ratings second, and the
other half completed the tasks in the opposite order. Each jury judged
only one case, which was the subject of both its punishment rating (on a
scale of 0 to 8) and its dollar award. Six juries (out of a total of 480) had
only five members because an insufficient number of participants showed
up at a given appointment time. A pilot test of twenty-nine juries was
conducted in Phoenix to test the materials and procedure. Because adjustments were very minor, these juries were added to the main sample
and the combined sample was analyzed together. Therefore, a total of
3,048 citizens participated in 509 juries.

Summary of Experiment

Description: Citizen subjects (1) viewed a videotaped narration of a personal injury case summary; (2) read the same text; (3) gave the defendant a punishment rating on a bounded scale (0–8); and (4) chose a punitive damages dollar award. They then participated in six-person juries that deliberated to unanimous verdicts on the same two questions. Law students only took individual surveys on *rhetorical asymmetry.*

Number of subjects: 3,048 jury-eligible citizens in 509 mock juries; 87 law students.

Location: Phoenix, Arizona; Chicago, Illinois.

Decisions: Individual and six-person mock-jury deliberation.

Stimuli: Videotaped narration and written case summary and instructions.

B. Procedure and Materials

The procedure consisted of four parts. In part 1 all participants in a given session viewed a videotape for the case they would consider, read the corresponding written materials, and recorded their personal judgment of the appropriate punitive damages award or punishment rating (fig. 3.1). In part 2 participants were randomly assigned to a jury of six members and given thirty minutes to deliberate on and reach a unanimous verdict on a punitive damages amount or a severity of punishment

---

Punishment

How much should the defendant be punished because of their actions and to deter the defendant and others from similar actions in the future? Note that the compensatory damages that the defendant must pay do not count as part of the punishment. Please circle the number that best expresses the *jury's* judgment of the *appropriate level of punishment.*

None		Mild		Substantial		Severe		Extremely Severe
0	1	2	3	4	5	6	7	8

$ Damages

What amount of punitive damages (if any) should the defendant be required to pay as punishment and to deter the defendant and others from similar actions in the future? Note that the compensatory damages that the defendant must pay do not count as part of the punishment. Please write the *amount of punitive damages* that the *jury* agreed on in the blank below.

$ _____

Fig. 3.1. Response-Mode Manipulation

rating. In part 3 a new individual response form was distributed, which asked participants to record a second personal judgment for the same case, using the complementary type of verdict (punishment rating or dollar damages) to the one they had already used. In part 4 the jury again deliberated to reach a unanimous verdict on this second type of judgment for the same case. Thus, for each individual and for each jury, we have *both* a dollar award *and* a punishment rating for the case they considered. We use the terms *dollar judgments* and *punishment judgments* to refer to the dollar awards and punishment ratings made by individuals. For juries, we will refer to these as *dollar verdicts* and *punishment verdicts*. For purposes of understanding real-world behavior, the dollar awards are, of course, most important. We inquired into punishment ratings both to understand the relation between punishment judgments and dollar awards, and to see the effect of deliberation on both of these.

The case materials consisted of fifteen personal injury scenarios (summarized in table 3.1). A videotape was prepared for each case, in which a professional actor read the text of the case and all instructions aloud. To maximize comprehension, participants were required both to view the videotape and to read the written version. The size of the defendant firm (annual profits of $100 to $200 million) and compensatory damages ($200,000) were the same for all cases. Thus, the variability we observe cannot be accounted for by a model that depends on variability in compensatory damages awards or the defendant's ability to pay.

III. Results
A. *Preliminaries*

Notwithstanding the half-hour time limit for deliberation, 91% of juries reached a unanimous verdict on a punishment rating (a total of 461 verdicts), and 82% of juries reached a unanimous verdict on a dollar award (a total of 416 verdicts). The remainder had not reached a verdict when the time limit expired; these were treated as hung. All further analyses were conducted on the 401 juries that reached both a punishment verdict and a dollar verdict. Because there were no statistically significant differences between the verdicts of juries that judged dollars first and those who judged punishment first, we analyzed verdicts made by dollars-first juries and dollars-second juries together.

Table 3.1. Summary of Personal Injury Scenarios

Case	Description
Williams v. National Motors	Motorcycle driver injured when brakes fail
Smith v. Public Entertainment	Circus patron shot in arm by drunk security guard
Douglas v. Coastal Industries	Auto air bag opens unexpectedly, injuring driver
Sanders v. A&G Cosmetics	Man suffers skin damage from using baldness cure
Stanley v. Gersten Productions	Elderly woman suffers back injuries from using exercise video
Glover v. General Assistance	Child ingests large quantity of allergy medicine, needs hospital stay
Lawson v. TGI International	Employee suffers anemia due to benzene exposure on the job
Newton v. Novel Clothing	Small child playing with matches burned when pajamas catch on fire
West v. MedTech	Disabled man injured when wheelchair lift malfunctions
Windsor v. Int. Computers	Secretary chronically ill due to radiation from computer monitor
Reynolds v. Marine Sulphur	Seaman injured when molten sulfur container fails
Crandall v. C&S Railroad	Train hits car at crossing, injuring driver
Dulworth v. Global Elevator	Shopper injured in fall when escalator suddenly stops
Hughes v. Jardel	Store employee raped in mall parking lot
Nelson v. Trojan Yachts	Man nearly drowns when defective boat sinks

B. Overview

How do the verdicts of deliberating juries compare to those of statistical juries? Our basic topic is the effect of deliberation on juror judgments, assessed by comparing the jury's verdict to the median predeliberation judgment of the individuals who composed that jury. We will refer to the median predeliberation judgment of the individuals in a jury as the verdict of the *statistical jury*. For purposes of understanding the effects of deliberation, we compare the verdicts of deliberating juries with those of statistical juries.

The results observed for the fifteen cases are shown in table 3.2. (The columns labeled *DSM* are explained later.) The cases are arranged in the

Table 3.2 Median Verdicts for Deliberating and Statistical Juries

	Punishment Verdicts			Dollar Verdicts		
Case	Statis-tical Juries	Delib-erating Juries	Average DSM	Statistical Juries	Delib-erating Juries	Average DSM
Reynolds	5.5	6.0	15%	1,875,000	10,000,000	54%
Glover	5.0	5.0	1	1,000,000	4,000,000	52
Lawson	4.3	4.5	4	475,000	2,000,000	53
Williams	5.0	5.0	14	550,000	1,500,000	46
Smith	5.5	6.0	19	325,000	1,000,000	52
Nelson	5.0	5.0	20	450,000	1,000,000	48
Hughes	5.0	5.0	12	450,000	1,000,000	45
West	4.5	5.0	9	500,000	1,000,000	34
Douglas	4.0	4.0	11	225,000	500,000	40
Crandall	4.0	4.0	−8	200,000	500,000	35
Sanders	3.5	3.0	−8	50,500	100,000	25
Windsor	3.0	2.0	−26	37,500	50,000	38
Stanley	1.0	1.5	0	0	0	0
Dulworth	0.3	0.0	−15	0	0	17
Newton	0.0	0.0	3	0	0	23
Mean of Top 5	5.1	5.3	11	845,000	3,700,000	51
Mean of Middle 5	4.5	4.6	9	365,000	800,000	40
Mean of Bottom 5	1.6	1.3	−9	17,600	30,000	21
Overall Mean	3.7	3.7	3	409,200	1,510,000	37

table in descending order of the median dollar verdict of deliberating juries. Note first that the median verdicts of deliberating and statistical juries produce very similar rankings of the cases. For dollars, there is a Spearman rank correlation[1] of .88 between the deliberating and statistical jury verdicts in table 3.2; for punishment verdicts, the average rank correlation is even higher, at .98. Furthermore, the correlation between punishment verdicts and dollar verdicts is also high, at .87. These results confirm an essential finding of chapter 2: Judgments of punitive intent

1. The Spearman rank correlation is an index of agreement between rankings that is analogous to first converting each column to ranks (from 1 to 15 in this case) and then computing the correlation between the two sets of ranks. It is interpreted similarly to conventional correlations.

and of dollar awards share the same core of moral outrage and, therefore, produce the same ordering of cases, at least in the aggregate.

While there is agreement on the *ordering* of cases, the *level* of verdicts tells a different tale. Punishment verdicts are, on average, quite close for statistical and deliberating juries, but dollar verdicts show a dramatic difference: Deliberating juries produce much higher awards, especially at, but not only at, the high end. Indeed, 83% of the 330 nonzero dollar verdicts are above the median individual for that jury. This is the most important finding in the study: the severity shift in dollar verdicts.

In summary, then, aggregate verdicts from deliberating and statistical juries show strong agreement on the relative egregiousness of the cases; and for punishment verdicts, they do not dramatically diverge. Deliberating juries, however, produce dollar verdicts that far exceed the median of the jurors who composed them. We now try to understand how this pattern might occur. To do so, we divide decisions into three parts: (1) the decision about whether to punish at all; (2) the decision about the appropriate punishment verdict; and (3) the decision about the appropriate dollar verdict. As we shall see, the effects of deliberation are quite different for the three decisions.

C. Punish or Not Punish: A Majority Model

The first decision for a jury is, presumably, to determine whether to punish or to reject punishment by a verdict of $0 in damages or a zero punishment rating. Table 3.3 shows the percentage of nonzero verdicts that were made by juries, depending on the initial distribution of judgments among the jurors. The pattern is identical for punishment and dollar verdicts: When a majority of juror judgments is zero (i.e., four or more), the jury verdict is virtually certain itself to be zero. When a majority of jurors has nonzero judgments, the jury verdict is virtually certain not to be zero. Finally, if the jury is evenly split, the chance of a zero

Table 3.3. Percentage of Nonzero Verdicts as a Function of Predeliberation Judgments

Individual Predeliberation Judgments	Jury Verdicts	
	Nonzero Punishment Ratings	Nonzero $ Awards
Majority nonzero	99%	98%
Even split	48%	45%
Majority zero	8%	4%

verdict is about fifty-fifty. Without detailed analysis of the deliberation transcripts, we do not know whether juries actually voted or explicitly agreed to adopt a majority-decision rule. We observe only that the pattern of results is very consistent with the adoption of such a rule. In contrast to other phases of the jury decision that we consider later, there is no evidence of any systematic effect of deliberation on outcomes (i.e., juries were no more or less likely to punish than their jurors). Thus, for the decision of whether or not to impose punitive damages, there is no indication of any asymmetry of power or influence between jurors who were initially inclined to say "yes" and those who were inclined to say "no."

D. Deliberation-Shift Analysis

We now turn to the severity of punishment verdicts chosen by the juries that determined that some punishment was appropriate. We wish to examine the relationship between the postdeliberation verdict of a jury and the predeliberation distribution of judgments among its members. For this purpose, we introduce a *deliberation-shift analysis,* which we will apply to both punishment ratings and dollar awards. The predeliberation judgments of jurors are first ranked, from the most lenient to the most severe; the eventual verdict of the jury is then inserted in that ordering, and its rank is computed. For example, suppose that the individual jurors had predeliberation judgments of $0, $200,000, $300,000, $500,000, $1 million, and $5 million, and that the jury verdict was $750,000. The jury verdict ranks fifth in the distribution of individual judgments of its members. In this instance the jury was more severe than four of its original members and less severe than two of its members, indicating that overall deliberation made judgments more severe.

If the outcomes of deliberation were determined by a simple voting model, the jury verdict would always be in the middle of the distribution of initial judgments, at the median. There would be no shift toward greater leniency or more punishment. With no shift for a jury of six (with the jury verdict added as the seventh member), the predicted position of the jury in the distribution of the opinions of its members is always fourth. The deliberation-shift measure (DSM) is the *difference* between the observed and the predicted rank of the jury verdict, as a percentage of the maximum possible shift in that direction. To continue our dollar example above, since the jury ranks fifth among its jurors, the difference would be $5 - 4 = 1$. For a jury of six, the maximum possible upward shift is $7 - 4 = 3$, and the DSM would be $\frac{1}{3} \times 100 = 33\%$. This means that the rank of the jury verdict was 33% of the way from the rank of the median juror (4) to the rank of the maximum juror (7).[2] DSM is positive if the jury is more severe than its median member; it is negative if the jury is more lenient than its median member. If the jury verdict was higher than the maximum juror, DSM would be 100%; if it was lower than the minimum juror, DSM would be −100%. To study the systematic effects of deliberation, we computed DSM for every nonhung jury, separately for punishment verdicts and for dollar verdicts. Table 3.2 shows the mean values of DSM for each of the fifteen cases for both punishment and dollar verdicts.

E. Punishment Ratings Either Up or Down

For punishment verdicts, there is a clear pattern in the results, which can be observed both in the column of DSM values and by comparing the statistical and deliberated verdicts: Deliberation increased the severity of punishment for high-punishment cases and reduced it for low-punishment cases. Reading down the table, DSM is positive for nine of the top ten cases and negative for four of the bottom five cases. There was a severity shift for the high-punishment cases and a leniency shift for the low-punishment cases.

Because the table is arranged roughly in decreasing order of punitive intent, we can see that DSM is positive for high-punishment cases (average for the top ten cases is 10%) and negative (−9%) for low-punishment cases. Further, the correlation between DSM and the median statistical jury verdicts is .67, which means that the more severe the individual predeliberation judgments, the greater the shift. We therefore observe systematic *choice shifts,* in which deliberation generally increases differences among cases, by making severe verdicts more severe and lenient verdicts more lenient, relative to the predeliberation judgments of jurors.

F. Dollar Awards and the Severity Shift: Deliberation Increases Punitive Damages

We now turn to the more important task of understanding the remarkable difference between the dollar awards obtained from deliberating juries and from a statistical pooling of the predeliberation opinions of jury members. The basic result is that deliberation causes awards to

---

2. Because the DSM is formulated as a percentage, it can be computed for, and has the same interpretation for, a jury of any size.

increase, and it causes high awards to increase a great deal. As extreme but actual illustrations of the severity shift, consider a few examples from the raw data:

- A jury whose predeliberation judgments were $200,000, $300,000, $2 million, $10 million, $10 million, and $10 million reached a verdict of $15 million.
- A jury whose predeliberation judgments were $200,000, $500,000, $2 million, $5 million, and $10 million reached a verdict of $50 million.
- A jury whose predeliberation judgments were $2 million, $2 million, $2.5 million, $50 million, and $100 million reached a verdict of $100 million.

Now consider the DSM column for dollar verdicts in table 3.2. Recall that the value of DSM is positive if the jury verdict is more severe than the median judgment of its jurors, and negative if the jury is more lenient. The pattern of results is very clear: DSM is generally positive, indicating that deliberation generally produced a severity shift. Furthermore, DSM for dollar verdicts is much higher for high-punishment cases than for low-punishment cases: The correlation between the median punishment verdict and DSM for dollar verdicts is .95.

The difference between deliberating and statistical juries is very large, especially for the high-punishment cases: For the top ten cases in table 3.2, the average DSM of 46% means that the jury verdict is about halfway between the second-highest and third-highest individual judgments. Even more surprising, for the ten high-punishment cases, 10% of jury verdicts were *even higher* than the highest individual judgment (i.e., the DSM was 100% for these juries). A further 17% of verdicts were equal to the highest individual judgment (i.e., a DSM of 83%). These extreme verdicts were less common for the five low-punishment cases: 15% of verdicts equaled the highest individual judgment, and none exceeded this maximum. The pattern is clear: Deliberation made dollar verdicts more severe, especially for high-punishment cases.

Notably, we did not find that the degree of dispersion between individual predeliberation judgments contributed to greater or lesser shifts as a result of deliberation. For example, for juries with nonzero verdicts for the same case, the average correlation between the standard deviation of individual judgments (a measure of dispersion) and the DSM was $-.05$ for dollars and .08 for punishment (neither correlation is statistically different from zero). In other words, juries whose members were in rough agreement (i.e., had a low standard deviation) about dollars or punishment did not show a different shift from groups whose members were in substantial disagreement about dollars or punishment.

G. Do People from Arizona Agree with People from Texas? The Effects of Geography, Race, Gender, Education, Age, and Wealth

A subsidiary but nonetheless important question is whether the findings of chapter 2 are replicated under the current study's changes in stimuli, procedure, and sample. The answer is that the previous results were replicated in every essential respect. The findings in Texas were replicated in Arizona, despite evident differences between the two regions, and people from the two areas evaluated cases in the same way. As before, dollars and ratings produce very similar rankings of the cases (a rank correlation of .90 compared to .91 in the previous study[3]). Different demographic groups again produced very similar average evaluations, as indicated by the extremely high correlations in table 3.4.

In addition, the ordering of case evaluations closely matches that in chapter 2. There are ten cases that are common to both studies, and evaluations made by Texans in the previous study are highly predictive of those made by Arizonans in the current study—the rank correlation between the two samples is .90 for punishment ratings and .98 for dollar awards. Thus, the current larger study, with several nontrivial changes, confirms the conclusion that individual moral judgments are predictable and shared, but that expressing them in dollars produces unpredictability and confusion, and especially so in juries.

H. With Respect to Dollars, How Predictable Are Jury Verdicts?

An important goal of the legal system is to treat the similarly situated similarly. Chapter 2 showed that both the dollar judgments of individuals and the dollar verdicts of statistical juries would probably fail this test of procedural justice because of a high degree of unpredictability in damages awards for the same case, as well as inconsistency in distinguishing between cases of more and less egregious conduct. Among

---

3. Cass R. Sunstein et al., "Assessing Punitive Damages (with Notes on Cognition and Valuation in Law)," 107 *Yale L.J.* 2071 (1998); Daniel Kahneman et al., "Shared Outrage and Erratic Awards: The Psychology of Punitive Awards," 16 *J. Risk Uncertainty* 49 (1998).

Table 3.4. Correlations between Demographic Groups
on Intended Severity of Punishments

Gender		Men		
	Women	.99		

Ethnicity		White	Hispanic	
	Hispanic	.92		
	Other	.88	.81	

Household Income		< 30K	30–50K	
	30–50K	.98		
	> 50K	.99	.99	

Age		< 30	30–39	40–49
	30–39	.97		
	40–49	.96	.97	
	> 50	.96	.97	.97

Note: Entries are correlations between mean responses to scenarios by respondents in the indicated demographic categories.

many in the legal community, there is the hope, and indeed the conviction, that deliberation by a group of jurors will overcome individual biases and produce more just and more predictable verdicts. As will be seen, our findings lend no support to this view.

The simplest and most practical criterion for predictability is reflected in the distribution of possible verdicts for a given case (a criterion that asks the extent to which the *identically* situated are treated identically). This is, of course, a critical piece of information for a lawyer advising a client about whether or not to settle a dispute, or for an actor contemplating liability for a potentially tortious course of conduct. In our sample we have multiple independent juries rendering punitive damages verdicts for the same case, and this information can be used to estimate verdict distributions.

Table 3.5 presents selected distributional statistics for each case. The range of possible dollar verdicts is strikingly large. For example, each of the top five cases has a minimum award of $500,000 or less, and yet the average maximum award for these cases is over $83 million. Further, the maximum verdicts are ten to five hundred times as large as the median verdicts (for cases with nonzero medians). Even for the three cases at the bottom with zero medians (i.e., a majority of juries for that case awarded no punitive damages), plaintiffs could still be awarded $500,000. Also, although there is considerable noise (in part because the number of juries

Table 3.5. Percentiles of Jury Dollar Verdicts, by Case (in thousands of dollars)

	Minimum			Median			Maximum
Case	0th	10th	25th	50th	75th	90th	100th
Reynolds	250	1,000	3,500	10,000	17,500	50,000	100,000
Glover	500	1,000	1,250	4,000	10,000	50,000	100,000
Lawson	200	250	1,000	2,000	6,000	15,000	100,000
Williams	100	200	700	1,500	5,000	10,000	15,500
Smith	0	100	300	1,000	7,000	20,000	100,000
Nelson	100	250	500	1,000	5,000	5,000	100,000
Hughes	0	200	850	1,000	2,000	20,000	40,000
West	1	200	500	1,000	2,000	4,000	10,000
Crandall	0	50	250	500	1,450	2,000	100,000
Douglas	0	1	250	500	1,000	25,000	50,000
Sanders	0	0	0	100	500	1,000	50,000
Windsor	0	0	0	50	400	5,000	25,000
Newton	0	0	0	0	75	200	500
Dulworth	0	0	0	0	40	300	500
Stanley	0	0	0	0	25	250	500
Mean of Top 5	210	510	1,350	3,700	9,100	29,000	83,100
Mean of Middle 5	20	140	470	800	2,290	11,200	60,000
Mean of Bottom 5	0	0	0	30	208	1,350	15,300
Overall Mean	77	217	607	1,510	3,866	13,850	52,800

for each case is relatively small), the range of verdicts for a given case tends to increase in proportion to the median verdict. Note that these variations between juries occurred on identical presentations of identical facts, unaffected by differences in, for example, compensatory awards or lawyers' presentations.

To make the uncertainty of these dollar verdicts more concrete, imagine that a statistically sophisticated and greatly experienced lawyer is advising a defendant about a possible punitive damages award on the basis of the data illustrated by table 3.5. For the purpose of the illustration, assume that the lawyer is known to be not only sophisticated but also wise and able to make unbiased predictions of jury decisions: When she states that her best guess is an award of X, the actual award is equally likely to be above or below X (this is her estimate of the median award). On the basis of our data, the lawyer would be able to provide the client with the following information:

> My best guess is that you will face a judgment of $X. There are equal chances that it will be higher or lower than this amount. However, there is a lot of uncertainty about how much higher or lower it will be: There is a 10% chance that you will have to pay more than a times that amount —and there is a 10% chance that you will have to pay less than $1/b$ of that amount.

Averaging across cases, the best estimates[4] of a and b, respectively, are 7.74 and 6.61. On the basis of these values, a lawyer who predicts a verdict of $2 million should also estimate that there is a 10% chance that the actual verdict will be over $15.48 million and a 10% chance that it will be less than $300,000. Because the range increases proportionately with the mean (except for noise), the same values of a and b apply for any value of X.[5] Finally, these estimates assume a jury of six. The uncertainty would very likely be reduced somewhat with a larger jury.[6]

I. Are Deliberating Juries More Predictable than Statistical Juries?

In the introduction to this chapter, we asked whether deliberating juries would produce dollar verdicts that are more predictable than those of statistical juries. We can now use the a and b analysis above to answer this question. As with the verdicts of deliberating juries, variability in the

---

4. These estimates are obtained in two steps: (1) Compute the following ratios for each case—90th percentile/median and median/10th percentile. (2) Compute the geometric mean across cases for each ratio. The geometric mean is the standard method for averaging ratios. The estimates reported here are for the nine cases that have neither a median of zero or a 10th percentile of zero (see table 3.4).

5. To test for proportionality, we run a regression of the difference between the 90th and 10th percentiles for a given case on the median for that case. If the range goes up proportionately with the median, then this regression should have a good fit, and the constant in the regression should be close to zero. In fact, the line fits quite well ($R2 = .66$) and the constant is not significantly different from zero ($p > .05$).

6. Because statistical uncertainty is proportional to the size of the jury, we can approximate how much smaller a and b would be for a jury of twelve, under the assumption that uncertainty in deliberating juries would reduce at the same rate as in a statistical jury. In this case, since the jury would be twice as large, we divide a and b by the square root of 2. The resulting estimates are $a = 4.67$ and $b = 5.47$, which in the lawyer advice example would produce a predicted verdict range of $430,000 to $10.94 million.

verdicts of statistical juries is roughly proportional to the median verdict. We can apply the same procedure as before to estimate the factors *a* and *b*, which measure the estimated relationship of the 10th and 90th percentiles for each case to the median award for that case.

For statistical juries, our estimates of *a* and *b* are 2.88 and 4.11, which are both far less than the corresponding figures of 6.61 and 7.74 for deliberating juries. In our example above, the lawyer's predicted range for a statistical jury verdict would be from $690,000 to $8.22 million compared to the range for a deliberating jury verdict of $300,000 to $15.48 million. Obviously, there is far less uncertainty about the verdicts of statistical juries than about those of deliberating juries.

This pattern is remarkably consistent across cases. There is greater uncertainty in deliberating jury verdicts for each of the ten cases for which *a* can be calculated (those with nonzero medians) and greater uncertainty for eleven of the twelve cases for which *b* can be calculated (those with nonzero 10th percentiles). It is important to note that this estimation procedure effectively controls for the severity shift, and, therefore, that these differences are not due merely to the generally higher level of verdicts by deliberating juries. We conclude, rather to our surprise, that deliberation is a significantly poorer way of aggregating opinions than is statistical pooling—at least if the goal is to decrease the arbitrary unpredictability of awards.

IV. What Happened?

By far the most striking finding in our data is the severity shift produced by deliberation. What mechanism causes a jury to decide on an award that exceeds the initial judgment of its median member—and sometimes to exceed the highest predeliberation judgment of all its members?

Some of our findings seem connected with the well-known finding of group polarization.[7] After deliberation, groups tend to end up in a more extreme position in the same direction as their predeliberation tendency. For example, group members who tend to approve of affirmative action programs are likely after deliberation to approve of affirmative action programs all the more; group members who tend to oppose gun control

7. See Roger William Brown, *Social Psychology* (2nd ed., 1986); and Cass R. Sunstein, "Deliberative Trouble? Why Groups Go to Extremes," 110 *Yale L.J.* 71 (2000).

are likely after discussion to oppose gun control with some vehemence. With respect to punishment ratings, our study seems to have found group polarization, with high rankings (those over 3) increasing as a result of deliberation and low rankings decreasing.

The mechanisms that underlie group polarization have been extensively studied, and those mechanisms bear directly on what we have observed. When a group is inclined in a certain direction, most of the publicly expressed arguments will be made in that same direction, thus heightening people's sense that the original tendency makes sense. Informational influences will therefore move people to think that evidently egregious wrongdoing was egregious indeed. Social influences matter, too: People generally do not want to be seen as being mildly disapproving of conduct that most people find abhorrent, or as being severely disapproving of conduct that most people do not greatly mind. These points help explain what we have found with respect to punishment ratings. They also seem to explain why small awards increased less than large awards: With the latter, members were generally in favor of strong dollar punishment, and discussion increased the strength of that inclination. But what explains the generality of the severity shift? Why do dollar awards increase across-the-board?

We hypothesize that a feature of deliberation, a rhetorical asymmetry, helps produce the one-way movement that we observe. Specifically, once the jury has agreed that there will be a nonzero dollar award, the arguments for a larger award have a rhetorical advantage and are more persuasive. If this is the case, then a jury would be drawn disproportionately toward the larger predeliberation judgments of its jurors. No such asymmetry would be expected for the punishment scale, if it is hypothesized that social norms give the advantage not to anyone arguing that the conduct of a corporate defendant was "worse" in the abstract, but to anyone arguing for a higher dollar award against a corporate defendant. The key point has to do with the translation of a punishment judgment into a dollar award; those who argue that "more" money is necessary to punish a corporation appear to have an upper hand. The unbounded dollar scale affords great latitude in the expression of what "more" means.

To examine the hypothesis of rhetorical asymmetry more directly, we conducted a small follow-up test, asking eighty-seven University of Chicago law students whether it would be harder to argue for a smaller or a larger award. In this study respondents were simply told that they were deliberating about punitive damages awards and were given no details of any case. They were first asked to generate arguments for a higher or lower award, and then asked which award (higher or lower) would be easier to justify. Half of the students were asked to argue for a higher award; half were asked to argue for a lower one. After generating the relevant arguments, they were asked to complete a second task, which went as follows:

> Imagine that a jury in a civil trial is deliberating about a personal injury case in which the defendant is a large corporation (with annual profits of approximately $200 million). The jury has already (a) unanimously ordered the defendant to pay an amount of compensatory damages that fully compensates the plaintiff, and (b) unanimously concluded that while the underlying conduct was not truly horrendous, it was sufficiently reckless to justify an award of punitive damages as well (in addition to compensatory damages).
>
> In general, which position would you expect to be harder for a juror to argue for in a deliberation? (Please circle the letter of your answer.)
> a) It is harder to argue that damages should be higher. [15%]
> b) It is harder to argue that damages should be lower. [55%]
> c) The positions are equally hard to argue for. [30%]

The students were expressly told not to begin the second task (assessing the comparative difficulty question) until after they had completed the first (making arguments one way or the other).

The results supported our hypothesis: A clear majority (55%) thought that arguing for a lower award would be the more difficult rhetorical position. Further, of those who showed a preference, the margin was almost four to one that arguing for a larger award is easier. Moreover, there was no effect of being asked to justify a higher or lower award; both groups agreed that it is harder to argue for a lower award. It seems likely that a rhetorical asymmetry played a substantial role in producing jury verdicts consistently above the median individual, and sometimes even above the highest individual.

Another explanation for the severity shift would suggest that groups move toward the mean of individual dollar judgments, rather than the median. Because individual dollar judgments are skewed to the right and include many extreme judgments, the mean will be above the median (this is true for 91% of juries) and could account, in theory, for the higher level of verdicts. From an analysis of the data, our basic conclusion is that while it is possible that movements toward the mean may have played some role in producing severity shifts, this cannot be the fundamental explanation. The simplest demonstration of this comes from the fact that 27% of nonzero jury dollar verdicts were as high as or higher than that of the highest predeliberation dollar judgment of individuals. But a fuller explanation requires a more detailed analysis.

To examine the hypothesis that the mean of individual awards would predict jury dollar verdicts and hence the severity shift, we recomputed the statistical jury results using the mean individual judgment, rather than the median.[8] As expected, the mean juror produces higher dollar verdicts than the median juror, although it is still lower than 64% of nonzero jury verdicts (albeit an improvement over the 83% figure for the median juror). This partial success, however, comes at a high price. Even though the mean juror is consistently higher than the median juror (and seemingly closer to jury verdicts), it is less reliable and is actually a worse predictor of jury verdicts on the conventional measures of predictive success: It explains less of the variance in jury verdicts (4% vs. 26%) and has larger prediction errors on average (compared to the median juror predictions, the root-mean-square error[9] for the mean juror is 2.21 times larger, and the mean absolute error is 1.53 times larger). The choice between the median and the mean primarily means choosing between types of errors—with the median juror, the statistical jury's verdict is almost always too low but almost never disastrously wrong. With the mean juror, the signs of the errors are more balanced (⅔ too low and ⅓ too high), but there can occasionally be huge positive errors (i.e., mean juror far above the jury verdict).[10] Thus, even if the mean juror with its higher overall levels did fit jury verdicts better (and it does not), we would still need to account for a consistent upward movement in jury verdicts, relative to the mean juror, and for those verdicts that are at or above the maximum individual judgment in that jury.

8. For punishment verdicts (not depicted here for clarity), switching to the mean as the basis for statistical juries has little effect because of the low level of skewness in the distribution of punishment judgments.

9. The root-mean-square error (RMSE) is calculated by first computing the differences between the predicted verdict (i.e., the median or average of predeliberation jurors) and the actual verdict (the jury verdict), taking the square of each difference, and then taking the square root of the average squared difference. In regression the predicted value of the regression equation plays the same role as the mean or median do here, and the RMSE is thus analogous to the standard error of a regression (the estimate of σ). The mean absolute error (MAE) is computed by taking the average of the absolute values (i.e., the magnitude, regardless of its sign) of the differences.

10. This is usually due to the presence of one or two extremely high individual judgments in a jury.

V. Conclusion

We have found that as compared with the median of individual judgments, deliberation makes low-punishment judgments decrease and high-punishment judgments increase. It also makes—and this is our most important finding—dollar awards generally increase, while making high-dollar awards substantially increase, in a general severity shift. We have also found, somewhat to our surprise, that deliberating juries produce more unpredictability than would be found by taking the median of pre-deliberation judgments from jurors.

These findings have four major implications. First, moral judgments about personal injury cases are very widely shared over diverse communities and demographic categories. Second, those shared moral judgments do not produce predictable dollar awards. Third, dollar awards reflect a systematic severity shift, apparently a result of a rhetorical asymmetry in which arguments for higher awards have a general advantage over arguments for lower awards. Fourth, the problem of unpredictable and erratic dollar verdicts is increased, not alleviated, by the fact that juries are deliberative bodies.

4

Do Plaintiffs' Requests and Plaintiffs' Identities Matter?

Reid Hastie, David A. Schkade, and John W. Payne

I. Introduction

The prior two chapters make it clear that punitive damages amounts are highly unpredictable due to the use of the dollar scale, and that deliberation makes the problem worse. Is there, however, any predictability to the magnitudes of dollar awards for the same basic legal case? Further, are dollar amounts systematically higher or lower as a function of variables that should not matter from the standpoint of the legal system? This chapter presents experimental data showing that the answers to those two questions are "yes" and "yes!" Specifically, the following results were found:

- The dollar amounts that are requested by plaintiffs in their closing arguments to a jury have a dramatic effect on the size of the punitive damages award: the higher the request, the higher the awards. Almost half of the jurors said that the plaintiff's award request influenced their judgment process; analysis of the data indicates that the greater their reliance on the plaintiff's request, the higher the awards. Judges' instructions that arguments by the plaintiff's lawyer are not evidence did not eliminate this effect.
- Local plaintiffs are awarded more than geographically remote plaintiffs, while the location of the defendant company does not have reliable effects on awards. The local-plaintiff effect occurred even though the lead plaintiff in the case studied was a profit-seeking company, not an individual.

II. Background and Hypotheses

As suggested earlier in this volume, the processes involved in the awarding of punitive damages can usefully be broken down into two stages. First, the juror decides whether the defendant's behavior was sufficiently egregious or reprehensible that punitive damages are warranted. Factors that influence the reprehensibility of an injurious action are summarized in the law (and jury instructions) on punitive damages: causality, foreseeability, intentionality, and malicious attitude.[1] Previous research has shown that these factors are considered,[2] although both individuals and juries are far from thorough in their evaluations.[3]

Second, the juror attempts to translate the desire to punish into a dollar value. As noted in chapter 2, this constitutes the mapping of an internal judgment onto an unbounded magnitude scale. Translation of punitive intent to a dollar award appears to be very unreliable, as would be predicted from prior research involving magnitude scales. Further, the use of an unbounded dollar scale (a magnitude scale) is often subject to anchoring effects. Anchoring effects follow from a natural judgmental process of starting from an initial value for a response and then adjusting to yield a final decision. Typically, however, adjustments from the initial value are insufficient. Consequently, judgments tend to be anchored on the initial values, regardless of their reasonableness.[4] However, one would expect anchoring effects to be particularly strong in the case of punitive damages awards because of the need to use a magnitude-type scale (dollars) to translate punitive intent into a response, and because of the complex and unfamiliar nature of this judgment task. In particular, an *ad damnum* request by a plaintiff is likely to serve as an anchor in assessing punitive damages awards even when jurors are instructed that arguments by the plaintiff's lawyer are not evidence. Thus, the experiments reported in this chapter are designed to extend the extensive literature on anchoring effects to the domain of punitive damages awards, and to test the hypothesis that punitive damages awards will shift predictably toward the salient reference point provided by the plaintiff's request.

1. Neal Feigenson et al., "Effect of Blameworthiness and Outcome Severity on Attributions of Responsibility and Damage Awards in Comparative Negligence Cases," 21 *Law & Hum. Behav.* 597 (1997).

2. Corinne Cather et al., "Plaintiff Injury and Defendant Reprehensibility: Implications for Compensatory and Punitive Damage Awards," 20 *Law & Hum. Behav.* 189 (1996).

3. See chapter 5.

4. See John W. Payne et al., "Behavioral Decision Research: An Overview," in *Measurement, Judgment, and Decision Making* 303 (Michael H. Birnbaum ed., 1998), for a review of anchoring effects in the behavioral decision research literature; and Gretchen B. Chapman and Brian H. Bornstein, "The More You Ask for, the More You Get: Anchoring in Personal Injury Verdicts," 10 *Applied Cognitive Psychol.* 519 (1996), for evidence of anchoring in compensatory awards.

Another factor that has been suggested as influencing punitive damages awards is the identities of parties in a lawsuit. The distinctively high plaintiff's verdicts associated with some geographical locations (e.g., the Bronx, Alabama and Texas state courts, and rural Illinois) have led commentators to hypothesize that some juries are motivated by their power to redistribute wealth from remote (usually corporate) accounts into local (usually individual citizens') pockets.[5] This *wealth-redistribution* hypothesis implies that it is not just a corporation's "deep pockets" that promote high awards, but also the plaintiff's "empty pockets."[6] A recent Supreme Court ruling also suggests that defendant identity might matter: "We agree with TXO that the emphasis on the wealth of the wrongdoer increased the risk that the award may have been influenced by prejudice against large corporations, a risk that is of special concern when the defendant is a nonresident."[7] Our hypotheses are that geographically local (rather than remote) plaintiffs will receive larger awards and that remote defendants will be assessed larger awards.

III. Study Design: Experiment 1
A. *Participants*

One hundred and seventy-four mock jurors (jury-eligible adult citizens) were sampled from the Reno, Nevada, area and were paid for participation.

---

5. Arthur S. Hayes, "Bronx Cheer: Inner-City Jurors Tend to Rebuff Prosecutors and to Back Plaintiffs," 219 *Wall St. J.,* March 24, 1992, at A1; Linda Himelstein, "Jackpots from Alabama Juries: A String of Mammoth Awards Has Insurers Starting to Flee," *Bus. Wk.,* March 24, 1992, at 83; Gregory Jaynes, "Where the Torts Blossom: While Washington Debates Rules about Litigation, Down in Alabama, the Lawsuits Grow Thick and Wild; Excessive Lawsuits and Damage Awards in Barbour County, Alabama," 145 *Time,* March 20, 1995, at 38; George L. Priest, "Punitive Damages Reform: The Case of Alabama," 56 *La. L. Rev.* 825 (1996).

6. Robert J. MacCoun, "Differential Treatment of Corporate Defendants by Juries: An Examination of the 'Deep Pockets' Hypothesis," 30 *Law & Soc'y Rev.* 121 (1996); John C. Turner et al., "Self and Collective: Cognition and Social Context," 20 *Personality & Soc. Psychol. Bull.* 454 (1994).

7. *TXO Prod. Corp. v. Alliance Resources Corp.,* 1993, at 2723. See also Paul H. Rubin et al., "BMW v. Gore: Mitigating the Punitive Economics of Punitive Damages," in *Supreme Court Economic Review,* vol. 5, 179 (Harold Demsetz et al. eds., 1997).

Summary of Experiment

Description: Subjects saw a videotaped narration, then read the same written summary of an environmental accident case and instructions. There were six different versions, identical except for two manipulations of each of three variables: high and low punitive damages award requested by the plaintiff lawyer; local and distant domicile of the plaintiff; and local and distant domicile of the defendant.

Number of subjects: 375 jury-eligible citizens in two experiments.

Location: Reno, Nevada.

Decisions: Individual.

Stimuli: Videotaped narration and written case summary and instructions.

B. Materials

An environmental accident was selected as the basis for stimulus materials (the 1990 accident in which a Southern Pacific train derailed and dumped toxic herbicide into the Sacramento River near Dunsmuir, California). The materials included a detailed description of a train derailment and the spilling of a toxic herbicide into the "Durango River" in northern Nevada. The herbicide polluted a thirty-eight-mile stretch of the river, killing wildlife and destroying a fish hatchery. The plaintiffs were described as "about 150 individuals and businesses," including the owners of the fish hatchery as the lead plaintiff. Extensive expert testimony was presented that demonstrated the multiple causes of the accident, including "string-lining" as the train rounded a curve on a dangerous section of track. Detailed information about the defendant railroad company's financial status was included and abbreviated, but realistic closing arguments were presented. Mock jurors were told that liability for the accident had been established in a prior legal proceeding and that the defendant had paid $24.5 million in compensatory damages and fines. Furthermore, it had been determined that the company's actions constituted reckless conduct and so the consideration of punitive damages was warranted.

Jury instructions based on the punitive damages instructions from one of the actual trials that had ensued after the Sacramento River spill were presented to the mock jurors.[8] The instructions included a discussion of the factors that should be considered and the goals (punishment and deterrence) toward which the award should be directed. The case summary

---

8. They are almost identical to the instructions in Ronald W. Eades and Graham Douthwaite, *Jury Instructions on Damages in Tort Actions* 98–101 (3rd ed., 1993).

and instructions were used as scripts for a thirty-five-minute videotape; written versions of the case and instructions were also provided to each mock juror.

Two award-anchor conditions, low and high, were created by varying the plaintiff's closing argument request for a relatively low level of punitive damages (concluding, "So the range you may want to consider is between $15 million and about half a year's profit, $50 million") or a relatively high level (concluding, "So the range you may want to consider is between $50 million and about a year's profit, $150 million"). The identity of the lead plaintiff was manipulated to create remote-plaintiff and local-plaintiff conditions. In half of the treatments, the plaintiff was described as the Maple Leaf Hatchery, a division of Monarch Foods, headquartered in Toronto, Canada (remote plaintiff); in the other treatments, the plaintiff was described as the Durango River Hatchery (local plaintiff). Finally, the identity of the defendant was manipulated to create a remote defendant and a local defendant. In half of the treatments, the defendant was the Chicago Western Railroad headquartered in Chicago (remote); in the other half, the defendant was the Nevada Pacific Railroad headquartered in Las Vegas (local). The eight possible combinations of the three two-level variables were realized in eight videotaped case summaries. Individual subjects were assigned at random to one of the eight versions of the case.

C. Procedure

Participants were introduced to the mock-jury task and then shown the videotaped stimulus case. They were told that the judge's instructions on the tape were the law and that they should adhere to them in making their individual decisions. The participants were given as much time as they wanted to study the written case materials and instructions and to take handwritten notes (an average of fifteen minutes was used studying the written materials).

After the mock jurors finished studying the case, they completed a verdict form that first asked them if they thought a punitive damages award should be awarded. If they answered "yes" to this question, they were asked to assess an award amount in dollars. After rendering their verdicts, the mock jurors completed a second questionnaire that probed the reasons for their judgments. They were asked for a percentage rating of the amount of their award (if any) that was intended to punish the defendant versus to deter the defendant or others. They were also asked to indicate, "What particular actions by the defendant did you intend to punish . . . and what particular actions by the defendant did you intend to deter?" In addition, they were asked to identify the parties or individuals whom they believed would receive and pay out money from any awards and the degree to which an award would benefit or cost the residents of the state of Nevada. Memory for the judge's instructions was also measured (and, consistent with the results of other studies reported in this book, was poor). Finally, demographic information and political preference information was obtained from each mock juror.

IV. Results: Experiment 1
A. Punitive Damages Awards

The distributions of dollar awards from the individual jurors, separated into high- and low-anchor conditions, are displayed in figure 4.1. The dollar awards are distributed asymmetrically, with a long "tail" of high values and a large "lump" of zero values (27% indicated no award should be made). A few high awards stand out against the rest as outliers: one at $275 million, one at $500 million, and one huge award at $1.06 billion dollars. This last outlier response value will be eliminated from most of our statistical analyses (however, the mock juror's source of this specific value is clear: $1.06 billion was the amount of the defendant company's net worth, described in a financial report presented as evidence). Overall, the present results are consistent with other research in this volume, and elsewhere, showing large variability in punitive damages awards.

There are several popular values in the distribution that can be associated with numbers that were salient in the case materials (e.g., $24 million was the amount of compensatory damages already paid). The $15 and $50 million values, the median awards in the low- and high-anchor conditions, are especially interesting because they appear to be compromise judgments: the lower dollar figure requested by the plaintiff's attorney in the low- and high-anchor conditions respectively.

The mean values with the single highest value deleted are reported in table 4.1 along with other descriptive statistics. The manipulated variables all produced effects in the predicted directions, however, only the plaintiff's request (low vs. high anchor) had statistically reliable effects on the dollar-award amounts. Note that the mean (and median) awards

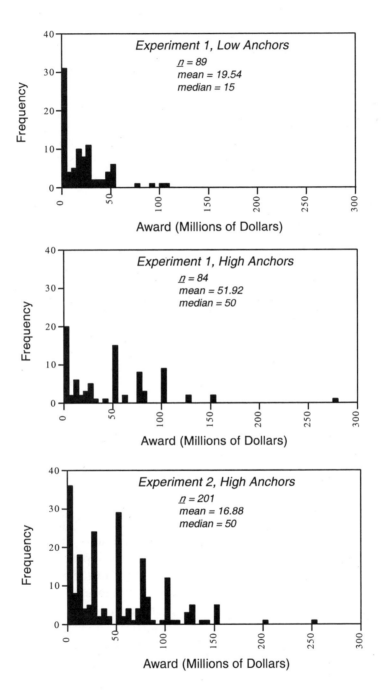

Table 4.1. Results of Experiment 1

Anchor	Low ($15–50 million)				High ($50–150 million)			
Defendant	Local		Remote		Local		Remote	
Plaintiff	Remote	Local	Remote	Local	Remote	Local	Remote	Local
n	23	25	21	20	18	22	20	23
Mean	15.22	17.06	24.49	22.40	39.06	64.73	43.10	57.39
Median	5.00	15.00	20.00	13.50	45.00	50.00	15.50	50.00
Std. deviation	21.92	16.93	20.98	30.66	34.31	104.75	65.34	45.57
Proportion of zero awards	.48	.24	.24	.20	.28	.23	.30	.17

were about two and a half times larger when the request was high ($50 to $150 million) versus low ($15 to $50 million). Thus, there is some order in the highly variable dollar awards. In particular, the results underscore the central role of salient anchor values in mock jurors' reasoning about awards. The numbers highlighted in the plaintiff's closing argument and the amount of the compensatory award dominated the process of transforming punishment intent into a dollar value. The power of the plaintiff's request is especially impressive given the large collection of numbers that were presented to the mock jurors as evidence to describe the defendant's financial status (two tables containing approximately forty numbers plus accompanying exposition).

Finally, there was a burst of eleven zero awards (48% of the awards) in the remote plaintiff, local defendant, and low-anchor experimental conditions, which would seem to be less favorable to the awarding of punitive damages. However, statistical analyses did not identify this condition as significantly different from the others.

We also asked mock jurors a few questions about their reasoning processes when they set awards. We looked only at mock jurors who set an

Fig. 4.1. Distributions of the dollar awards in the low- ($15 to $50 million) and high- ($50 to $150 million) anchor conditions from the two experiments. (Three outlier values were excluded to make these displays more comprehensible: values of $500 million and $1.06 billion from the experiment 1, high-anchor display, and a value of $4.5 billion from the experiment 2 display.)

award (and excluded the one highest award value). We found considerable diversity across respondents in individual tastes for punishment versus deterrence. The modal response was "fifty-fifty," with a large standard deviation (21 points on the 100-point scale). The motive to punish was associated with higher awards. Finally, punishment was mentioned approximately one and a half times as often as deterrence when jurors described their reasoning processes. Taken together, the results suggest that punishment plays a larger role in thoughts about punitive damages awards than does deterrence.

While there was a slight tendency to redistribute wealth, with larger awards assessed against remote defendants and larger awards assessed for local plaintiffs, neither effect was statistically significant. On the other hand, local plaintiffs received 36% higher awards than remote plaintiffs on average, a difference in median awards of $4.2 million. Therefore, we conducted a second experiment to provide more sensitive tests of the mock jurors' tendency to redistribute wealth from remote defendants to local plaintiffs. We also collected more extensive measures of the participants' considerations in setting their awards as well as more measures of judgment-relevant attitudes, to see if we could develop a clearer picture of the reasoning process and account for more individual difference variance in the awards.

V. Study Design: Experiment 2

A second experiment was conducted—essentially a systematic replication of the four high-anchor conditions from experiment 1 (in which the plaintiff's attorney requests an award in the range between $50 million and $150 million). A more extensive questionnaire was designed to explicate the reasoning processes leading to a punitive judgment. Two experimental variables, plaintiff's geographic location and defendant's geographic location, were manipulated, creating four experimental conditions implemented with the same toxic-spill case materials from the first experiment.

A. Participants and Materials

Two hundred and three jury-eligible adults were sampled from the Reno area by a marketing research firm and were paid for participation in the study. The same stimulus materials and procedures from experiment 1 were repeated in experiment 2. Four of the original experimental conditions (the high-anchor conditions) were included in a between-subjects design.

B. Procedure

Participants were randomly assigned to one of the four experimental conditions and viewed the videotaped trial summaries in groups ranging in size from forty-six to fifty-six participants. An average of approximately fifteen minutes was spent by the participants studying the written case materials after viewing the videotapes, and an additional twenty minutes completing verdict forms and questionnaires.

Following the verdict form, the mock jurors completed a questionnaire that was designed to provide information about their decision processes. Their memories for details from the case materials were tested (e.g., "Who was the defendant in this case [and] where was its headquarters located?"). They responded on a series of scales inquiring about their beliefs concerning specific causes of the accident and motives of the parties at trial (e.g., "The accident was caused by stupidity or carelessness of the company's employees"; "The plaintiff's company seems to be greedy and mostly interested in making money off this lawsuit"). An open-ended question asked them to describe their thinking when they set the dollar award: "Write down a list of instructions that you could tell to someone else so that they would think about an award the same way you did and reach the same conclusion about what the amount should be." Follow-up questions inquired about specific strategies and factors considered (e.g., "I made a lot of numerical calculations to decide on an award"; "I used my personal knowledge about award amounts in other trials to tell me how much to award in this case"; "[I considered] the amount of compensatory damages that had already been paid out"). Finally, respondents were asked for a percentage rating of the amount of their award (if any) that was intended to punish the defendant versus to deter the defendant or others.

VI. Results: Experiment 2
A. Punitive Damages Awards

The distribution of award values is similar to the distributions obtained in experiment 1: asymmetric with long "tails" of higher values and a prominent "lump" (14%) of zero-award values. The zero-award values were distributed evenly across the four experimental conditions. Several

Table 4.2. Results of Experiment 2

Defendant	Local		Remote	
Plaintiff	Remote	Local	Remote	Local
n	48	46	54	55
Mean	37.27	49.44	42.06	58.01
Median	25.00	50.00	25.00	50.00
Std. deviation	33.74	39.31	50.50	47.16
Proportion of zero awards	.17	.07	.21	.13

award values "attracted" many responses—including $50 million and $150 million, the numbers mentioned in the plaintiff's award requests. In addition, "round" values such as $10, $25, $75, and $100 million were used often (see fig. 4.1). One mock juror assessed a damages award that was far higher than the others, $4.5 billion—approximately equal to the total assets of the defendant company (the next highest award was $250 million), and his response was excluded from our statistical analyses.

Table 4.2 presents summary statistics for the four experimental conditions. The magnitude of the significant plaintiff's location effect, awards to the local Durango River Hatchery, is significantly higher than to the remote Maple Leaf Hatchery. The magnitude of this location effect is even larger than in our first study (a 35% difference in the average awards; a 100% difference in the median awards, or a $25 million difference; and remote plaintiffs receive nothing 90% more often than do local plaintiffs). A remote defendant was, on average, assessed a slightly higher dollar value, however, the effect was not significant.

Turning to measures of the reasoning processes, jurors who viewed the accident as caused by the defendant's "desire to make as much profit as possible" and who believed that "the defendant company has caused other accidents but was not caught" gave higher awards. On the other hand, jurors who viewed the defendant as unlucky gave lower awards.

Considering only mock jurors who made awards (dropping the twenty-nine zero-award respondents), 47% indicated that the plaintiff's award requests influenced their judgment process; the greater their reliance on the plaintiff's requests, the higher their awards. Mock jurors who indicated that they relied more heavily on the compensatory damages amount (i.e., $24 million) gave lower awards.

VII. Conclusion

To summarize, in the first experiment, we observed a large effect of the plaintiff's award request. The more the plaintiffs requested, the more they got. The difference in median awards between the low-anchor and high-anchor conditions was $35 million for an identical fact situation. Our various rating and open-ended report measures indicated that the requested values were the second most popular anchor mentioned, while the compensatory damages amount, $24 million, was the most popular.

In the second experiment, punitive damages award amounts were influenced by the plaintiff's location. This finding is not inconsistent with wealth redistribution, but it may be better described as a bias to favor local recipients. On the other hand, we did not find statistically reliable effects due to defendant location. It is possible that our manipulation of defendant location was simply too weak to produce a detectable effect (e.g., the local defendant company was headquartered in Las Vegas, not Reno, where our mock jurors resided, while the local plaintiffs were located near Reno and included private individuals as well as a profit-seeking company).

In addition, we were interested in our mock jurors' reactions to the distinction between the goals of punishment and deterrence articulated in the judge's instructions. In open-ended reports of their decision strategies, participants emphasized punishment over deterrence.

Taken together, our results are consistent with the two-stage framework for the punitive damages judgment process presented in chapter 2. The first stage of that framework involves an evaluation of the reprehensibility of the defendant's actions—actions that may be judged as more severe when a similar (local) person has been harmed. This first stage leads to a judgment (intention) to award punitive damages. The second stage involves a transformation of this intention to punish into a specific dollar-award value. This second stage can best be described as an *anchor-and-insufficient-adjustment process*.[9] Consequently, an arbitrary anchor value can sometimes exert a large influence on the final judgment. In the present research, we interpret the large effect of the plaintiff's dollar-award request as due to its influence as an anchor in mock jurors' judgment processes.

9. Amos Tversky and Daniel Kahneman, "Judgment under Uncertainty: Heuristics and Biases," 185 *Science* 1124 (1974).

The jurors' ratings of their judgment strategies and their open-ended reports on their strategies support the view that the anchor-and-adjust strategy was the most common award-setting strategy. What is less clear, and very important, is the manner in which jurors selected an anchor from the collection of numbers that were available in the evidence and arguments presented at trial. Anchors ranged from thousands of dollars to billions of dollars with little apparent rhyme or reason. They were not highly correlated with mock jurors' backgrounds or attitudes, with their ratings of responsibility (even with their felt anger), or with their intentions to punish versus deter. The selection of an anchor appears to be a somewhat haphazard event that injects great variability into the award-setting process.

In conclusion, the present results reinforce the description of punitive damages awards as highly variable and arbitrary. The broad distribution of individual awards for identical fact situations and the variety of reported award-setting strategies in the two experiments described in this chapter are disturbing. At the end of the process of judging a single fact situation, dollar awards ranged from zero to $4.5 billion. However, the two experiments reported in this chapter do point to the fact that punitive damages awards can be influenced by predicable factors. Specifically, punitive damages awards were influenced by the geographical location of the lead plaintiff and by plaintiffs' requests. With identical evidence and financial circumstances, the awards averaged $14 million higher for the local plaintiffs (much larger, a $59 million difference, if the largest outlier award is included in the data; and the difference in medians was $25 million, a doubling from the case for the remote plaintiffs), even though from the standpoint of the legal system, punitive damages award amounts should not be affected by geography. Similarly, with identical evidence circumstances, the awards were two and a half times larger when the plaintiff's lawyer requested a larger amount. Of course, the plaintiff's request is at least to some extent an arbitrary amount. At a more theoretical level, this effect of the plaintiff's request on the dollar awards is consistent with an anchor-and-insufficient-adjustment process that is likely to be involved in the use of an unbounded-magnitude dollar scale to reflect the reprehensibility of conduct.

B. To Punish or Not?

Introduction

Cass R. Sunstein

Thus far we have been emphasizing jury judgments about dollar awards, because these judgments have received so much attention, and because in the view of most observers, dollar awards are the central ground for concern. But before juries award any amounts at all, they have to make an initial determination, to the effect that a punitive damages award is appropriate. How do juries make that determination?

Recall that under the law, punitive damages generally cannot be awarded merely because the defendant has been negligent, in the sense that the defendant has failed to follow the proper standard of care. The plaintiff must show that the defendant has either (1) intentionally harmed the plaintiff, as in a case of murder, rape, or battery; or (2) recklessly harmed the plaintiff, by engaging in actions with knowledge that the harm would occur, or with a gross deviation from ordinary standards of care. In most of the interesting cases in the real world, the question is one of recklessness: Did the defendant's conduct go beyond negligence, to suggest the level of misconduct that warrants special punishment?

In this section we investigate how jurors answer this question. We find that juries do not carefully follow judicial instructions, and indeed that they are willing to ignore a large number of the legally necessary conditions for punitive damages verdicts. Perhaps most important, we find that juries use everyday habits for the assessment of blame, and that they often substitute those habits for the standards suggested by the legal system. The substitution of *everyday morality* for legal standards, documented here, might well be a pervasive phenomenon in the legal system.

We also find that like everyone else, jurors show hindsight bias: They tend to think that what happened was overwhelmingly likely to happen. In the psychological literature, and to a growing extent within law, it is well-known that people suffer from hindsight bias. We study that bias here because it is centrally important to the determination of liability for punitive damages, and because it has not previously been established in the context of punitive damages awards. The bias can produce mistaken judgments about liability because it inclines jurors to find recklessness in defendants when engaging in the acts that ultimately caused harm.

Whether these findings present problems and, if so, how those problems should be solved are not our concerns here. Our emphasis, instead, is on the extent to which jurors assessing liability for punitive damages proceed like ordinary people—overstating the extent to which unfortunate events were bound to occur and using common moral reasoning to assess recklessness, sometimes at the expense of legal requirements.

5

Judging Corporate Recklessness

Reid Hastie, David A. Schkade, and John W. Payne

I. Introduction

How do individual jurors comprehend evidence, instructions on the law, and then reason to a verdict regarding liability for punitive damages? This chapter reports on a study of juror and jury decision processes when making the liability decision regarding whether punitive damages are warranted or not. A special feature of the study was the use of video-tapes of the mock-jury deliberations to examine the relationships that may exist between the processes of group deliberations and the liability judgments that were reached. We offer the following conclusions:

- Many of the mock juries decided that punitive damages were warranted, although appellate and trial judges had concluded that they were not warranted. Analysis of jury decision processes suggests that the tendency to find the defendant liable was partly due to juries' failure systematically to consider the full set of legally necessary conditions for the verdicts they rendered. Specifically, the typical jury failed to consider even half of the five legally prescribed conditions for a finding that punitive damages are warranted. Nonetheless, approximately 65% of these same juries concluded that the defendant was liable. Significantly, the juries concluding "yes, punitive damages are warranted" were reliably less thorough in their coverage of the legally prescribed conditions than juries concluding that punitive awards were not justified.
- At the individual level, jurors were generally not very good at remembering and comprehending the judge's instructions. Those jurors who were better able to comprehend and recall the instructions were also more likely to decide "not liable."

II. Background and Hypotheses

In a typical jury trial in which punitive damages are sought, there is an initial determination of liability with three possible outcomes: The defendant is not liable for any damages; the evidence demonstrates the defendant's conduct was negligent and only compensatory damages may be warranted; or the defendant's conduct was more than negligent and reached levels of reckless or malicious conduct, and both compensatory and punitive damages may be warranted.[1] A typical set of requirements to conclude that a defendant's conduct was reckless enough to warrant punitive damages includes subjective consciousness of a foreseeable and probable grave danger consequent on the conduct, conscious disregard for the danger by the defendant, conduct that was a gross deviation from an ordinary level of care, and the occurrence of the dangerous outcome. These criteria for punitive damages require jurors to make several cognitively difficult judgments.

As discussed earlier in this book, the explicit goals of punitive damages awards are to deter *and punish* the defendant's conduct. Thus, they are a mixture of civil and criminal law traditions. Jurors can be expected to have a variety of interpretations of these concepts, and this problem is compounded by the lack of clear instructions on these concepts or the provision of examples or standards for award amounts. Supreme Court Justice Stevens has expressed a related concern about punitive damages awards: "The problem that concerns us . . . is that a jury will not follow those instructions and may return a lawless, biased, or arbitrary verdict."[2]

The present research is designed to study the jury's decision of whether a defendant has engaged in malicious or reckless conduct that would warrant a punitive damages award. In particular, we study the behavior of jury-eligible citizens making decisions in realistic, representative civil cases that turn on the question of whether a defendant's conduct is reckless or not. We use a mock-jury simulation method that has proven useful in studies of jurors' decision processes and in providing accurate projections to the outcomes of a real jury.

The four stimulus cases were based on cases that had been subjected

---

1. James D. Ghiaridi and John J. Kircher, *Punitive Damages: Law and Practice* (1995); Arthur F. Roeca, "Damages," in *Toxic Torts: Litigation of Hazardous Substance Cases* 494 (Gary Z. Nothstein ed., 1984).

2. *Honda Motor Co. Ltd. et al. v. Karl L. Oberg,* 114 S. Ct. 2331 (1994), at 2341.

to judicial review, so we can assess the extent to which our mock jurors' verdicts match the legally endorsed verdicts. Because we have the conclusions from judicial review, we will attempt to identify the differences in processes that discriminate between juror decisions that are consistent and inconsistent with the decisions of judges. The cases we selected are difficult. We hoped that the cases would generate a range of opinions. As discussed more fully below, this happened. The proportion of "yes" verdicts by the mock juries for punitive damages ranged from 35% to 71%. Given the range of expressed judgments, we then relate differences in the judgments about punitive damages to jurors' self-reported reasons for their verdicts and the contents of their discussions in deliberation. In other words, we examine the cognitive and social decision processes of jurors that may have led to the different judgments about liability for punitive damages.

Our basic hypothesis is that jurors in punitive damages cases face a very difficult cognitive task and that a common approach to deal with this cognitive difficulty is to use everyday concepts of liability, punishment, and deterrence that do not map neatly onto their legal counterparts. In particular, everyday habits of assessing blame do not match the legal requirements in some states that a series of requisite "elements" each have to be present in order to justify a finding of liability for punitive damages.

III. Study Design
A. Participants

Participants, jury-eligible adult citizens, were sampled from the Denver area by a marketing research firm and paid $50 for participation in the study. The participants were sampled representatively by residential address and contacted by mail. A final sample of 726 deliberating mock jurors was obtained. Fifty-five percent of the jurors were women. The average age of the sample was 47 with a range from 25 to 77 years. The modal educational level was a high school diploma with some vocational training. Seventy percent of the sample was white (European American), 15% African American, 12% Hispanic, and 3% other ethnicity.

Summary of Experiment

Description: Subjects saw a videotaped narration, then read the same written summary of a personal injury accident case and instructions. They were exposed
to one of four different cases, all based on real cases in which punitive damages
had been denied. First individually and then by unanimous verdict of six-person
juries, subjects were asked to assess liability for punitive damages.

Number of subjects: 726 jury-eligible citizens in 121 mock juries.

Location: Denver, Colorado.

Decisions: Individual and six-person mock-jury deliberation.

Stimuli: Videotaped narration and written case summary and instructions.

B. Materials

Four legally significant cases that required jurors to distinguish between negligent and reckless conduct were selected as the basis for stimulus materials.[3] The *Anderson v. Whittaker Corp.* (1987) case involved
four boaters lost in a powerboat after an inadequate recall. The *Harper
v. Zapata Off-Shore Co.* (1983) case involved an injured seaman denied
part of his maintenance pay after hiring a lawyer. The *Jardel Co., Inc. v.
Hughes* (1987) case involved a shopping mall owner that failed to prevent
the abduction and rape of an employee in the parking lot. Finally, the
In re Marine Sulphur Queen (MSQ) (1972) case involved thirty-nine sea-
men lost in a dangerously designed and operated molten sulfur carrier.
These cases were selected because they are frequently cited as precedents, and because the proper action on the issue of punitive damages
had been decided as a matter of law by trial or appellate court review of
the original proceedings. In each case the trial court or a higher court established that the facts did not warrant the consideration of action on punitive damages. Of course, one could argue that the higher courts were
wrong, and punitive damages were warranted in these cases. Our focus,
however, is not so much on the right or wrong of the decision as it is on
the extent to which juror reasoning considered the necessary conditions
for the verdicts rendered, and the relationship between instructions and
juror judgments.

Judge's instructions (approximately five hundred words long) on liability and on procedures such as the standard of proof, the unanimity
quorum requirement, and the selection of a presiding juror were derived

---

3. *Anderson v. Whittaker Corp.*, 692 F. Supp. 734 (W.D. Mich., 1987); *Harper v. Zapata Off-
Shore Co.*, 563 F. Supp. 576 (1983); *Jardel Co., Inc. v. Hughes,* Del. Supr., 523 A.2d 518 (1987);
In re Marine Sulphur Queen 460 F.2d 89 (1972).

primarily from the instructions in *Jardel Co., Inc. v. Hughes*. The instructions provide a detailed prescription of the standards for finding "reckless disregard," and they are not an unusual description of legal standards for deciding this issue (see appendix). The instructions include definitions of malicious conduct and reckless or callous disregard for others, carefully specifying the differences between negligent and reckless conduct. Specifically, the instructions made it clear that in order for conduct to be in reckless or callous disregard of the rights of others, four factors must be present. First, a defendant must be subjectively conscious of a particular grave danger or risk of harm, and the danger or risk must be a foreseeable and probable effect of the conduct. Second, the particular danger or risk of which the defendant was subjectively conscious must in fact have eventuated. Third, a defendant must have disregarded the risk in deciding how to act. Fourth, a defendant's conduct in ignoring the danger or risk must have involved a gross deviation from the level of care which an ordinary person would use, having due regard to all the circumstances. The judge's instructions also made it clear that negligence is the failure to use such care as a reasonable, prudent, and careful person would use under similar circumstances. The jurors were instructed that reckless conduct requires a conscious choice of action, either with knowledge of serious danger to others or with knowledge of facts that would disclose the danger to any reasonable person.

The case summaries and instructions were used as scripts for videotapes representing the four cases. (An example case, *Jardel Co., Inc. v. Hughes,* is included at the end of this chapter. Copies of all case materials are available from the authors.) One of these summaries served as the stimulus case for each mock jury. Jurors watched the videotape (durations ranged from eleven to fifteen minutes) and then read a written summary before beginning deliberation.

C. Procedure

Participants were brought to a central location in groups ranging in size from thirty-eight to fifty-two participants and were introduced to their mock-jury task. They completed a short background information questionnaire and were instructed that they would be asked "to make a legal decision just like the ones that jurors make in legal trials." Then they were shown one of the videotaped stimulus cases on a projection screen. The mock jurors were told that the judge's instructions on the tape were the law and that they should adhere to them in making individual and group decisions. They were provided with a written copy of the to-be-judged case, including judge's instructions, note pads, and pencils. After the videotape they were given ten minutes to study the written script and to take handwritten notes. Then they completed a questionnaire indicating their individual predeliberation verdicts by checking "yes," proper to award punitive damages; "no," not proper to award punitive damages; or "undecided." They were also asked to indicate their confidence in the decision on a six-point scale labeled from "50%, No idea I am just guessing" to "100%, Absolutely certain my verdict is correct." We should note one difference between our method and the procedures in actual trials: Our mock jurors did not first decide on compensatory damages awards before deciding on punitive damages, as they usually would in trials that involve punitive damages.

Following the trial presentation, the mock jurors were grouped into six-person mock juries and went to separate conference rooms to deliberate. (Note that this study, like that reported in chapter 3, involves deliberating mock juries.) The mock juries were provided with a copy of the judge's instructions and reminded that their verdict must be unanimous. Their deliberations were videotaped, with their knowledge and permission (one videotape was lost due to an equipment malfunction, so that jury is excluded from content analyses of the deliberation process). They completed deliberation, with a verdict or by declaring their jury deadlocked. (Four of the 121 juries were unable to reach a conclusion after two hours of deliberation but did not declare themselves deadlocked. Their deliberations were terminated by the experimenters, and they will be classified as "hung" in our analyses.) After concluding deliberation, jurors were asked to complete a second questionnaire that asked for their personal verdicts, probed the reasons for their judgments, and tested their memories for information from the judge's instructions (copies of the original instructions were not available at this time). Then jurors were paid for their participation and excused.

IV. Results
A. Verdicts

Table 5.1 provides a summary of the individual verdict preferences measured before and after deliberation. The 95% confidence intervals on the proportions of "yes" verdicts are listed for the individual pre- and post- and group verdicts. Table 5.2 presents the group jury verdicts. The best estimate of the rates at which the mock juries rendered "yes, liable

Table 5.1. Juror Verdicts

	Predeliberation Individual Juror Verdicts				
	Anderson	*Harper*	*Jardel*	*MSQ*	Overall
Yes	62% (116)	53% (98)	59% (99)	76% (142)	63% (455)
No	30% (56)	33% (62)	33% (55)	17% (31)	28% (204)
Undecided	8% (14)	14% (26)	8% (14)	7% (13)	9% (67)
95% confidence intervals (around "yes")	55–69%	46–60%	52–66%	70–82%	60–67%

	Postdeliberation Individual Juror Verdicts				
	Anderson	*Harper*	*Jardel*	*MSQ*	Overall
Yes	52% (97)	67% (124)	60% (101)	81% (150)	65% (472)
No	43% (83)	32% (59)	39% (65)	16% (30)	33% (237)
Undecided	3% (6)	1% (3)	1% (2)	3% (6)	2% (17)
95% confidence intervals (around "yes")	45–59%	60–74%	53–67%	75–87%	62–69%

Table 5.2. Jury Verdicts

	Jury Verdicts (Including Hung Verdicts)				
	Anderson	*Harper*	*Jardel*	*MSQ*	Overall
Yes	35% (11)	68% (21)	57% (16)	71% (22)	58% (70)
No	42% (13)	32% (10)	29% (8)	13% (4)	29% (35)
Hung Juries	23%	—	14%	16%	13%
Undecided	(7)	(0)	(4)	(5)	(16)

	Jury Verdicts (Excluding Hung Verdicts)				
	Anderson	*Harper*	*Jardel*	*MSQ*	Overall
Yes	46% (11)	68% (21)	67% (16)	85% (22)	67% (70)
No	54% (13)	32% (10)	33% (8)	15% (4)	33% (35)
95% confidence intervals (around "yes")	23–66%	52–84%	48–86%	71–99%	58–76%

for punitive damages" verdicts is based on the proportions of "yes" juries out of the total number of verdict-rendering juries, excluding undecided juries. The assumption is that undecided juries would tend to split
according to the proportion represented by verdict-rendering juries or,
should the cases be retried, decide at the rate estimated by the other
verdict-rendering juries. Thus, we have calculated 95% intervals around
the proportions of "yes" jury verdicts with the "undecided" verdicts excluded from the totals. The rate at which individuals and juries favored
"yes" verdicts is far above zero for all cases: Over 50% of individual jurors favored "yes" after deliberation, and the "yes" jury verdict rates were
over 50% for three of the four cases. Recall that in each case a trial court
or appellate review concluded that the facts did *not* warrant a finding of
reckless or malicious conduct. Note that the percentage of "yes" verdicts
by the mock juries varied by case from 35% *(Anderson)* to 71% *(MSQ)*.
Thus, across juries there were distinctions made based on the case facts.

There was substantial disagreement among the mock juries on every
one of the four cases. In terms of individual differences among the jurors, jurors with higher incomes were likelier to decide "not liable," and
white jurors were more likely to favor a "no liability" verdict than minority jurors.

While the numbers of juries that rendered verdicts discrepant from
those reached on appeal is perhaps disturbing, that was not the primary
focus of this study. Instead, the focus was the nature of the jury deliberations as they related to jury verdicts. In particular, we focused on the extent to which jury deliberations considered the conditions necessary for
a punitive damages liability judgment, as contained in the instructions
given to the jury.

B. The Dynamics of Jury Deliberation

Jury deliberation times ranged from 5 minutes to 99 minutes, with an
average time of 43 minutes (median of 42 minutes). Four jury deliberations were terminated by the researchers because the end of the session
had been reached but no verdict had been rendered. The individual pre-
and postdeliberation verdict preferences and confidence ratings show
that deliberation had the general effect of shifting jurors from the "undecided" state of mind to a verdict preference. Similarly, confidence ratings moved up from pre- to postdeliberation: Average predeliberation
confidence was 83% (on the 50% to 100% scale), and postdeliberation
it moved up to 90%.

There was also a general tendency for jurors to shift to the "yes, liable for punitive damages" verdict during deliberation. Jurors were about twice as likely to shift from "undecided" to "yes, liable for punitive damages" than to "no, not liable" (of the sixty-seven initially "undecided" jurors, 60% shifted to "yes" and 33% to "no," and 7% remained "undecided"). This shift may be a result of coalition size effects during deliberation: Larger factions tend to prevail in deliberation (the larger the coalition favoring "yes" at the start of deliberation, the higher the probability of a "yes" jury decision), and "yes" factions were larger at the start of deliberation in most juries. On the other hand, when the "no" and "yes" fractions were equal, the jury tended to conclude with a "no" verdict. However, this global conclusion needs to be qualified for the particular case being judged. For the *Anderson* case, there was a tendency for the shift across deliberation to favor the "no" verdict: The probability of a "yes" juror changing to "no" was .25, versus the probability for a "no" juror changing to "yes" of .14. For the other cases, the probabilities of changing favored the "yes" verdict.

C. Jury Deliberation

To allow a detailed analysis of the nature of group deliberations, the videotaped jury deliberations were transcribed into written text. Each statement by a deliberating juror was "coded" into one of sixty-three categories designed to capture the essential decision-relevant elements of the deliberation process (a summary of the coding system is available from the authors). The categories covered the following topics: beliefs and inferences about the case fact situation; legal requirements for consideration of punitive damages (presented in the judge's instructions); expressions of sympathy for the plaintiffs; causal attributions including blame and responsibility; personal attitudes and experiences relevant to the case; statements of conclusions on legal issues; and group-management directives (e.g., voting, admonitions to follow instructions, etc.).

First, a coder segmented each transcript into statements (61,104 statements total, approximately 509 statements per jury). Second, each statement from every transcript was separately classified independently by two coders; the assignment of coders to juries was counterbalanced so every coder and pair of coders analyzed equal numbers of juries, and order of jury coding was determined randomly for each coder separately. Coders agreed with one another on classification of over 70% of the individual statements across the full set of sixty-three coding categories.

Table 5.3. Percentage of Statements
in Major Coding Categories

Facts and inferences about the case	36.0%
Discussion of legal issues	14.6
Sympathy for the plaintiff	.3
Attributions of blame	4.4
Group process issues	10.4
General attitudes	1.6
Experiences, examples, analogies	6.3
Evaluations and conclusions	7.1
Miscellaneous/uncodable	19.3
Total	100.0%

Disagreements between coders were dealt with by randomly selecting one of the two assigned codes.

Not surprisingly, the most common topic of discussion was recalling and interpreting the specific details of the cases' fact situations (table 5.3). It is no exaggeration to note that these civil juries, much as in criminal juries, spent most of their time in deliberation trying to construct a common narrative story summary of the evidence.[4] Juries also spent a large portion of their time discussing legal issues (including the judge's instructions) and drawing conclusions about these legal issues. However, the coverage of legal conditions for punitive damages presented in the judge's instructions was usually incomplete; on average groups discussed 3.13 out of 5 and drew conclusions about 2.78 out of the 5 legally relevant conditions. The other most frequent activities were various group-management activities (who should speak next, taking votes, etc.) and sharing examples, personal experiences, and speculating about hypothetical situations.

1. Predicting jury verdicts from the contents of deliberation.

We performed a series of statistical analyses in which the unanimous jury verdict was the criterion dependent variable ("yes, award punitive damages" vs. "no, do not award punitive damages," with the hung

4. Nancy Pennington and Reid Hastie, "A Cognitive Theory of Juror Decision Making: The Story Model," 13 *Cardozo L. Rev.* 519 (1991); and Nancy Pennington and Reid Hastie, "A Theory of Explanation-Based Decision Making," in *Decision Making in Action: Models and Methods* 188 (Gary A. Klein et al. eds., 1993).

Table 5.4. Deliberation Content Categories Related to Group Verdicts

Coding Category*	Regression Coefficients**
Purpose of punitive damages is to deter others	+.139 (.147)
Defendant is to blame for a specific event	+.033 (.268)
Conclusions about whether the defendant was malicious	+.038 (.225)
Discussion of third-party motives (motives of someone other than plaintiff or defendant)	−.163 (−.216)
Discussion of meaning of negligence	−.048 (−.269)
Discussion of required burden of proof	−.046 (−.164)
Admonition to follow the judge's instructions	−.104 (−.181)
Acknowledgment of uncertainties	−.016 (−.160)

*Frequency of each category-verdict relationship consistently significant at or beyond $p < .05$.
** + means a jury was more likely to award punitive damages as the number of statements in the category increased; − means the inverse relationship was observed; standardized coefficients are in parentheses; the complete regression equation also included a constant term (−1.089).

juries excluded) and the predictors were the frequencies of statements classified into each of the coding categories. Control variables were included in every analysis representing the average predeliberation verdict of the individual jurors on each jury and case factors *(Anderson, Harper, Jardel,* or *Marine Sulphur Queen)*. Thus, the analysis accounts for the variance in the group verdicts that remains after these two control variables have been entered into the predictive equation.

Nine of the initial fifteen coding categories appeared repeatedly and always had significant coefficients with the same signs (table 5.4). The directions of influence of most of these predictors are no surprise; in a sense they function as face-validity checks on the coding categories. For example, a jury that spent more time blaming the defendant for bad outcomes was more likely to vote for punitive damages. In contrast, juries that questioned the motives of other parties and stated that more information was needed were more likely to conclude that punitive damages were not warranted.

2. Legally significant predictors of verdicts.

The most striking differences between juries rendering "yes" verdicts and those concluding with "no" or "hung" was how thoroughly their deliberations considered the legally necessary conditions for punitive damages stated in the judge's instructions. Under the judge's instructions

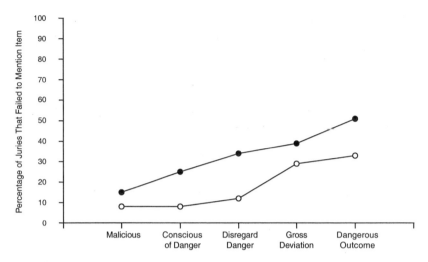

Fig. 5.1. The percentages of "yes" *(filled circles)* and "no" *(open circles)* verdict-rendering juries that mentioned (discussed or reached conclusions) during deliberation the legally required conditions for a judgment that punitive damages were warranted.

given to the jurors, there are two general justifications for awarding punitive damages: (1) finding that the defendant was *malicious* or (2) finding that the defendant's actions exhibited *reckless or callous disregard* for risks to others. The first justification is sufficient by itself, but the second requires that a conjunction of four conditions be present. Figure 5.1 summarizes the percentages of juries that discussed *or* drew conclusions about each of these five conditions, separated into "yes" and "no" verdict-rendering juries. For each of the five legal conditions, "yes" juries were *less* likely to either discuss or state conclusions about each of the conditions. On the other hand, juries were significantly less likely to award punitive damages if someone simply suggested that the judge's instructions should be followed (see table 5.4).

The relationship between thoroughness of deliberation on the law and verdicts is also observed when summary measures of jury thoroughness are examined. A measure of thoroughness was created by indexing whether each jury discussed or reached conclusions about each of the five legally required conditions and adding up these numbers to obtain a measure of thoroughness of coverage (ranging in value from 0 [no coverage] to 10 [both discussion and a stated conclusion for every condition]).

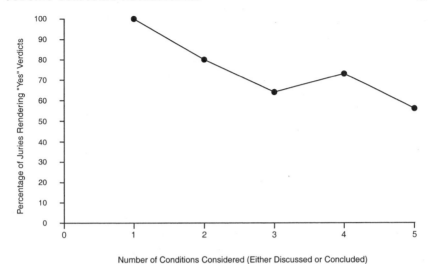

Fig. 5.2. The relationship between the percentages of juries awarding punitive damages and the thoroughness of their coverage during deliberation of the legally required conditions for a judgment that punitive damages were warranted.

No juries received a perfect thoroughness score of 10 for discussion and conclusions on each of the five legal issues. By this measure, "yes" juries were significantly less thorough (mean = 5.17) than "no" and "hung" juries (mean = 6.92, $p < .001$). Figure 5.2 depicts the relationship between thoroughness indexed as *either* discussion *or* conclusions on each of the five legal elements and the percentage of juries rendering "yes" verdicts. The pattern is again dramatic, with 100% of the juries who did not cover any legal issues rendering "yes" verdicts, dropping to 45% "yes" verdicts for the most thorough juries.

Reinforcing this theme of cursory treatment of legal issues, our analyses of the contents of discussion showed that greater discussion of the required burden of proof also led to fewer punitive damages awards (see table 5.4). In contrast, more discussion of extralegal reasons to award punitive damages (i.e., considerations not mentioned in the judge's instructions) led to more "yes" verdicts.

Jurors may have difficulty in separating the different legal concepts that apply to punitive and compensatory damages and therefore may treat them as interchangeable, especially when the plaintiff is the recipient of a potential punitive award. In our juries, when someone commented in deliberation that compensatory damages had already been paid to the plaintiff (a fact that was stated in each case description), the jury was less likely to award punitive damages. Similarly, negligence (relevant to compensatory damages) and recklessness (relevant to punitive damages) may be confused in the minds of jurors. We found that when the meaning of negligence was discussed, the jury was less likely to award punitive damages. In both of these cases, confusion about the distinctions between compensatory and punitive damages and between negligence and recklessness would be likely to produce a bias against the defendant. Overall, discussion of issues that were legally relevant reduced the tendency to decide, incorrectly, that punitive damages were warranted.

Finally, we examined individual jurors' written postdeliberation explanations for their verdicts and rated the extent to which each juror relied on the judge's instructions when justifying his or her verdict. A score of 0 indicated no reference to the instructions, 1 indicated some reliance, and 2 indicated heavy reliance on the instructions. The overall rate of reliance on the judge's instructions was surprisingly low. Forty-nine percent of the jurors made no reference at all to the judge's instructions when justifying their verdicts. The extent to which individual jurors referred to the judge's instructions when justifying their verdicts was strongly correlated with their juries' verdicts ($r = -.43$, $p < .001$); jurors who relied more heavily on the instructions were more likely to be on juries reaching a "no" verdict.

D. Comprehension of the Judge's Instructions

Given the clear relationship between reliance on the judge's instructions and verdicts, we now turn to the question of how well individual jurors comprehended and remembered the judge's instructions. Participants were asked to recall portions of the judge's instructions on liability by means of specific questions on each important element relevant to their decisions—for example, "What is the legal definition of 'reckless or callous disregard for the rights of others'? (If you cannot remember the legal terms, try to state this definition in your own words.)" Written responses to these questions were "scored" based on accuracy of recall of nine elements or legal distinctions from the instructions. Two research assistants were trained to code the responses in terms of lenient criteria in which recall of the gist of each element was scored correct if paraphrases preserved the approximate meaning of the original instruction.

These scores were converted to a percent correct metric with possible scores ranging from 0% to 100% correct. Intercoder reliability was $r = +.86$; 90% of the paired scores were within 5% of one another for the two coders.

The overall level of performance on this recall-comprehension test was low: The median score was 5% correct (the mean was 9%), 30% of the participants received a score of zero correct, and the high score was 67% correct. These low scores cannot be attributed to nonresponses due to low motivation to comply with the decision task; there were almost no blank response forms and the zero-comprehension scores were usually assigned to lengthy but incorrect responses.

Several individual difference background factors predicted comprehension of the instructions: juror age (younger jurors' comprehension was better: $r = -.24, p < .001$), juror education (better-educated jurors' comprehension was better: $r = +.32, p < .001$), juror income (higher-income jurors' comprehension was better: $r = +.16, p < .001$), and juror ethnicity (white jurors' comprehension was better than minority jurors: $r = +.14, p < .001$).

The instruction recall–comprehension score was significantly correlated with the confidence-weighted predeliberation verdict preference for only the *Anderson* case ($r = -.21, p < .01; r = -.23, p < .01$, for the simple verdict preference with undecided jurors excluded from the analysis). Participants who were better able to comprehend and recall the instructions were also likelier to decide "not liable."

V. Conclusion

The present study provides insight into juror and jury decision processes when making an important liability decision. Importantly, our content analyses of the deliberation process show that the typical jury failed to consider even half of the five legally prescribed conditions for a finding that punitive damages were warranted, even though approximately 65% of these same juries concluded that the defendant was liable. And we found that juries concluding "yes, punitive damages were warranted" were reliably less thorough in their coverage of the legally prescribed conditions than juries concluding that punitive awards were not justified.

A related finding was the low level of comprehension and memory for information conveyed in instructions on the law. Overall comprehension, indexed with a relatively lenient coding scheme, was low; less than 10% of the most relevant portions of the judge's instructions could be correctly recalled within minutes of the conclusion of deliberation. Furthermore, in the present study the instructions were relatively clear, succinct, and realistic; they were distinctively prominent in the context of our summarized cases; and written instructions were available during deliberation. Poor comprehension and memory for instructions is the usual finding in studies of real and mock-jury decision making, even when researchers provide more specific recall cues or use multiple-choice or recognition-memory test formats.[5] We believe that the essential finding, disturbingly poor comprehension, is a valid description of what occurs in actual jury trials, although this conclusion is based on our mock-jury simulation, which is far from courtroom conditions.

The low levels of comprehension by individual jurors and the lack of thoroughness in jury deliberation imply that juries rely on legal concepts only partly in making their decisions on liability for punitive damages.[6] Furthermore, the less they rely on the law, the more likely they are to render verdicts that disagree with judges' opinions in these cases.

We do not believe that the failure to adequately consider all the relevant legal requirements is because the juries were not motivated to perform their task. Instead, we believe that the incomplete processing of case information and the limited following of the judge's instructions reflect the several difficult cognitive judgments that are part of a decision on liability for punitive damages. Given the difficulty of those judgments, it should not be surprising that we find evidence for cognitive simplifications that may not track the law.

Jurors' everyday concepts of liability, punishment, and deterrence clearly do not map neatly onto their legal counterparts; their everyday habits of assessing blame do not match the legal procedures of verifying that a series of requisite "elements" have each been established to a specified (and unfamiliar) "standard of proof"; and when they get to the jury deliberation part of their task, they discover that there is substantial disagreement among their fellow citizens about conceptual and factual issues. Finally, there is a complex structure of conjunctive and disjunctive

5. E.g., James Luginbuhl, "Comprehension of Judge's Instructions in the Penalty Phase of a Capital Trial," 16 *Law & Hum. Behav.* 203 (1992); Alan Reifman et al., "Real Jurors' Understanding of the Law in Real Cases," 16 *Law & Hum. Behav.* 539 (1992); and Richard L. Wiener et al., "Comprehensibility of Approved Jury Instructions in Capital Murder Cases," 80 *J. Applied Soc. Psychol.* 455 (1995).

6. Cf., Richard L. Wiener et al., "The Social Psychology of Jury Nullification: Predicting When Jurors Disobey the Law," 21 *J. Applied Soc. Psychol.* 1379 (1991).

relationships on elements that must be decided to properly render the general verdict. Under these circumstances, the jurors fall back on their rough-and-ready everyday reasoning habits, probably influenced by their sympathies for one party or the other, and they fail to complete the task presented to them in their instructions from the judge.

Example Stimulus Case
Jardel Co., Inc. et al. v. K. Hughes[7]

This case involves the following two parties: the plaintiff, Kathleen Hughes, a shopping mall employee who was abducted from the mall parking lot, beaten, and raped; the defendant, Jardel Co., Inc., owner and operator of the shopping mall.

The specifics of the case are as follows:

On July 18, 1980, shortly after the 9:00 P.M. closing time, the plaintiff, an employee of the Woolco store in the Blue Hen Mall, left her place of employment. She walked through the interior arcade of the mall and exited through the rear entrance adjacent to the parking lot where her vehicle was located. Near the entrance to the Fox Theater, the plaintiff was accosted by two scruffy-looking young men who had been denied entrance to the theater because Fox personnel believed them to be intoxicated. When these individuals asked the plaintiff for a cigarette, she briefly spoke with them, gave them a cigarette, and walked on. The men followed the plaintiff to her car, which was parked approximately fifty feet from the mall entrance. When she attempted to enter her car, they forced their way into her car with her and drove away.

After being driven to a remote site adjacent to the mall, the plaintiff was beaten and raped by both assailants. While she was unconscious and lying on the ground, her assailants attempted to run her over with her car and later set fire to the car while she was lying in it. The plaintiff regained consciousness and staggered nude and bloodied onto a nearby highway, where a passing motorist found her and took her to a nearby hospital.

The plaintiff remained hospitalized for six days. She was treated for severe contusions to the face and scalp, a cerebral concussion, and a permanent skull fracture. This latter injury has resulted in a permanent displacement of her left eye and double vision. In addition to her physical injuries, the plaintiff, at the time of the trial four years later, still suffered psychological effects from her traumatic experience.

Since 1979 Jardel had contracted with Globe Security Systems, Inc., to provide guards for the mall exterior. Jardel paid according to the number of guards provided by Globe. Jardel decided to use one guard for each nightly shift beginning at 9 P.M. Globe personnel testified that they had suggested to Jardel that the

---

7. *Jardel Co., Inc. v. Hughes,* Del. Supr., 523 A.2d 518 (1987).

mall exterior was too large for one guard and that more guards were needed. Jardel denied receiving a specific recommendation but did acknowledge that Globe requested, on more than one occasion, an increase in the number of guards. In response, Jardel asked Globe to justify the additional expense.

Globe said they wanted an additional guard because there was no radio contact with the Dover police. The police allowed direct radio access only to police officers. Globe wanted a second guard inside the mall, who would be in radio contact with the outside guard and could telephone the police. Jardel countered that maintenance personnel who already worked inside the mall throughout the night could contact the police if necessary.

When Hughes was forced into her vehicle in the rear parking lot, the single Globe guard was in his patrol vehicle, parked in the front parking lot.

Mall owners are not compelled to provide security. But Jardel chose to provide security, presumably to render the mall more attractive to its tenants and their customers and employees. Once Jardel did provide a security program, Jardel became obligated to do it in a reasonable manner, with a view toward the dangers to which the program was directed. The standard that governs this situation says, "A possessor of land who holds it open to the public for business purposes is liable to the public while they are on the land for such purpose, for physical harm caused by . . . intentionally harmful acts of third persons. If past experience is such that the owner should reasonably anticipate criminal conduct on the part of third persons, either generally or at some particular time, he may be under a duty to take precautions against it, and to provide a reasonably sufficient number of servants to afford reasonable protection."

A Dover police officer presented evidence of the number of police responses to the Blue Hen Mall in the two and a half years preceding the incident. Of 394 incidents reported, over 90% were property or nonpersonal crimes. The remaining incidents, however, involved a kidnapping at gunpoint, an armed robbery, a sexual molestation, indecent exposures, and purse snatchings, with approximately one-half of these incidents occurring in the mall parking lot.

The court concluded that under the circumstances, the protection provided by Jardel was an insufficient response to the known history of criminal activity.

Hughes was compensated in full for her expenses, lost income, and pain and suffering. In addition, Hughes claimed she was entitled to punitive damages.

Plaintiff Argument in Favor of Punitive Damages

Despite the history of violent crimes in the Blue Hen Mall, and despite the repeated requests from Globe Security to add another guard because of the large size of the parking lot, Jardel chose to save money by having only one exterior guard on duty. Punitive damages should be awarded against Jardel to punish them for flagrantly avoiding their duty of protecting mall employees and customers, and to deter them, and other mall owners, from such future behavior.

Defendant Argument against the Award of Punitive Damages

Although we all wish crime could be prevented, we know it cannot be. In this case Jardel voluntarily provided a reasonable level of security, consistent with the history of crime on their mall property. Jardel's behavior was not even close to the malicious or reckless and callous disregard for the rights of others that is required by the judge's instructions for the award of punitive damages.

Judge's Instructions
(See appendix.)

Question

Kathleen Hughes (the plaintiff), a shopping mall employee who was abducted, beaten, and raped while going to her car after work in the mall, has sued the mall's owner, Jardel Co., Inc. (the defendant), asking for punitive damages. You have been given a legal definition of when punitive damages are proper. You must use that definition whether you agree with it or not. Based on that definition, would it be proper to award punitive damages against Jardel Co., Inc., yes or no?

Answer: Yes _____ No _____

6

Looking Backward in Punitive Judgments: 20-20 Vision?

Reid Hastie, David A. Schkade, and John W. Payne

I. Introduction

In the last chapter we investigated the processes involved in a jury decision to award punitive damages and the role of judicial instructions in those processes. In this chapter we explore a common judgmental phenomenon that is likely to play a particularly important role in judging recklessness: the hindsight effect.

As noted earlier in this book, when a claim is made for punitive damages on the grounds of reckless conduct, the plaintiff must prove there was a grave danger or risk of harm that was a *foreseeable and probable* effect of the action, and that the defendant decided to act with conscious indifference to the potential consequences.[1] Thus, the law asks the fact finder to attempt to recover a naive, *ex ante* view of once-future events and to judge the defendant's conduct in light of what he or she did know or should have known in the past. Unfortunately, much research suggests that it is difficult to recover a naive, *ex ante* view of events in hindsight and that there is a tendency in hindsight to judge that one "knew it all along."[2] Because liability for punitive damages can depend so heavily on inferences about the defendant's *ex ante* state of mind, this chapter reports on an experimental investigation of the hindsight bias within the context of jurors' judgments of liability for punitive damages. We also extend prior work on hindsight bias by examining whether such a bias is

1. W. Page Keeton and William Lloyd Prosser, *Prosser and Keeton on the Law of Torts* (5th ed., 1984); Ronald W. Eades and Graham Douthwaite, *Jury Instructions on Damages in Tort Actions* (3rd ed., 1993).

2. Baruch Fischhoff, "Hindsight ≠ Foresight: The Effect of Outcome Knowledge on Judgment under Uncertainty," 1 *J. Exper. Psychol.: Hum. Percep. & Perform.* 288 (1975); Scott A. Hawkins and Reid Hastie, "Hindsight: Biased Judgments of Past Events after the Outcomes Are Known," 107 *Psychol. Bull.* 311 (1990); Kim A. Kamin and Jeffrey J. Rachlinski, "Ex Post ≠ Ex Ante: Determining Liability in Hindsight," 19 *Law & Hum. Behav.* 89 (1995).

found for other specific judgments that are important in the context of punitive damages: foreseeability of an accident, conscious awareness of grave danger, and gross deviation from an ordinary level of care. In addition to the basic question of a hindsight effect on various punitive damages judgments, the study also investigates the following questions: Does the magnitude of the harm that was caused by an accident affect the size of any hindsight bias? Does asking a person to assume the role of a juror as compared to a citizen whose personal judgment is being elicited reduce the size of any hindsight bias?

To preview, the following results were obtained:

- Participants' judgments showed dramatic hindsight effects. For instance, *ex ante* two-thirds of the participants approved of a request by a railroad to continue operations, but *ex post* (jurors given exactly the same case description but also told that an accident had occurred) two-thirds judged that the railroad's behavior was reckless and that the railroad was liable for punitive damages.
- Participants in the juror role exhibited slightly smaller hindsight effects when judging liability than did those in the citizen role. However, substantial amounts of a hindsight bias were still observed, particularly with regards to judgments of *recklessness,* a key judgment in deciding liability for punitive damages.
- The magnitude of the damage caused by the accident had no effect on any measures of hindsight.

II. Background and Hypotheses

A number of researchers have suggested that legal judgments may be subject to a hindsight bias.[3] Further, in the context of criminal cases, Bodenhausen demonstrated a hindsight effect even though the mock jurors were told to disregard information about a prior trial outcome.[4] On the civil side, Kamin and Rachlinski (1995) asked college students to judge negligence before or after a barge collided with a drawbridge causing damage to property along a river (their fact situation was based on a

3. Hal R. Arkes and Cindy A. Schipani, "Medical Malpractice v. the Business Judgment Rule: Differences in Hindsight Bias," 73 *Or. L. Rev.* 587 (1994); Susan J. LaBine and Gary LaBine, "Determinations of Negligence and the Hindsight Bias," 20 *Law & Hum. Behav.* 501 (1996); Jeffrey J. Rachlinski, "A Positive Psychological Theory of Judging in Hindsight," 65 *U. Chi. L. Rev.* 571 (1998); David B. Wexler and Robert F. Schopp, "How and When to Correct for Juror Hindsight Bias in Mental Health Malpractice Litigation," *Behav. Sci. & L.* 485 (1989).

4. Galen V. Bodenhausen, "Second-Guessing the Jury: Stereotypic and Hindsight Biases in Perceptions of Court Cases," 20 *J. Applied Soc. Psychol.* 1112 (1990).

classic tort case, *Petition of Kinsman Transit Co.*).[5] In foresight, participants were asked to decide if a city should hire a bridge operator during winter months when the danger of flooding was relatively low. In hindsight, the participants were presented with an accident that would certainly have been averted had an operator been hired and were asked to judge retrospectively whether the city was negligent for not hiring the operator. In foresight, only 24% of the participants chose to hire the operator, but in hindsight, 57% believed the city should have hired the operator. The participants were also asked to estimate the probability that an accident would occur prospectively or retrospectively. Retrospective probabilities (.13) were slightly higher than their prospective counterparts (.09). Thus, there is evidence of hindsight effects in both criminal and civil cases. The present research extends prior research and investigates the potential for hindsight effects in judgments of whether a defendant's "conduct was in reckless or callous disregard of the rights of others," the focal issue in many punitive damages verdicts.

As mentioned earlier in this book, the juror is frequently asked in some states to decide if four factors were present in punitive damages cases:

> First, a defendant must be subjectively conscious of a particular grave danger or risk of harm, and the danger or risk must be a foreseeable and probable effect of the conduct. Second, the particular danger or risk of which the defendant was subjectively conscious must in fact have eventuated. Third, a defendant must have disregarded the risk in deciding how to act. Fourth, a defendant's conduct in ignoring the danger or risk must have involved a *gross* deviation from the level of care which an ordinary person would use, having due regard to all the circumstances.

Note that these standards for liability for punitive damages are different from those for compensatory damages—although state law varies on when people are liable for injuries they cause. Liability for compensatory damages sometimes follows from the mere fact of harm. Sometimes liability for compensatory damages requires negligence, where "negligence" is the failure to use such care as a reasonable, prudent, and careful person would use under similar circumstances. Kamin and Rachlinski's study investigated judgments of negligence.[6] Liability for punitive damages, on the other hand, involves judgments of malice or "recklessness," which invokes different considerations. *Reckless* conduct differs from negligence in that it requires a conscious choice of action, either with knowledge of serious danger to others or with knowledge of facts (or facts that anyone would have) that would disclose the danger to any reasonable person. Thus, the legal judgment of recklessness might be particularly influenced by hindsight if the juror's knowledge of outcome leads to a projection of foreseeability onto the defendant.

We also extended the scope of prior studies by asking for evaluations of the quality of a decision that preceded and permitted the actions that resulted in harm. Did our participants evaluate the decision in terms of only the information available *ex ante* before the accident, or was their evaluation colored by the outcome that was unknown to the hypothetical *ex ante* jury? In addition, we varied the role that the participants in our research were assigned when making their judgments. Half of the participants were asked to respond as private citizens and to express their opinions about some newsworthy events as they might if questioned in a survey interview. The others were asked to assume the role of jurors who had been asked to make a legal judgment relevant to the same events. Our hypothesis was that participants would be more motivated to overcome hindsight biases when playing a well-defined social role as a juror and that the detailed instructions concerning the elements of the legal judgment would help them overcome hindsight biases. Nonetheless, we hypothesized that there would still be hindsight effects in our judgment situation for people in the juror role. Finally, we also varied the magnitude of the harm that was caused by the accident described in our case materials. It has been suggested that people have a need to believe that the world is orderly and predictable.[7] When an outcome is dramatic, people will "need to believe" it is predictable and therefore there will be large hindsight effects. In the present experiment, we manipulated the magnitude of the damage caused by a train derailment to provide a direct test of the hypothesis that larger outcomes produce larger hindsight effects.

III. Study Design
A. Participants

A representative group of 227 jury-eligible citizens was sampled from the Reno, Nevada, area and paid for participation. One-third of the

---

7. Elaine Walster, " 'Second Guessing' Important Events," 20 *Hum. Rel.* 239 (1967).

participants were given foresight materials, and two-thirds were given hindsight materials, as described below.

Summary of Experiment

Description: Subjects viewed a videotaped narration and then read a written environmental accident case summary and instructions. They were exposed to one of two versions differing only in whether or not subjects were told there had been an accident. "No-accident" subjects were asked if the company should be compelled to fix a hazardous facility. "Accident" subjects were asked if the company must pay punitive damages.

Number of subjects: 227.

Location: Reno, Nevada.

Decisions: Individual survey.

Stimuli: Videotaped narration and written case summary and instructions.

B. Materials

The fact situation from an environmental damage accident was selected as the basis for stimulus materials (the 1990 accident in which a Southern Pacific train derailed and dumped toxic herbicide into the Sacramento River near Dunsmuir, California). Two versions of the materials were prepared: In the foresight version, the participants learned about the situation along a mountainous section of railroad track that the National Transportation Safety Board (NTSB) had declared hazardous. Extensive expert testimony was presented to identify causes of potential train accidents. The participants were told that the railroad had appealed the NTSB order to stop operations and that the NTSB was to decide whether or not to lift the order, to allow the railroad to continue operations.

In the hindsight conditions, the materials included a brief description of a train derailment and the spilling of a toxic detergent into the "Durango River" in northern Nevada. The detergent polluted a thirty-eight-mile stretch of the river, killing wildlife and damaging a fish hatchery. The same details from the NTSB hearing were presented as evidence describing the conditions before the accident (some foresight information was made implicit in hindsight, as it would have appeared to be unnatural if presented explicitly), and the railroad's operations were described as continuing *pending* resolution of the dispute over the NTSB order (i.e., the railroad had not proceeded to disregard a legally binding order). The plaintiffs were described as "about 150 individuals and businesses," including the owners of the fish hatchery. The hindsight participants were asked to render a verdict or an opinion about whether the railroad should be held liable for punitive damages beyond compensatory damages for the accident.

One-half of the participants were instructed that they should assume the role of a juror asked to decide whether or not to lift the NTSB order to stop operations (foresight conditions) or to render a verdict on the railroad's liability for punitive damages (in hindsight). The juror-role participants were instructed to "make a legal decision just like the ones that jurors make in legal trials. . . . [Y]ou will watch a videotaped summary of a legal case. . . . [B]ased on the videotape, you will decide on your personal verdict for the case." The juror-role participants also heard attorneys' closing arguments and were told to follow the judge's instructions on the law when they decided on their verdicts. The other half of the participants were assigned to a citizen's role and were instructed to "give your opinions about a legal situation like the ones you hear about on television and read about in the newspapers. . . . [Y]ou will watch a videotaped summary of some events relevant to a legal decision. . . . [B]ased on the videotape, we will ask your opinions about the legal situation and related events." The citizen-role participants did not hear the attorneys' arguments or receive the judge's instructions. The distinction between juror and citizen roles was preserved in the labels used to refer to the participants and tasks in the questionnaires completed at the end of the experiment.

In the foresight juror-role conditions, the mock jurors were asked to decide if "from a preponderance of the evidence that the Chicago Western Railroad should be relieved of the National Transportation Safety Board order requiring changes to the track roadbed. . . ." To our knowledge there are no jury trial decisions that exactly parallel the circumstances of our foresight condition. So, in the foresight juror-role conditions, we manufactured instructions that were parallel to the hindsight punitive damages instructions. We instructed subjects that their decision to lift the NTSB order should depend on their judgment of whether there was a clear risk to the public; that is, whether "there existed a particular grave danger or risk of harm that is a foreseeable and probable effect of the existing condition [of the tracks]," and whether "leaving the existing condition unchanged involved a gross deviation from the level of care which an ordinary person would use, having due regard to all the circumstances." Thus, each of the four conditions that would be relevant to assessing liability for punitive damages after an accident had occurred (pending a decision on the request to lift the NTSB order) was cited as an element of the decision to lift the NTSB order before an accident had occurred.

In the hindsight juror-role conditions, the mock jurors were told that an accident had occurred, were given details of the damage, and then asked to decide if "from a preponderance of the evidence that an award of punitive damages against the Chicago Western Railroad is necessary in this case to achieve punishment and deterrence." In both cases the mock jurors were given instructions concerning the aspects of the situation that they should consider in rendering their judgments. In the hindsight conditions, these instructions were based on punitive damages instructions from one of the lawsuits that ensued after the Sacramento River train derailment. A final manipulation in the hindsight conditions concerned the magnitude of damages caused by the accident, reporting that either $240,000 (low damage) or $24 million (high damage) had already been paid by the railroad to compensate those injured for their losses.

The case summaries and instructions were used as scripts for six videotapes, one for each experimental condition. The six experimental conditions were created as follows: First, two foresight conditions were created, one in which participants were asked to play the role of a juror deciding on whether or not the NTSB order to stop operations should be lifted, and one in which they were asked to respond as a private citizen, that is, to give their opinions about the legal situation. The participants acting as jurors in the foresight condition were also told that their decision to lift the NTSB order should depend on whether there was a clear risk to the public defined in terms of a foreseeable and probable effect, and also whether leaving the existing condition unchanged would involve a gross deviation from the level of care that an ordinary person would use. Second, four hindsight conditions were created in which a train derailment was described following a jury decision to lift the NTSB order. All of the information from the foresight cases was presented as context for the derailment; the additional information described the train derailment and the payment of compensatory damages and restitution to those harmed by the derailment. In half of the hindsight cases, the impact of the accident was described as $240,000; in the other half, the compensatory damages amount was $24 million. In half of the hindsight cases, the participants were asked to play the role of jurors and in half to respond as private citizens. Individual subjects were assigned at random to one of the six versions of the case.

C. Procedure

Participants were introduced to the experimental task, and then shown the fifteen-minute videotaped stimulus case. All participants were provided with written copies of the videotaped script and pencils. After the videotape they were given as much time as they wanted to study the written case materials and instructions and to take handwritten notes (mock jurors spent an average of approximately twelve minutes studying the written materials).

The mock jurors then completed a response form rendering their verdict or expressing their opinion and then completed a questionnaire that probed the reasons for their judgments, obtained background demographic information, and measured some relevant attitudes.

IV. Results

A. Judgments of Liability and the Accident

The focus of the experiment was on the effects of the three independent variables on judgments and evaluations of the railroad's conduct. For most measures, only the foresight-hindsight manipulation affected participants' responses. We will consider the few measures on which the participant-role factor (juror vs. citizen) had an effect, after we discuss the foresight-hindsight differences. The magnitude of the damages factor ($240,000 vs. $24 million paid in compensatory damages) had no effect on any measure, so we will ignore it in the remainder of this results section.

The first question put to participants in the foresight condition was whether the NTSB order should be lifted, allowing the railroad to continue to operate; the parallel question in the hindsight conditions was whether the railroad should be held liable for punitive damages following the accident (see table 6.1 for a summary of primary judgment results). Since no participants viewed the railroad's actions as motivated by malice, we assume that the hindsight verdict or opinion reflects judgments of the degree to which the railroad's conduct, continuing to operate without improving the tracks, was judged as reckless.

In the foresight conditions, 33% of the participants judged that the railroad should not be allowed to continue operations; in the hindsight conditions, 67% judged that the railroad's actions were reckless enough to warrant the assessment of punitive damages, a highly significant dif-

Table 6.1. Decision and Confidence Measures

Temporal Perspective	Foresight		Hindsight			
Role	Juror	Citizen	Juror		Citizen	
Damage			Small	Large	Small	Large
n	51	51	41	46	41	47
Proportion of anti-RR judgments	37	29	61	57	76	75
Confidence scaled judgments (-100 to $+100$ scale)	-22	-37	$+19$	$+14$	$+47$	$+44$
Probability of serious accident (0 to 100 scale)	37	32	57	55	63	62

ference. When the judgments were indexed by participants' assessments of confidence on a -100 to $+100$ scale (with higher numbers indicating more confident judgments against the railroad), the same results were obtained. Prospective and retrospective estimates of the "probability that a serious accident would occur" also showed a dramatic foresight-hindsight effect; the average probability estimate in foresight was .34, and in hindsight it was .59 (the analysis was calculated on a 0 to 100 scale). Thus, the probability of a serious accident was more than 20 percentage points higher in the hindsight condition and went from "less likely than not" to "more likely than not."

Participants were posed a general liability question in foresight ("... is there a grave danger or risk of harm that is a foreseeable and probable effect of the existing condition of the railroad tracks?") and in hindsight ("... before the accident occurred, was there a grave danger or risk of harm that was a foreseeable and probable effect of the existing condition of the railroad tracks?") that they answered on a ten-point scale (see table 6.2 for summary of liability element ratings). Again, there was a significant and dramatic foresight-hindsight difference: Average rating in foresight was 3.50 versus an average rating in hindsight of 6.08. The general liability question was followed by questions on each of the elements underlying liability for punitive damages (the mock-juror-role participants had been given these instructions as part of their stimulus cases). There were substantial foresight-hindsight differences on the ratings for each of these elements, including "conscious of a grave danger" (average ratings of 4.95 vs. 5.93), "risk was foreseeable" (3.40 vs. 5.52),

Table 6.2. Ratings of Liability and Decision Quality

Significance	Foresight	Hindsight
Liability for an accident	3.50	6.08
Defendant was malicious	1.80	2.12
Defendant was reckless	2.89	5.12
Conscious of a grave danger	4.95	5.93
Risk was foreseeable	3.40	5.52
Disregarded the risk of a grave danger	3.36	5.59
Gross deviation from an ordinary level of care	2.99	4.91
Decision quality	+0.96	−.33
Decision maker's competency	66.55	53.00

"disregarded the risk of a grave danger" (3.36 vs. 5.59), and "gross deviation from an ordinary level of care" (2.99 vs. 4.91). Only the element of malice (". . . was [would] the conduct of the railroad be malicious in continuing to operate without modifying its tracks?") showed no foresight-hindsight effect (1.80 vs. 2.12). Forty-two percent of the participants rated this item a zero on the ten-point scale.

Participants were also asked to evaluate the quality of the decision of a hypothetical jury that had decided that the NTSB order should be lifted, allowing the railroad to continue its operations. When asked to "evaluate the decision itself, the quality of the thinking that went into it" on a seven-point scale (ranging from +3 to −3), foresight participants gave the jury an average rating of +.96 ("correct, but the opposite would be reasonable too"), while hindsight participants gave a significantly different rating of −.33 ("incorrect, but not unreasonable"). Similarly, participants were asked to imagine that the same jury might make more decisions: "Compared to other groups or persons who might make these decisions, how competent was the original jury?" Foresight participants gave average ratings of 66.55 (on a 0 to 100 scale) while hindsight participants gave a significantly lower rating of 53.00.

Participants' role (juror vs. private citizen) had a small but significant effect on liability judgments in the hindsight conditions, but not in the foresight conditions. On the primary judgment of liability for punitive damages (verdict or opinion), considering only hindsight conditions, participants in the citizen role were more likely to conclude against the railroad (74% favored punitive damages in the citizen role vs. 59% in the juror role); when the difference in judgments, scaled by confidence, was tested, it too was significant: ratings of 45.28 versus 16.61 on a -100 to $+100$ scale.

B. Correlated Variables

The measures of legally relevant judgments were all highly correlated in expected ways. For example, the primary decision ("Lift the order?" or "Is the defendant liable?") was correlated with judgments of probability that a serious accident would occur: the presence of a grave danger or risk of harm, the recklessness of the defendant's actions, the foreseeability of an accident, the degree to which the defendant exhibited disregard of the risk, and the extent to which the defendant's action was a gross deviation from the proper level of care.

V. Conclusion

The major result of the present study is an example of dramatic differences between judgments in foresight and in hindsight in the case of punitive damages decisions. Every measure of the probability of an accident, responsibility for the accident, and liability was sensitive to the manipulation of temporal perspective. For example, only 33% of one sample of jury-eligible citizens did not support the railroad's request to continue operations in foresight, but 67% of another sample judged the railroad's actions to warrant the assessment of punitive damages in hindsight after an accident had occurred. This dramatic shift occurred even though *ex post* no new information about the risks of an accident had been provided and the NTSB order to stop operations was not in effect. Similarly, the average estimate of the probability of a serious accident in foresight was .34, but in hindsight it was .59. The observed hindsight effect conforms to expectations based on common sense, and it is consistent with dozens of other experimental studies of legal and nonlegal judgments.

We also found that the hindsight effect was dispersed across several other inferences that are important in the context of the punitive damages liability decision. Participants rated the foreseeability of the accident and the defendant's conscious awareness of a grave danger as much higher in hindsight than in foresight. After the accident they also judged the decisions and decision makers who allowed the railroad to continue operations as substantially worse in quality.

Is the hindsight effect a bias and a defect of judgment? Kelman, Fallas, and Folger introduce a useful distinction among three varieties of hindsight effects.[8] The first refers to *ex post* adjustments in the perceived probability that an event would occur. Researchers have noted that under many conditions this form of learning from experience should not be called an error or a bias at all.[9] The second refers to people's mistaken belief that their *ex ante* and *ex post* judgments would have been more similar to one another than they would in fact have been (i.e., they represent the "I knew it all along" phenomenon). This second variety of hindsight is an error. The respondents are unaware of their altered perceptions, and it is descriptively inaccurate to believe that the *ex ante* judgment would have been similar to the *ex post* judgment.

The third form of hindsight effect refers to the projection of the "knew it all along" effect onto a third party; to judge that another person *ex ante* would have made judgments consistent with the *ex post* judgments. This third variety of hindsight effect is also an error of judgment, and it is most relevant to our empirical findings. The substantial effects of information about the accident on ratings of foreseeability, on conscious disregard of a grave danger, and on decision quality of a hypothetical *ex ante* decision maker are all clear-cut examples of the third variety of hindsight effects, and they are highly relevant to the distinctive differences between judgments of negligence and recklessness as set forth in the jury instructions on punitive damages: as noted earlier, reckless conduct requires a conscious choice of action, either with knowledge of serious danger to others or with knowledge of facts that would disclose the danger to any reasonable person. That is, the conclusion that the defendant was reckless requires an inference about that party's subjective state of mind, what the defendant knew, or what "anyone" should have known.

Unfortunately, there are no known general remedies for hindsight bias. The difficulty of ameliorating the effects of common judgment habits has been illuminated by the mostly unsuccessful efforts to design debiasing procedures. Kamin and Rachlinski, for example, tried a direct warning instruction, but it had no effect on their mock jurors' judgments.[10] More generally, Wilson and Brekke provide a catalog of the conditions that must be met by an effective debiasing procedure: (1) the

8. Mark Kelman et al., "Decomposing Hindsight Bias," 16 *J. Risk & Uncertainty* 251 (1998).

9. E.g., Scott A. Hawkins and Reid Hastie, "Hindsight: Biased Judgments of Past Events after the Outcomes Are Known," 107 *Psychol. Bull.* 311 (1990).

10. Kamin and Rachlinski, *supra* note 2.

person making the judgment must be aware of the bias; (2) the person must know the magnitude and direction of the biasing effect; (3) the person must be motivated to correct the bias; and (4) the person must have some means to correct the bias.[11] Since only the first condition can be guaranteed in many situations, including juror judgments, it is difficult to imagine a generally effective debiasing method.

Will the "crucible" of jury deliberation eliminate hindsight effects? We doubt it. If there are substantial hindsight effects in individual decisions, we would expect those effects to be reflected in group decisions.[12]

In conclusion, we believe that a hindsight bias is almost inevitable when jurors make punitive damages decisions. Further, we believe that this behavioral fact has important implications for the principles and procedures that should apply when juries make decisions concerning the liability of defendants for punitive damages. Some of the alternatives for dealing with hindsight in the context of punitive damages judgments are discussed later in this book.

11. Timothy D. Wilson and Nancy Brekke, "Mental Contamination and Mental Correction: Unwanted Influences on Judgments and Evaluations," 116 *Psychol. Bull.* 117 (1994).

12. Norbert L. Kerr et al., "Bias in Judgment: Comparing Individuals and Groups," 103 *Psychol. Rev.* 687 (1996); Dagmar Stahlberg et al., "We Knew It All Along: Hindsight Bias in Groups," 63 *Org. Behav. & Hum. Decision Processes* 46 (1995). ·

C. Jurors and Judges as Risk Managers

Introduction

Cass R. Sunstein

We now turn to some broader issues. Our principal interest is in the role of juries and judges as managers of risk. Do jurors attempt to ensure that punitive damages awards will contribute to sensible management of social risks? How, if at all, do they approach the question of risk regulation? Are judges better?

To understand these questions, a little background is in order. From the economic point of view, a key task of regulation, including regulation from courts and juries, is to produce *optimal deterrence*—neither too much nor too little deterrence of private conduct. Suppose that companies are in the business of producing medicine for children, and that the relevant medicine sometimes have harmful side effects. If those companies are entirely free to give children medicine that makes them sicker still, there will be too little deterrence. Clearly some kind of penalty is needed to ensure that companies have an adequate incentive to make sure that children are being helped, not hurt. But if the penalty is extremely high, there might be a problem. If companies that produce medicine are faced with extremely high awards from juries, there may be over-deterrence—companies might be deprived of the incentive to put good medicines on the market at all, for fear of a costly lawsuit. For those skeptical of this point, simply imagine punitive damages awards that are high enough to make it unprofitable for companies to be in this line of business at all.

These ideas are controversial, and we do not, as a group, intend to take a position on them here. Some people insist that the purpose of punishment is to ensure retribution rather than optimal deterrence. We suggest only that many policy analysts believe that the task of the legal system is to create penalties that are high enough to produce adequate deterrence, but not so high as to produce overdeterrence.

If this is our basic goal, punitive damages sometimes seem to make a great deal of sense. From the economic point of view, one problem with a system of compensatory damages is that even if they are hurt, some people will not obtain compensation at all. Perhaps they do not know that a particular product was responsible for their injury. Perhaps they lack the resources and the knowledge to bring suit. If so, punitive damages can make up for the shortfall in compensatory damages—ensuring that the defendant pays an amount equal to the total cost of the harms that it has caused. In fact, this is a standard economic approach to punitive damages awards.

It should be clear that a form of cost-benefit analysis is playing a central role in this approach. The goal is to use the legal system to ensure that the benefits of what companies are doing will outweigh the costs of what companies are doing. From this it follows that from the standpoint of managing social risks, it is desirable for companies to be conducting their own cost-benefit analysis before they market products, at least if the analysis is done honestly and accurately.

With this background, we ask in this section about jurors' attitudes toward the key questions. Chapter 7 finds that jurors do not respond favorably to corporate cost-benefit analysis. In fact, it finds that punitive damages awards increase, rather than decrease, when companies have done such an analysis, even when a high value is placed on the key variables (such as life). Sound cost-benefit analysis, of the sort that the legal system wants to encourage, can increase punitive damages awards.

In chapters 8 and 9, we explore a related question: Do jurors decrease punitive awards when the probability of detection is high, and increase such awards when the probability of detection is low? Chapter 8 shows that they do nothing of the sort—even when information about probability of detection is expressly provided, people tend to ignore it. In addition, people object to awards that go up or down with the probability of detection. Chapter 9 goes further. It shows that many people fail to follow a jury instruction (expressly urged by economic analysts) that asks them to take probability of detection into account.

Chapters 10 and 11 explore broader issues, of general interest and with relevance to how the law approaches punitive damages awards. Chapter 10 shows that ordinary people do not think very well about risks.

They are subject to various cognitive biases, leading them to overstate and understate hazards. These biases are highly likely to affect punitive damages awards, because such awards depend on judgments about risks. Chapter 11 shows that judges suffer from similar biases, but to a significantly smaller degree. How and whether these points bear on legal reforms are issues that we take up in chapter 13.

7

Corporate Risk Analysis: A Reckless Act?

W. Kip Viscusi

I. Introduction

In 1999 a Los Angeles jury imposed a $4.8 billion punitive damages award on General Motors for a case involving severe burns to passengers in a 1979 Chevrolet Malibu.[1] This award, which was the largest punitive award ever in a personal injury case,[2] arose in part because the company had undertaken an explicit analysis of the types of fire risks and design-change costs associated with burn injuries.[3] Even though a judge subsequently reduced the punitive damages award to $1.2 billion and the total award to $1.3 billion, the financial stakes remained at a level that was wildly disproportionate to the extent of the harm.[4] This and other instances of juror responses to what could be considered routine corporate product-safety decision making raise questions about how jurors think about punitive damages awards in products liability cases.

Trading off risk against cost is not foreign to any of us. Indeed, it is implicit in our daily lives. We face numerous prospects posing various levels of risk. To decide which risks to bear and which to avoid, we attempt to get a sense of how consequential the risks are and whether there is some offsetting advantage that makes bearing the risk reasonable. In designing their products, corporations also must make similar judgments

1. Andrew Pollack, "$4.9 Billion Jury Verdict in G.M. Fuel Tank Case," *N.Y. Times,* July 10, 1999, at A7; and Andrew Pollack, "Paper Trail Haunts G.M. after It Loses Injury Suit," *N.Y. Times,* July 12, 1999, at A12.

2. Ann W. O'Neill et al., "G.M. Ordered to Pay $4.9 Billion in Crash Verdict Liability," *L.A Times,* July 10, 1999, at A1. Subsequently, on July 14, 2000, a jury made a $145 billion award in a Florida tobacco class action case.

3. See Pollack, *supra* note 1.

4. See Frederic M. Biddle, "GM Verdict Cut $3.8 Billion in Suit over Explosion," *Wall St. J.,* Aug. 27, 1999, at B5. Also see "GM Vows to Appeal California Judge's Order Cutting Record Punitive Award to $1.2 Billion," 27 *BNA Product Safety & Liability Reporter* 866 (Sept. 3, 1999).

regarding the character of their products. To do so, they try to anticipate how their products will be used and what risks will be incurred in that usage. Another factor they must consider is consumer preferences, especially how much customers value safety as opposed to other product attributes, including its price.

The formal mechanism for making safety trade-off judgments is a risk analysis that outlines the costs and benefits of different safety options. Such an analysis usually proceeds in a series of steps. First, risk analysis involves identifying risks or hazards and then assessing their magnitudes. Is it a serious threat or a minor background risk? Second, how can each risk be reduced, and what would be the cost of changing the product design to achieve the risk reduction? Finally, comparing all the opportunities for safety improvement, which of them on balance do the most for consumer welfare and for the company's effort to market the product? Will consumers be willing to pay the price increases associated with these safety improvements? These decisions will be subject to market tests, policy tests, and the courts, as a company may have to defend itself against charges of negligence if there are accidents.[5]

We want companies to think systematically about safety rather than leaving such matters to more haphazard guesswork. Moreover, when companies place a value on safety, we want it to be sufficiently high—at a level commensurate with how those of us who will suffer the risk consequences value safety. It is therefore somewhat surprising that jurors do not appear to be receptive to such analyses.

To some, a corporation's decisions that ultimately must balance cost against risk may appear to some as a "cold-blooded calculation" invented by economists.[6] Indeed, as suggested by a number of actual cases, jurors in products liability cases appear to have a tendency to adopt that view. This tendency may be linked to anticorporate bias and a general suspicion

5. See A. Mitchell Polinsky, *An Introduction to Law and Economics* (2nd ed., 1989); Stephen G. Breyer, *Breaking the Vicious Circle: Toward Effective Risk Regulation* (1993); Richard A. Posner, *Economic Analysis of Law* (5th ed., 1998); and John W. Wade, "On the Nature of Strict Liability for Products," 44 *Miss. L.J.* 825, 837 (1973).

6. See The State of Mississippi Memorandum, *The State of Mississippi Tobacco Litigation,* Aug. 11, 1995. They variously describe my analysis for monetizing the health costs of cigarettes as "No court of equity should countenance, condone, or sanction such base, evil, and corrupt arguments . . . [*id.* at 21]. Seeking a credit for a purported economic benefit for early death is akin to robbing the graves of the Mississippi smokers who died from tobacco-related illness. . . . It is an offense to human decency, an affront to justice, uncharacteristic of civilized society, and unquestionably contrary to public policy" (at 23).

of corporate motives.[7] Explicit risk-cost trade-offs, which in effect balance lives lost and environmental damage against monetary costs, seem to offend juror sensibilities.

Whether undertaking a risk analysis actually leads a jury to add a sizable punitive damages award to the compensatory damages is largely a speculative matter if one relies solely on observation of court cases where we know that a company undertook a risk analysis and that punitive damages were awarded. Moreover, often the post-trial interviews single out the risk analysis as a pivotal concern. However, what is needed is a controlled experiment that isolates the role of different kinds of risk analyses and assesses their link to punitive damages awards. Does a risk analysis truly make a company more vulnerable to punitive damages, controlling for other aspects of the case?

While jurors might not consider all forms of risk analysis as a worthwhile corporate exercise, presumably they should view sound analyses that conform to the procedures used by government safety agencies positively. Moreover, analyses that value life more highly presumably should make corporate safety decisions less vulnerable to punitive damages sanctions. The experimental results in this chapter will show that these reasonable expectations are not always borne out, and in many respects, juror behavior is quite puzzling.

Whether the existence of a risk analysis by itself makes jurors more likely to award punitive damages cannot be assessed using actual case data. The apparent evidence of such a linkage in actual court cases is confounded by many variables and case differences. Using such data to assess the influence of any particular factor is elusive. To explore the incremental effect of risk analysis, I conducted an original survey of almost five hundred jury-eligible citizens, holding everything constant except the risk-analysis issue. In my survey, subjects were asked whether punitive damages were warranted, and in what magnitude, against a corporation that did a risk analysis showing that the benefits of the safety improvement did not exceed the costs. Two main themes emerged. First, risk analyses did not help a company's prospects with respect to punitive

7. A 1998 National Law Journal-DecisionQuest poll found that people often may think the worst of corporate actions: "Three out of four people said they believe executives of big companies often try to cover up the harm that they do, and more than one in five said they could not be a fair juror if a tobacco company were one of the parties to a case they were considering." See Peter Aronson et al., "Jurors: A Biased, Independent Lot," *Nat'l L.J.,* Nov. 2, 1998, at A1.

damages. Second, and even more puzzling, is that use of a high value of life by the company boosts the award level.

II. Hypotheses and Structure of the Juror Judgment Survey

To explore how jurors react to the presence of corporate risk analyses of product hazards, I constructed a survey in which jury-eligible citizens considered alternative accident scenarios. Some mock jurors considered cases in which no cost-benefit analysis was performed by the company, whereas other jurors considered variants of a case in which the company did perform such an analysis. By comparing the responses of the jurors across the different case treatments, one can ascertain the incremental influence of undertaking an economic analysis.

Summary of Experiment

Description: Each subject read one variation of a summary of a products liability/ personal injury case and then was asked to choose a punitive damages award against the defendant. The summaries were identical except for manipulation of whether or not the defendant company had done a cost-benefit analysis, whether or not the analysis contained an error, and the implied amount the company was willing to spend on product safety.

Number of subjects: 489 jury-eligible citizens.

Location: Phoenix, Arizona.

Decisions: Individual survey.

Stimuli: Written case summary and instructions.

A. Participants

The sample consisted of 489 adult participants, two-thirds female, with a mean age of forty-five and a median education level involving some college. Subjects were recruited to participate in the study by a survey research firm in Phoenix, Arizona, which reimbursed the participants for taking part in the study. Detailed multiple-regression analyses, which control for the influence of demographics, yield similar results to the overall sample comparisons.[8]

B. Materials and Procedure

The study examined a variety of hypotheses, leading to the five different scenarios that will be discussed further below. Here I will outline

---

8. These analyses are reported in W. Kip Viscusi, "Corporate Risk Analysis: A Reckless Act?" 52 *Stan. L. Rev.* 547 (2000).

Table 7.1. Juror Risk Survey Variations

	Description
Scenario	No Cost-Benefit Analysis
1	No analysis performed, $4 million cost per life saved
2	No analysis performed, $1 million cost per life saved
	Cost-Benefit Analysis Performed
3	Analysis using $800,000 compensatory damages amount to value life, $4 million cost per life saved
4	Analysis using NHTSA value-of-life figure of $3 million to value life, $4 million cost per life saved
5	Erroneous analysis using NHTSA value-of-life figure of $3 million to value life, estimated cost per life saved of $4 million but actual amount was $2 million
Survey Waves	Lives Lost
1	Total lives lost was ten
2	Total lives lost was four

the experimental structure and the principal hypotheses related to the scenarios, which are summarized in table 7.1. All scenarios involved a similar auto accident context. Scenario 1 is the baseline scenario, which will serve as the initial reference point. In that scenario the company performs no analysis and the cost per life saved is $4 million. By comparing the results in the other scenarios with this control group, one can ascertain the incremental effect of the risk-analysis manipulations as compared to the no-analysis case.

Table 7.2 outlines the following series of five hypotheses that can be tested using the juror results.

• Scenario 2 involves auto risks in which the cost per life saved for greater safety is less than in scenario 1, as it is now $1 million rather than $4 million. However, there is no corporate risk analysis in either case. Jurors should have a more favorable view of decisions in which the safety measures not undertaken by the company have a higher cost per life saved because increasing safety is more expensive. Thus, scenario 2 should be less favorable to the company than scenario 1.
• Comparing the results of scenario 1 with scenarios 3 through 5 in which the company did a risk analysis indicates whether a corporate

risk analysis is viewed as a responsible act or a red flag that leads jurors to punish the corporation.

• Comparing scenarios 3 and 4 provides a test of whether the type of corporate risk analysis matters, as scenario 3 values life based on compensatory damages and scenario 4 uses the statistical value of life of $3 million. Does it matter whether corporations use court awards as the reference point for assessing the cost of death or instead use a higher value consistent with government regulatory analyses? A higher value based on willingness to pay for safety should be regarded more favorably. However, the cognitive processes by which respondents think about appropriate punitive damages levels may lead them to focus on dollar figures in the case description as a means of thinking about the punitive damages value. If jurors believe that a company undervalued life and wants to set a punitive damages level that "sends the company a message," a higher value of life in the company's analysis may serve as an anchor that raises liability awards.

• Comparison of scenarios 4 and 5 indicates whether there is any effect of company errors in the risk-assessment component of the analysis.

• All scenarios were run using both four deaths and ten deaths as the accident context to see whether higher absolute-risk levels would lead jurors to impose greater sanctions on the company. Presumably more accidents for any given level of operations should be viewed more adversely.

The focal point of the risk-analysis cases is on whether the mock jurors would levy punitive damages and the amount of punitive damages they would choose to award. The substantive context of this decision is exemplified by the following case scenario that was used in the situation in which no analysis was performed (scenario 2). Respondents considered an analogous scenario in which only four people would die, as opposed to the ten given below:

> A major auto company with annual profits of $7 billion made a line of cars with a defective electrical system design. This failure has led to a series of fires in these vehicles that cause 10 burn deaths per year. Changing the design to prevent these deaths would cost $10 million for the 100,000 vehicles affected per year, or $100 each. The company thought that there might be some risk from the current design, but did not believe that it would be significant. The company notes that even with these injuries, the vehicle has one of the best safety records in its class.

Table 7.2. Summary of Experimental Structure, Hypotheses, and Results

Experimental Test	Hypothesis	Finding
Scenario 1 vs. scenario 2	Jurors will impose greater sanctions (i.e., increased frequency and magnitude of punitive damages) if safety improvements are cheaper or a lower cost per life saved is used.	No significant effect ($t_{PROB} = 1.58$; $t_{AMT} = 0.100$)
Scenario 1 vs. scenarios 3, 4, 5	Jurors will impose greater sanctions if firms undertake a risk analysis related to subsequent accidents.	Significant effect with large influence on award level ($t_{PROB} = 2.78$***; $t_{AMT} = 1.85$*)
Scenarios 1–2 vs. scenarios 3–5	Jurors will impose greater sanctions if firms undertake a risk analysis related to subsequent accidents.	Significant effect with influence on both probability and award level ($t_{PROB} = 2.11$**; $t_{AMT} = 2.45$**)
Scenario 3 vs. scenario 4	Jurors will not be as likely to punish corporate risk analysis using a higher value of life and in line with government regulatory practices. Alternative hypothesis: Higher value-of-life measures by the company serve as an anchor that boosts damages awards.	Insignificant effect in the "wrong" direction as awards increase with value of life used ($t_{PROB} = 0.08$; $t_{AMT} = 1.05$)
Scenario 4 vs. scenario 5	Juries will impose greater sanctions if corporations make errors in their risk analysis.	No significant effect ($t_{PROB} = 0.50$; $t_{AMT} = 0.60$)
Scenarios 1–5 (10 deaths) vs. scenarios 1–5 (4 deaths)	Juries will impose greater sanctions if the number of lives lost is greater.	No significant effect ($t_{PROB} = 0.80$; $t_{AMT} = 0.43$)

Note: t_{PROB} is the t-statistic for the difference in punitive-award probability means.
t_{AMT} is the t-statistic for the difference in award-level geometric means.
*statistically significant at 10% level, two-tailed test.
**statistically significant at 5% level, two-tailed test.
***statistically significant at 1% level, two-tailed test.

The courts have awarded each of the victim's families $800,000 in damages to compensate them for the income loss and pain and suffering that resulted. After these lawsuits, the company altered future designs to eliminate the problem.

By indicating that the product was "defective," the intent of the question was not to draw a legal conclusion but simply to indicate that the system failed to operate in a completely safe manner.[9] Moreover, even if the respondents concluded that a defect existed from a legal standpoint, that would be consistent with the award of compensatory damages. As indicated in the survey text, the court already awarded compensatory damages, and the only concern is whether punitive damages are warranted.

Respondents then considered two questions. The first was whether or not punitive damages should be awarded "to punish the company for reckless behavior." Second, the respondents were asked for a dollar amount of punitive damages if they chose to award such damages to the survivors, where they picked from the following possibilities: $100,000, $1 million, $10 million, $100 million, and some other amount selected by the respondent.

Different groups in the sample considered the five different scenarios summarized in table 7.1. In much of the discussion below, these different scenarios will be pooled into broader categories since there were no statistically significant differences among many of the major component groupings. The first broad category consists of the two scenarios in which the company performed no cost-benefit analysis of the product hazard. In scenario 1 the company did not perform the analysis, but the cost per life saved would have been $4 million. In scenario 2, which is the one that was reproduced in the text above, the details of the scenario were the same except the cost per life saved was $1 million.

The fact that jurors are unresponsive to the cost per life saved is consistent with what will turn out to be the broader theme in these results, which is that the key substantive concerns that one would expect to drive the jurors' views do not in fact have a statistically significant influence. One would expect that jurors should be more likely to levy punitive

9. For example, *Black's Law Dictionary* 376 (5th ed., 1979) defines defect as "the want or absence of some legal requisite; deficiency; imperfection; insufficiency." This terminology is not substantially different from popular usage, "an imperfection that impairs worth or utility," as defined in *Webster's Ninth New Collegiate Dictionary* 333 (9th ed., 1990).

damages if the cost per life saved is lower than if it is higher because companies are presumably more remiss if it is cheaper to provide a safe product. The expense that the company needs to incur to provide for greater product safety is less when the cost per life saved is low, making safety expenditures more attractive. However, in all of the statistical tests using regression results, the level of the cost per life saved did not have any significant effect on juror decisions to levy punitive damages or on the amount of the award.

The second set of scenarios—scenarios 3 through 5—consists of those in which the company performed a cost-benefit analysis of some kind. In scenario 3 the company performed the analysis in much the same manner as did Ford and GM, in cases to be discussed below, by using an amount that is comparable to the compensatory damages amount for such cases. In particular, this scenario assumed that the company used an $800,000 amount to value the lives lost. In this as well as in the two subsequent scenarios, the cost that the company would have had to incur to save a statistical life was $4 million.

In scenario 4 the company instead undertook the analysis in a manner that follows the approach taken by government regulatory agencies. Rather than use the compensatory damages amount, it used a value-of-life figure based on society's willingness to pay to prevent small risks of death. This measure consequently goes beyond the value of a person's earnings or the usual amount of a compensatory damages award. Rather, it reflects the risk-cost trade-off based on the individual's own willingness to pay for greater safety. This approach is suggested for use throughout the federal government by the U.S. Office of Management and Budget.[10] As described by the survey:

> To determine whether the safety improvement was worthwhile, the company used a value of $3 million per accidental death, which is the value used by the National Highway Traffic Safety Administration in setting auto safety standards. The company estimated that the annual safety benefits of this safer design would be $30 million (10 expected deaths at $3 million per death), while the cost would be $40 million. As a result, the company believed that other safety improvements might save more lives at less cost.

10. See U.S. Office of Management and Budget, *Regulatory Program of the United States Government, April 1, 1992–March 31, 1993* (1993).

By comparing the results for scenario 4 with those in scenario 3, we can ascertain whether undertaking a systematic analysis patterned after those used by the government has any beneficial influence on how the jurors view a cost-benefit analysis of product-safety designs. Some may question whether the efficiency test embodied in that standard is appropriate.[11] However, even if one does not accept it, surely the company is being more responsible by valuing lives more highly in scenario 4 than scenario 3. Alternatively, comparing scenario 4 with scenario 1 makes it possible to ascertain whether performing an analysis helps or hurts the company's position in the eyes of the jury, holding constant the cost-per-life-saved value.

The final survey variant in scenario 5 is that in which the company makes a mistake in assessing the risk component in the analysis by underestimating the number of deaths by a factor of two. Under this analysis the company estimates that the cost per life saved would be $4 million, whereas in fact it turns out to be $2 million. Because the reference value of life used by the National Highway Traffic Safety Administration (NHTSA) is $3 million per life, this error represents the difference between the analysis passing a cost-benefit test and failing such a test. The company believed that it passed, but because of the error it did not. Comparison of the results in scenario 5 with scenario 4 enables us to determine whether such errors in a cost-benefit analysis affect juror attitudes toward corporate risk analysis.

The bottom rows in tables 7.1 and 7.2 indicate the different waves of the survey. One set of respondents considered the set of five scenarios in which the total lives lost was ten. A second set of respondents considered the identical scenarios, except that the total lives lost was four. The scale of the risk in terms of the number of lives lost did not have any statistically significant influence on the responses. Thus, within the ranges examined, neither the cost per life saved nor the absolute level of the risk had any statistically significant influence on jurors' propensity to award punitive damages.

11. See Steven Garber, "Punitive Damages and Deterrence of Efficiency—Promoting Analysis: A Problem without a Solution," 52 *Stan. L. Rev.* 1809 (2000). He suggests the possibility that people might prefer that companies value safety by more than market forces would dictate. This hypothesis is certainly true if people undervalue or underestimate the risk. But if risks are well-known, the result will be that people will pay higher prices for more safety devices than they would want if choosing themselves. Do people really want the subcompact Ford Focus to have the same expensive safety features as the Mercedes ML320 sport utility vehicle?

III. Results: Findings for the Risk-Analysis Scenarios

Table 7.3 reports the overall mean values of the jurors' reactions to the five different scenarios both in terms of their propensity to award punitive damages as well as the dollar value of such awards. The different versions of the survey are listed in the first column of table 7.3, where in addition to presenting each of the different scenarios, I also summarize the results for the combined group of two scenarios in which no cost-benefit analysis was performed, the three scenarios in which there was such a cost-benefit analysis, and all five scenarios.

Consider first the frequency with which punitive damages were

Table 7.3. Jurors' Reactions to Automotive Negligence Case

Panel A: Scenarios with No Cost-Benefit Analysis by Company			
Version of survey	Sample Size	Proportion Favoring Punitive Damages	Geometric Mean of Awards ($ millions)	Median Award
$4 million/life (scenario 1)	97	.845	2.95	1.0
$1 million/life (scenario 2)	97	.918	2.86	1.0
Combined no analysis by company	194	.881	2.91	1.0
Panel B: Scenarios with Cost-Benefit Analysis by Company			
Version of survey	Sample Size	Proportion Favoring Punitive Damages	Geometric Mean of Awards ($ millions)	Median Award
Court costs as value (scenario 3)	97	.928	4.02	3.5
NHTSA value of life (scenario 4)	102	.931	5.31	10.0
NHTSA value of life, error (scenario 5)	96	.948	4.50	10.0
Combined analysis by company	295	.936	4.59	10.0
Panel C: Full Sample Results			
Version of survey	Sample Size	Proportion Favoring Punitive Damages	Geometric Mean of Awards ($ millions)	Median Award
Total for all five scenarios	489	.914	3.85	5.0

Note: t-test (punitive damages frequency): $t = 2.0958*$
    t-test (in punitive damages amount): $t = 2.4431*$
*Statistically significant at 5% level, two-tailed test.

awarded. In scenario 1, which is the reference scenario in which the cost to save a life was $4 million but no analysis was performed, 85% of these subjects were willing to award punitive damages. This figure rises to 92% for scenario 2 in which no analysis is performed but the cost to save a life drops to $1 million.[12] Overall, the two versions of the survey in which there is no analysis performed had 88% of the subjects awarding punitive damages. Because of this high base level, the incremental effect of the corporate analysis scenarios will largely be manifested in damages levels.

Presumably, one would expect jurors to be more lenient if the company could justify its actions based on a cost-benefit analysis. The opposite turns out to be the case. In the three scenarios in which the company did perform a cost-benefit analysis using either compensatory damages amounts or the willingness-to-pay-for-safety measure for the value of life, the probability of awarding punitive damages ranges from 0.93 to 0.95, where these differences are not statistically significant across the different cases.[13] Thus, the character of the analysis that the company performs does not have a statistically significant effect. There is, however, a statistically significant difference between the pooled scenarios 3 through 5 in which a company did an analysis and the pooled scenarios 1 and 2 in which it did not. Overall, the scenarios in which a company performed an analysis led to a punitive damages award 94% of the time, which is 6% higher than the two cases for which no analysis was performed and 9% higher than when no analysis was performed and the cost per life saved is $4 million per life (scenario 1). The extent of the overall variation in the award frequency is not great because of the high propensity of jurors to award punitive damages for all these scenarios.

One might be tempted to conclude that the small but statistically significant increase in the frequency of punitive damages after a company performs a risk analysis is not a strong effect. However, that conclusion misses the essence of what should have happened. If a corporation performs a risk analysis that shows that the costs of greater safety measures exceed the benefits, then the company's behavior passes the traditional Learned Hand test for negligence. It does not seem to be a form of reckless behavior that would warrant punitive damages. One consequently would have expected risk analysis to decrease the frequency of punitive damages, but no negative influence was observed. The absence

12. These values are not, however, statistically different from each other, as is indicated by the associated *t* value of 1.58.

13. In particular, the highest *t*-statistic is 0.545.

of a reduction in the likelihood of punitive damages is in itself a strong effect that goes against theoretical predictions. However, matters are in fact much worse, as undertaking a risk analysis raises rather than lowers the frequency of punitive damages awards. The direction of the effect is disturbing because jurors are doing the opposite of what juries should be doing if corporations are to be encouraged to think systematically about risk and cost trade-offs.

Considerably more variation is displayed with respect to the magnitude of the awards. As in the case of punitive damages frequency, the hypothesis is that risk analyses should reduce punitive damages. The last two columns in table 7.3 present the geometric mean of the award value and the median award amount. Because of the strong influence of high award outliers, these two measures provide a more reliable index of the award levels than does a standard arithmetic mean. There is a remarkable difference across the no-analysis and risk-analysis scenarios. For the two scenarios in which the company did not undertake a cost-benefit analysis, the value of the awards is almost identical. The geometric mean value ranges from $2.86 million to $2.95 million, or an average across the two groups of $2.91 million. The median value is identical for both scenario 1 and scenario 2, as it is $1 million.

As is indicated by the bottom rows of panels A and B of table 7.3, the award amount is roughly 50% greater in situations in which the company performed a cost-benefit analysis, as compared to the no-analysis scenarios. Overall, the scenarios in which an analysis was performed led to damages with a geometric mean value of $4.59 million, as compared to $2.91 million in punitive damages when no analysis was undertaken. A similar and more dramatic pattern is characterized by the median values, which are $1 million when no analysis is performed and $10 million when the company does a cost-benefit analysis.

The theoretical hypothesis is that performing a risk analysis should *decrease* punitive damages awards. That hypothesis is not borne out. However, once again matters are much worse than would be the case if we did not find the expected influence. Risk analyses led jurors to boost the award level, thus having the effect that is opposite of theoretical predictions.

It is interesting to compare how the company's performance changes when it performs a cost-benefit analysis following government norms, as in scenario 4, rather than simply using the value of compensatory damages as the measure for the value of life, as in scenario 3. Based on the economic merits, the company should fare better when it values life correctly and at a higher amount than when it simply uses the compensatory damages value. Moreover, respondents also are told that the company's approach follows that used by the National Highway Traffic Safety Administration. However, undertaking a sound risk analysis does not prove to be beneficial to the company's prospects. The propensity of the respondents to award punitive damages is almost identical—0.93— in each case. However, the level of punitive damages awarded turns out to be greater when the company performed the analysis correctly than when it simply used the compensatory damages value. The geometric mean award value increases from \$4.0 million to \$5.3 million in scenario 4 as compared to scenario 3, and the median award value is \$10 million for scenario 4, which is more than twice as great as the \$3.5 million median value for scenario 3.[14]

Performing the analysis more responsibly and valuing life at a higher amount leads juries to impose greater sanctions than when the company does the analysis but places a lower value on improvements in safety. This effect is exactly counter to expectations, because a higher value of life used by the company reflects a greater level of concern for safety for which the company should be rewarded, not punished. How might such an effect that is opposite of any reasonable pattern of behavior arise? The mock jurors seem to make little distinction with respect to whether there should be an award of punitive damages. However, the higher value-of-life amount used by the company in scenario 4 as compared to scenario 3 provides a dollar anchor for the jury in thinking about the appropriate punitive damages award. Somewhat perversely, use of a higher value-of-life estimate for the company's internal analysis of what it is worth to save a life may raise the target award level in the minds of the jury as they seek to impose a damages amount that will provide more of an incentive for safety than the company exhibited in its own internal analysis. Companies are consequently in the bizarre position of increasing the potential damages award that the jury may levy the greater the weight they place on consumer safety, as is reflected in their internal value-of-life estimate.

Anchoring effects for punitive damages are not unique to this particu-

---

14. Using the geometric mean, this difference is not, however, statistically significant. The median award level does differ significantly. Using a median regression yields a t-value of 3.36.

lar context. As was found in chapter 4, requests by the plaintiff's attorney for larger damages amounts tend to increase the dollar value of the award. Such requests are not entirely arbitrary, as they are often accompanied by irrelevant but superficially plausible mathematical formulas, such as an arbitrary percentage of the firm's profits or sales, based on the purported need to send the company a message. Indeed, the results in chapter 2 indicate that jurors in fact may have very little idea as to how to map their concerns for the corporation's behavior into a dollar amount. My results are even more disturbing, as there is not only an anchoring phenomenon that is the opposite of the desired effect, but there should not even be punitive damages of any kind triggered by responsible risk analyses.

Finally, consider scenario 5 in which the company undertook a flawed cost-benefit analysis. Comparison with the counterpart scenario 4 in which there was no such error suggests that errors are not that consequential. The jury was somewhat more likely to award punitive damages in the erroneous analysis case (0.95 probability vs. 0.93), but exhibited somewhat lower proclivities to penalize the firm ($4.5 million in punitive damages for scenario 5 vs. $5.3 million for scenario 4). Overall, there were no statistically significant differences between these two scenarios. Doing the analysis wrong is no better or worse than doing it right.

More detailed statistical analyses controlling for the different features of each scenario and respondent characteristics yield similar results.[15] Taking into account the influence of personal characteristics, undertaking a risk analysis increases the probability of a punitive damages award by 5%. It is somewhat noteworthy that the cost-per-life-saved amount and the absolute-risk level do not have a significant effect on the probability of a punitive damages award, as jurors seem to be unresponsive to variations in the underlying risk characteristics. Undertaking a cost-benefit analysis of risk does not help the company but instead boosts the value of punitive damages awarded by 47%. The cost-per-life-saved amount and the absolute-risk level do not play significant roles in affecting jury behavior.

IV. Synthetic Juries

The results for the corporate risk-analysis scenarios thus far have focused on individual responses and the determinants of these results. A

---

15. For a fuller report on these analyses, see W. Kip Viscusi, "Jurors, Judges, and the Mistreatment of Risk by the Courts," 30 *J. Legal Stud.* 107 (2001).

somewhat different question is how juries would actually perform in such cases. Instead of focusing on an individual, the issue becomes one of group decision making. The approach here will consider a series of synthetic juries drawn randomly from the 489 respondents on a scenario-by-scenario basis. As with the synthetic-jury analysis in chapter 2, these synthetic-jury results will give some indication of how the decision to award punitive damages and the determination of the level of punitive damages would have fared in a jury context. However, as the comparison of the synthetic-jury results in chapter 2 with actual group decision making reported in chapter 3 indicates, group decision making in practice may lead to more extreme awards rather than a moderation of outcomes.[16]

The procedure used to construct the synthetic juries is the following: For each of the five versions of the survey, a random sampling replacement procedure was used to draw a thousand juries of twelve individuals. For these thousand mock juries, it is possible to analyze the distribution of the number of jurors who favored the awarding of punitive damages as well as the level of punitive damages that they favored.

Consider first the distribution of the number of jurors favoring punitive damages. For scenario 1 in which the company undertook no analysis but there was a cost per life saved of $4 million, there were very few cases in which the jurors were unanimous in favoring a punitive damages award. In only 12.8% of the cases did all twelve jurors favor a punitive damages award, and in only 28.2% of the cases did eleven of the jurors favor punitive damages. If, however, the cost per life saved drops to $1 million as in scenario 2, the jurors become much more willing to levy punitive damages. Jurors unanimously recommended punitive damages 35.4% of the time, and all but one juror favored punitive damages 40.2% of the time. For the overall combined results of the two thousand synthetic juries for scenarios 1 and 2, 24.1% of the juries unanimously favored punitive damages, and an additional 34.2% had all but one juror in favor of punitive damages.

The results for the three analysis scenarios indicate a striking willingness of jurors to levy punitive damages. The instances in which all jurors unanimously favored punitive damages range from 39.0% for scenario 3 to 47.6% in scenario 5. The instances in which all but one juror favored

---

16. Indeed, this phenomenon may be more general, as is indicated by recent research by Cass Sunstein, e.g., Cass R. Sunstein, "Deliberative Trouble? Why Groups Go to Extremes," 110 *Yale L.J.* 71 (2000).

punitive damages average approximately 40.0% in all three scenarios. The combined analysis of the three thousand synthetic juries in scenarios 3 through 5 yields 42.3% of the synthetic juries that unanimously favored punitive damages, with an additional 40.6% having all but one juror in favor of punitive damages. Overall, 82.9% of the synthetic juries had eleven or twelve jurors favoring punitive damages in the three scenarios in which the companies did analysis, as compared to 58.3% of the juries for the two situations in which the company did not do analysis.

These results in the frequency of awarding punitive damages for the synthetic juries consequently magnify the differences that were found in individual responses above. Consideration of the frequency in which jurors awarded punitive damages on an individual basis did not yield as striking results for the probability of awarding punitive damages as it did for the level of punitive damages. However, once these individuals are placed within a group context, the role of these differences becomes very apparent. The greater willingness of jurors to levy punitive damages when the company performs a risk analysis dramatically shifts the balance within a jury to a level that is much more nearly unanimous or almost unanimously in favor of punitive damages.

The second issue pertaining to the role of synthetic juries is the level of punitive damages that they would award. Here I will focus on the award level favored by the median juror. As was indicated in chapter 3, the median award appears to be the most representative statistic for reflecting actual jury behavior.

The synthetic-jury results for the award levels reflect the patterns found earlier for the individual responses as well as the kinds of discrepancies reflected in the synthetic-jury results for the probability of awarding punitive damages. For the combined results for scenarios 1 and 2, the median award level is $1 million and the mean award level is $3 million. The three analysis scenarios each indicate higher award levels than in the no-analysis situations. The combined results for the three analysis scenarios indicate a median award level of $6 million. The highest awards occur not when the company used a low value of life based on court awards in scenario 3; nor does it occur in scenario 5 in which the company undertook erroneous analysis. Rather, it is for scenario 4 in which the company performed the analysis correctly and in line with the procedures used by the National Highway Traffic Safety Administration that the juries levied its greatest sanction—$7.5 million for a median award.

What these synthetic-jury results suggest is that the individual differences in the propensity to award punitive damages and the setting of the level of punitive damages may translate into considerable differences in terms of actual group decision-making outcomes. Moreover, as in the individual results, the results are the opposite of what one would hope to find. Performing a risk analysis is likely to tilt the jurors against the company in a manner that can have a demonstrable and substantial effect on jury outcomes.

V. Conclusion

The original mock-juror analysis done for this study made it possible to isolate which factors affected juror beliefs and how they were influential. The most consistent result across the different scenarios was that undertaking any type of risk analysis was harmful to the corporation's prospects both with respect to the probability of punitive damages and, more important, with respect to the magnitude of the award. Risk analyses consequently may trigger reactions consistent with the outrage model in chapter 2.

Another finding relates to the anchor effect described in chapter 4. Because jurors are basically left without guidance in setting a punitive damages award size, they grasp on to any numbers that are available. In my surveys I manipulated the value of life used by corporations in their cost-benefit analyses. Using a higher value of life as now recommended by the National Highway Traffic Safety Administration rather than the compensatory damages value means that a company is willing to spend more on safety. But in the mock-juror tests, the higher value had the perverse effect of inducing jurors to make larger punitive damages awards.

Another interesting finding from the test was what factors did not affect the likelihood and magnitude of punitive damages awards. Ideally, the expense of greater safety should be consequential. But what companies spent on safety had no significant effect on juror attitudes. Similarly, the number of deaths relative to the cost of eliminating a hazard would seem to be a determining factor in setting punishment, but it was not influential.

The recurring theme is that mock jurors reacted strongly and negatively when companies did cost-benefit analysis. Other factors had no influence on the jurors' punitive damages awards except for companies' willingness to spend more on safety, which increased award size.

Why do jurors punish corporations for risk-cost balancing? A variety of conjectures are possible. People may be averse to explicit balancing of costs and risks involving human lives. Money and lives are in different units that one may view as incommensurable. MacCoun has observed that these experiments may have generated the observed effects because they involve "taboo trade-offs" in which people simply don't want to explicitly trade off lives and money.[17] Thus, money and lives are not only measured using different metrics, but they also involve a comparison that some may believe is inappropriate to make.

The frame of reference that respondents use also may be retrospective rather than prospective. A respondent might not focus on the trade-off available at the time of the safety decision, which is between cost and small probabilities of an accident, not the certainty of an adverse outcome. In hindsight a small corporate expenditure would have prevented an identifiable death, whereas *ex ante* it is statistical lives that are at risk. Such pairwise comparisons involving identified victims and safety costs will be overwhelming, particularly for low-probability/high-loss events where the consequences are immense after the fact, but had a low expected value weighted by their small probability of occurrence. When corporations systematically attempt to identify all hazards, it will be economically prohibitive to eliminate all of them. Another way of saying this is that "zero risk" is unachievable. When an accident occurs due to a hazard that was identified but not eliminated, jurors may regard the corporate decision as "cold-blooded." This difficulty arises, in part, because of the well-documented role of hindsight bias with respect to retrospective risk judgments.

Hindsight alone surely is not the only factor at work. All the scenarios involved the same element of hindsight.[18] However, the role of hindsight may interact with what risk-analysis procedures the company took before the accident. If there was a careful analysis of a risk that was incurred before choosing to take the action generating the risk, respondents may feel quite differently about such analyses after the fact than if no analysis had been done. Indeed, that is what these results suggest. The role of hindsight consequently may not be uniform in all cases but may be quite different when interacting with a situation in which the company is making trade-offs that some may view as inappropriate.

17. See Robert J. MacCoun, "The Costs and Benefits of Letting Juries Punish Corporations: Comment on Viscusi," 52 *Stan. L. Rev.* 1821 (2000).
18. MacCoun, *id.,* makes this observation.

From an economic standpoint, what matters at the time of the corporate decision is the cost of the safety measure compared to the expected benefits. Benefits are expressed as the reduced probability of an accident multiplied by the value of the likely damage from an accident. But, as Judge Frank Easterbrook observed, hindsight bias is a "hydraulic force" compelling jurors not to compare the expected, probabilistic benefits and costs but to simply compare the loss to the victim before them against the costs to save that individual.[19] These types of influences may also contribute to the failure of risk analyses to be viewed as a worthwhile or necessary corporate effort.

19. See *Carrol v. Otis Elevator,* 896 F.2d 210, 215 (7th Cir. 1990) (Easterbrook, F., concurring).

8

Do People Want Optimal Deterrence?

Cass R. Sunstein, David A. Schkade,
and Daniel Kahneman

I. Introduction

For those interested in the effects of law on human behavior, deterrence is of course a central question. In this chapter we explore whether people seek *optimal deterrence,* as this idea is understood in the economic analysis of law. Our basic finding is that they do not. People appear to reject the view, widespread within economic analysis, that punishment should be increased beyond compensation where the probability of detection is low, and that compensation is adequate where the probability of detection is 100%. As throughout, our principal interest here is descriptive, not normative. Our central finding should be of interest both to those who accept and to those who reject the economic approach to punishment.

In the first and principal study, we focused people's attention on the probability that an objectionable action will be detected and punished, and examined whether they used this information in determining punitive damages. As we have noted at various points, the probability of detection is a key issue in economic analysis of deterrence; punitive damages are designed, in the economic view, to make up for the "shortfall" created when injured people do not obtain compensation. But in this first study we found that ordinary people do not pay attention to the probability of detection, even when it is explicitly drawn to their attention.

In the second study we asked the optimal deterrence question more directly. We presented respondents with the question of whether it is proper for a judge to refuse to allow punitive damages when the defendant is certain to be caught and required to pay compensation (i.e., the probability of detection is 100%). As we shall see, a strong majority of respondents rejected optimal deterrence in this context. Our findings here should be read in close concert with those in chapter 9, which finds that people do not conduct the mathematical operations recommended by those who seek optimal deterrence.

II. Background and Hypotheses

The economic theory of punishment in general, and of punitive damages in particular, is designed to ensure optimal deterrence of private and public misconduct. Emphasizing this point, many observers have suggested that participants in the legal system should be asked to choose among punishments by attempting to achieve optimal deterrence.[1] To take just one illustration, Polinsky and Shavell have gone so far as to offer a model jury instruction, one that would direct jurors to focus their attention on the probability that the defendant's act would be detected.[2]

Extending and elaborating on the standard law and economics wisdom on this topic, Polinsky and Shavell urge that a principal purpose of punitive awards is to make up for the shortfall in compensatory damages, a shortfall caused by the failure of potential plaintiffs to detect the injury and to seek compensation. Polinsky and Shavell would ask jurors to calculate a total award (compensatory plus punitive damages) by dividing the compensatory award by the probability that injured persons would detect and receive compensation for the injury.[3] Thus, for example, no punitive award should be permitted when the probability of

1. Robert D. Cooter, "Economic Analysis of Punitive Damages," 56 *S. Cal. L. Rev.* 79 (1982); Robert D. Cooter, "Punitive Damages for Deterrence: When and How Much?" 40 *Ala. L. Rev.* 1143 (1989); William M. Landes and Richard A. Posner, *The Economic Structure of Tort Law* 160–63 (1987).

2. A. Mitchell Polinsky and Steven Shavell, "Punitive Damages: An Economic Analysis," 111 *Harv. L. Rev.* 869 (1998).

3. *Id.* at 957–62. We emphasize the Polinsky and Shavell analysis because it is the most recent and detailed discussion of punitive damages from the standpoint of optimal deterrence. But note that they also discuss the possibility that punitive damages should be awarded to "punish" as well as to deter; see *id.* at 948–54, in particular by "imposing appropriate sanctions on blameworthy parties" (*id.* at 948). They suggest that this rationale is "significantly attenuated" when the defendant is a firm, because "the imposition of punitive damages on firms often penalizes individuals who are unlikely to be considered culpable, namely, shareholders and customers" (*id.* at 949). They also note that there is a question of how to determine the level of damages "when the objectives of deterrence and punishment have different implications" (*id.* at 955). Because we are interested in the deterrence question, we do not attempt to elicit the ingredients of punishment decisions here. But we observe that there is no evidence that people accept the plausible distinction offered by Polinsky and Shavell—between firms and the shareholders and consumers (or, for that matter, employees not responsible for the underlying harm) who may be adversely affected by punitive damages.

compensation is 100%, and the compensatory award should be doubled when the probability is 50%.[4] Polinsky and Shavell object that in the real world, jurors do not attempt to promote optimal deterrence; their jury instruction is designed to move juror performance in that direction.

An obvious question raised by proposals of this kind is whether jurors are able or willing to carry out the relevant tasks. In various places (see especially chapter 2), we have suggested that people's judgments about punitive damages awards are a reflection of outrage at the defendant's actions rather than of deterrence, a suggestion confirmed by other research as well.[5] This is not to say that people do not care about deterrence; of course they do. Our hypothesis here is that they do not seek to promote optimal deterrence; for this reason they do not make the kinds of distinctions that are obvious, even second nature, for those who study deterrence questions. Above all, they do not believe that in order to ensure optimal deterrence, the amount that a given defendant is required to pay should be increased or decreased depending on the probability of detection, a central claim in the economic analysis of law.

A. Relevant Psychological Research

Outside of the context of punitive damages, psychological work on punishment has suggested that when thinking about punishment, people's ideas diverge from what would be expected from an optimal deterrence approach. For example, Baron and Ritov studied people's judgments about penalties in tort cases involving harms resulting from the use of vaccines and birth control pills.[6] In one case, subjects were told that the result of a higher penalty would be to make companies try harder to make safer products. In an adjacent case, subjects were told that the

4. There are some qualifications here. As noted, Polinsky and Shavell offer a separate discussion of punishment, and they would also allow punitive damages to force the defendant to disgorge socially illicit gains; here the purpose would be to promote optimal deterrence by ensuring that the defendant, if an individual, is not able to profit from (illicit) hedonic gains from, say, an assault or rape (*id.* at 909–10, 954). It is also possible to imagine routes to optimal deterrence that diverge from the conventional "multiplier" approach. See Richard Craswell "Deterrence and Damages: The Multiplier Principle and Its Alternatives," 97 *Mich. L. Rev.* 2185 (1999). These and other qualifications are essentially irrelevant to our claims here.

5. Jonathan Baron and Ilana Ritov, "Intuitions about Penalties and Compensation in the Context of Tort Law," 7 *J. Risk & Uncertainty* 17 (1993); Jonathan Baron et al., "Attitudes toward Managing Hazardous Waste—What Should Be Cleaned Up and Who Should Pay for It?" 13 *Risk Analysis* 183 (1993).

6. Baron and Ritov, *supra* note 5.

consequence of a higher penalty would be to make the company more likely to stop making the product, with the result that less safe products would be on the market. Most subjects, including a group of judges, gave the same penalties in both cases. A related study found no reduction in penalty even when subjects were told that the amount of the penalty would have no effect on future behavior—because the penalty was secret, the company had insurance, and the company was about to go out of business. While not directly tied to the topic of optimal deterrence, these studies strongly suggest that intuitive punishment judgments are not tailored to consequentialist goals.

Another test of punishment judgments asked subjects, including judges and legislators, to choose penalties for dumping hazardous waste.[7] In one case the penalty would make companies try harder to avoid waste. In another the penalty would lead companies to cease making a beneficial product. Most people did not penalize companies differently in the two cases. Perhaps most strikingly, people preferred to require companies to clean up their own waste, even if the waste did not threaten anyone, instead of spending the same amount to clean up far more dangerous waste produced by another, now-defunct company.

These studies indicate that when assessing punishment, people do not focus solely on social consequences, at least not in any simple way. If this is true, it is reasonable to think that people also do not attempt to promote optimal deterrence. But this proposition had not been tested before. We attempt to make some progress on the question here, above all, by asking people to focus on a key variable: the probability of detection.

III. Experiment 1: The Irrelevance of Probability of Detection
A. Participants and Materials

The first study offered three personal injury cases to test the effect of explicitly varying the probability of detection on juror judgments. We examined whether people would offer different judgments about penalty

---

7. Baron et al., *supra* note 5. There is, in fact, a large literature documenting that deterrence considerations do not explain public opinion toward punishment, even when members of the public say that "deterrence" is their primary concern. See, e.g., Tom R. Tyler and Renee Weber, "Support for the Death Penalty: Instrumental Response to Crime, or Symbolic Attitude," 17 *Law & Soc'y Rev.* 21 (1982); Phoebe C. Ellsworth and Samuel R. Gross, "Hardening of the Attitudes: Americans' Views on the Death Penalty," 50 *J. Soc. Issues* 19 (1994).

levels when the probability of detection was altered. In one case, for example, the plaintiff suffered serious postoperative complications after surgery on his broken leg. He claimed that the surgeon was incompetent and sued the owner of the hospital. The hospital had previously received several complaints about the surgeon but had not disciplined him. Compensatory damages had already been awarded.

Summary of Experiment

Description: Each subject read one variation of a personal injury case summary and instructions and was then asked to choose a punitive damages award against the defendant. There were nine variations: three different cases and three values of the probability that the defendant's tortious behavior would be detected. This probability is a key factor in the optimal deterrence formula for punitive damages. Law students were given a case summary and asked if they agreed with the judge who denied punitive damages in accordance with optimal deterrence theory.

Number of subjects: 699 jury-eligible citizens; 84 law students.

Location: Phoenix, Arizona; Chicago, Illinois.

Decisions: Individual survey.

Stimuli: Written case summary and instructions.

B. Procedure

Three versions of each case were prepared. These differed only in the relative frequency of detection, which was set at 1 out of 100, 1 out of 10, or 1 out of 5. The level of compensatory damages was the same for all cases ($200,000) as was firm size (annual profits of around $150 million). Here, for example, is the relevant wording for one of the cases:

> In situations like this, victims who deserve compensation do not always receive it because (1) they don't know what caused their problem and therefore don't sue, (2) they don't know that they can sue, or (3) they sue and lose, even though they deserve to win under the law, because their lawyers are not good enough. Research has shown that in only 1 out of 100 situations where someone has an experience like Joan Glover is the company eventually required to pay compensation to the victim.

Note that several features of this design were specifically selected in order to enhance the likelihood that respondents would use, rather than ignore, the information provided on the probability of detection. Both firm size and compensatory damages were held constant; moreover, a quantitative response was required. Thus the design drew attention to the only number that varied between cases, the probability of detection, increasing the chance that it would be thought relevant. The probability information was also provided in the form of relative frequencies, which are more easily understood and processed than decimals. Respondents were specifically directed to deterrence (as well as retribution) in the jury instructions.

Respondents were randomly assigned to one of nine conditions, which were constructed to ensure that (1) each respondent judged all three cases, (2) each respondent judged all three levels of probability of detection, (3) across respondents, all nine combinations of case and probability of detection were equally represented in each of the three ordinal positions (first, second, third). The design is summarized in table 8.1.

A total of 699 jury-eligible citizens from Phoenix, Arizona, were recruited and paid by a survey firm. Participants were randomly assigned to one of the nine conditions described above, resulting in the sample allocation in table 8.1. Because the award distribution is severely right skewed, as is typical of punitive damages awards,[8] the natural log of awards was used as the dependent variable.

IV. Results: Experiment 1

The basic result was both striking and simple. Changes in the probability of detection did not produce significant changes in dollar awards, even though it was varied by a factor of 20; this was apparently irrelevant to these dollar judgments (table 8.2).[9] To be sure, there does appear to be a positive trend in the means, but this difference is not statistically significant—and even if it were, it is in the opposite direction of that required by the deterrence argument: the greater the likelihood of detection, the higher the award. The clear implications of this result are (1) that explicitly drawing people's attention to a low probability of detection does not by itself produce higher or materially different awards and (2) that optimal deterrence is, to that important extent, not promoted by people's spontaneous judgments about appropriate punishment.

8. See Cass R. Sunstein et al., "Assessing Punitive Damages (with Notes on Cognition and Valuation in Law)," 107 *Yale L.J.* 2071 (1998).

9. When interpreting a nonsignificant result as meaningful, it is important to be sure that enough statistical power was present. Note that we did find significant effects of case and sequence, and a case-by-sequence interaction (all significant $p < .01$). It is therefore clear that we had sufficient statistical power (with over two thousand total observations) to detect any significant effect of probability of detection if one in fact existed.

Table 8.1. Experiment 1 Design Summary

Order	Case	$P^{(detect)}$	Condition	N
1	*Glover*	1 in 100		
2	*Fredericks*	1 in 10	PD1	78
3	*Elegin*	1 in 5		
1	*Glover*	1 in 10		
2	*Fredericks*	1 in 5	PD2	78
3	*Elegin*	1 in 100		
1	*Glover*	1 in 5		
2	*Fredericks*	1 in 100	PD3	78
3	*Elegin*	1 in 10		
1	*Fredericks*	1 in 5		
2	*Elegin*	1 in 100	PD4	77
3	*Glover*	1 in 10		
1	*Fredericks*	1 in 100		
2	*Elegin*	1 in 10	PD5	77
3	*Glover*	1 in 5		
1	*Fredericks*	1 in 10		
2	*Elegin*	1 in 5	PD6	77
3	*Glover*	1 in 100		
1	*Elegin*	1 in 10		
2	*Glover*	1 in 5	PD7	78
3	*Fredericks*	1 in 100		
1	*Elegin*	1 in 5		
2	*Glover*	1 in 100	PD8	78
3	*Fredericks*	1 in 10		
1	*Elegin*	1 in 100		
2	*Glover*	1 in 10	PD9	78
3	*Fredericks*	1 in 5		

Nothing said thus far excludes the possibility that if specifically required to think about issues of optimal deterrence, as urged by Polinsky and Shavell, jurors might be willing and able to do so. (Chapter 9 describes tests of whether in fact people will apply such instructions.) It remains possible that people do care about deterrence but do not understand the relationship between probability of detection and (optimal)

Table 8.2. Mean $ Awards by Case and Probability of Detection

Case	Probability of Detection			
	$\frac{1}{100}$	$\frac{1}{10}$	$\frac{1}{5}$	Overall
Glover	677,399	736,139	929,608	773,987
Fredericks	1,139,891	906,100	920,564	983,423
Elegin	924,769	1,380,454	1,210,860	1,156,628
Overall	893,769	973,268	1,012,069	958,420

Note: These figures are derived from the mean log awards used in the analysis of variance. To make the figures more easily interpreted, the mean log award for each cell was
converted to $ by taking the inverse. For example, the mean log award for the *Glover*
case with a $\frac{1}{100}$ probability was 13.426, and $e^{13.426} = 677,399$.

deterrence; perhaps they are confused about how best to deter. Perhaps
they do not understand the risk of overdeterrence and underdeterrence
and might be willing to think in these terms if the concepts were explained. And while the first study tests whether jurors will take account
of the low probability of detection when prominently placed before
them, it does not ask for reactions to officials or institutions that have
done exactly that. Our second study sheds some light on whether people
want optimal deterrence; chapter 9 offers a more direct test of what jurors will do in the face of an optimal deterrence instruction.

V. Experiment 2: Do People Accept
Optimal Deterrence Policies?
A. *Participants and Procedure*

The first study did not expressly ask people whether optimal deterrence policies were appropriate or proper. In our second study we asked
University of Chicago Law School students to answer this question. The
general hypothesis was that most people would reject optimal deterrence
policies if chosen by a district court in the particular context of punitive
damages. The University of Chicago Law School, however, would seem
to be extremely unfavorable terrain for this hypothesis. University of
Chicago Law School students generally learn a great deal about deterrence theory in their first year of law school, and they study optimal deterrence in their required courses about the law of tort and criminal law.
Thus, training in the first year of law school alerts University of Chicago
students to the possibility of over- or underdeterrence and to the need
to consider both level and probability of penalty in achieving optimal
deterrence. It would therefore be reasonable to speculate that a large

percentage of students would accept optimal deterrence theory. But that speculation would be wrong.

A simple question was presented to eighty-four students in the first session of a general administrative law class, taken by both second-year and third-year students. The question was this:

> Tom Johnson, a construction worker, was severely injured as a result of grotesquely reckless safety practices by his employer. In the trial, uncontradicted experts testified that Johnson's employer "did not even try to take the most minimal and obvious precautions to protect workers against serious risks to life and health." The jury awarded Johnson $50,000 in compensatory damages and $300,000 in punitive damages. The trial judge set aside the punitive award on the ground that "there was essentially no chance that Johnson would not seek and receive compensation, and hence there is no need for punitive damages in this case." Assume that the trial judge was correct on his factual claim—and thus that there was no chance that Johnson would not seek and receive full compensation. Do you agree that punitive damages should not be awarded?

Respondents were asked to give one of four answers to this question: strongly disagree (1), somewhat disagree (2), somewhat agree (3), strongly agree (4). (Note that we did not ask whether the result was "fair," believing that this formulation might bias answers against optimal deterrence policies.) Since it seemed that an unusual number of respondents, having been schooled in optimal deterrence policies, would accept those policies, we also asked a follow-up question. The question was whether most other people would agree with the judge's decision.

VI. Results: Experiment 2

Very strong majorities of respondents rejected the optimal deterrence ruling (table 8.3). More particularly, 85% rejected the judge's decision to set aside the punitive damages award, and 67% of respondents said that most people would disagree with that decision. Apparently respondents believed that reckless or invidious behavior deserves to be punished, whatever deterrence theory may suggest. Hence the respondents' refusal to accept optimal deterrence theory provides some information about the content of punitive intuitions: In general, moral judgments about inappropriate behavior are affected little or not at all by the probability of detection.

Table 8.3. Experiment 2 Results Summary

Question	Person Rated	Strongly Disagree (1)	Some-what Disagree (2)	Some-what Agree (3)	Strongly Agree (4)	Mean Rating	Percent Disagree
Punitive Damages	Self	40	31	10	3	1.71	84.5%
Punitive Damages	Other	26	30	24	4	2.07	66.7%

It might be possible to respond, however, that the results in this study were driven by the relatively low compensatory award. Perhaps respondents rejected the judge's decision in the belief that $50,000 was too little to provide real compensation for the injury. To test for this possibility, a small follow-up study was done, also involving students at the University of Chicago Law School, using a substantially higher dollar award ($200,000). Essentially the same results were reached: Over 70% of the respondents rejected the judge's decision to set aside a punitive award on the ground that the probability of detection was high. The basic result is evidently driven by skepticism about the idea of optimal deterrence and about a judge's decision to set aside a jury's decision in the face of serious misconduct—not by the level of the compensatory award.

VII. Conclusion

People do not spontaneously think in terms of optimal deterrence, and their proposed punishments do not vary with the probability of deterrence, even when this factor is specifically drawn to their attention. In addition, law students trained in deterrence theory explicitly rejected judicial decisions based on conventional economic thinking about optimal damages awards. It seems clear that ordinary people would reject that conventional thinking as well—a proposition closely connected to the subject of the next chapter.

9

Deterrence Instructions: What Jurors Won't Do

W. Kip Viscusi

I. Introduction

Previous chapters demonstrated that people have considerable difficulty in applying conventional punitive damages instructions. Moreover, as chapter 8 indicates, people do not on their own develop punitive damages principles based on optimal deterrence concerns. Perhaps this failure could be remedied by giving jurors a simple formula for calculating the punitive damages amount. One such proposal is the deterrence-based approach advocated by Polinsky and Shavell. In particular, they have developed a model jury instruction to enable jurors to set punitive damages awards based on what they and many others believe are valid law and economics principles.[1] This influential article has already begun to receive attention as the most compelling available elucidation of the formal law and economics underpinnings of punitive damages.[2] However, as the results in the previous chapter indicated, people do not believe that such an approach is intuitively appealing or fair. However, could these qualms be remedied by giving people the Polinsky-Shavell instructions?

The punitive damages approach advocated by Polinsky and Shavell focuses principally on the observation that dates back to Jeremy Bentham that punishment levels should be related to the reciprocal of the probability of detection.[3] For example, if the chance of detection is 50%, then the total penalty must be twice the value of the harm in or-

1. See A. Mitchell Polinsky and Steven Shavell, "Punitive Damages: An Economic Analysis," 111 *Harv. L. Rev.* 869, 962 (1998).

2. *Perez v. Oldsmobile, Inc.,* Nos. 99-2742, 99-2854, 00-1701, and 00-1786, 2000 U.S. App. LEXIS 18281, at *7–8 (7th Cir. July 31, 2000).

3. See Jeremy Bentham, "Principles of Penal Law," in *The Works of Jeremy Bentham,* vol. 1, 365, 401–2 (John Bowring ed., 1962).

der to create the proper incentives for deterrence on an expected value basis.

The experimental method here is different than that in the previous chapter. Rather than asking whether people can develop the Polinsky-Shavell tests independently or are supportive of the general methodological approach, this chapter tests whether jury-eligible citizens can and will, in fact, apply the Polinsky-Shavell jury instructions. A sample of jury-eligible citizens considered a series of different case scenarios in which there was some nonzero probability that the environmental transgression would not be detected. They were then given the Polinsky-Shavell punitive damages instructions and asked to assess punitive damages for their case. This exercise consequently will provide a quite direct test of whether giving jurors an explicit formula for punitive damages will rationalize the punitive damages–setting process.

The results of this experimental test of the proposed punitive damages instructions were quite disturbing for those seeking a sound procedure for setting punitive damages awards. Very few of the 353 jury-eligible respondents in my sample carried out the basic elements of the deterrence calculation, even though they had the assistance of a table that gave them multipliers for translating compensatory damages values into deterrence values. Respondents were very insensitive to changes in the probability of detecting a violation, which should have been the key concern for setting deterrence values based on law and economics principles. Likewise, respondents were not sensitive to the degree of stealthiness of the defendant's behavior, which should have been a pivotal factor influencing the punishment value for damages. What mattered instead was the role of various anchoring effects based on, for example, suggested values for damages by the plaintiff's attorney. But such anchoring effects should be completely eliminated if people adhered to the Polinsky-Shavell formula. The mathematical formula for guiding jury behavior consequently achieves none of the purported objectives of the approach and remains vulnerable to the same kinds of contaminating influences that could distort punitive damages awards under the current regime.

II. Model Jury Instructions

Unlike the usual, quite general punitive damages instructions, the model jury instructions developed by Polinsky and Shavell are quite precise. I tested the effect of these instructions based on an original experimental design. As part of my study, each respondent was presented with a copy of punitive damages instructions that are almost identical to those advocated by Polinsky and Shavell for cases in which the defendant is a firm. These instructions are presented here as exhibit 9.1.

As the instructions indicate, there are three components to setting the level of punitive damages in the case of losses inflicted by firms, which is what the experimental cases in my study design focus on. The first component focuses on the deterrence amount for punitive damages. In situations of imperfect enforcement, the total penalty should equal the level of damages divided by the probability of detection. Thus, the punitive damages amount should equal this value less the amount of compensatory damages. Polinsky and Shavell summarize this formula in their article as follows: "This discussion suggests a simple formula for assuring that injurers will pay for the harms they cause: *the total damages imposed on an injurer should equal the harm multiplied by the reciprocal of the probability that the injurer will be found liable when he ought to be.*"[4] Indeed, more generally, Polinsky and Shavell believe that this should be the dominant concept used in setting punitive damages, though their article is stronger in this regard than are the jury instructions. More specifically, they characterize their overall finding regarding punitive damages as: "In summary, *punitive damages ordinarily should be awarded if, and only if, an injurer has a chance of escaping liability for the harm he causes.*"[5]

Consider the first component of the damages instructions pertaining to deterrence in part A of exhibit 9.1. These instructions give respondents an economic rationale for imposing a sanction that will provide for deterrence as the first part of the deterrence discussion. The second component of the deterrence discussion focuses on determining the probability that the defendant would have escaped detection. The third component provides respondents with a table for determining the appropriate amount of punitive damages from the standpoint of deterrence, which Polinsky and Shavell call the "base punitive damages amount." The fourth component emphasizes that this amount should not be adjusted for a variety of other factors, such as the role of litigation costs. The question then asks respondents what the base punitive damages amount should be.

4. See Polinsky and Shavell, *supra* note 1, at 889.
5. See Polinsky and Shavell, *supra* note 1, at 874.

Part B of the instructions is with respect to punishment. The Polinsky and Shavell article is hesitant to recommend an explicit role for punishment in the case of corporate offenses, as punishment is more appropriate for individual actions in which the blameworthy parties can be identified. Indeed, the instructions provided to respondents to assist them in calculating the appropriate punishment value for part B of the punitive damages determination emphasize some of these caveats, such as the importance of keeping in mind that compensatory damages have already been paid and will lead to some punishment already. The survey then asks respondents what their punishment value will be, which is the second component of punitive damages.

Part C of the instructions in exhibit 9.1 asks respondents to determine the level of punitive damages. The instructions indicate some kind of averaging process in which the punitive damages amount should be between the deterrence answer and the punishment answer, though the weight need not be one-half. The character of the scenarios and how salient the deterrence and punishment objectives are within the context of these scenarios will determine what the appropriate weight should be.

It is clear from the inspection of the Polinsky-Shavell approach in exhibit 9.1 that juries have a much more precise guide than existing instructions provide as to what their task should be in determining punitive damages. The instructions give them a rationale for the deterrence objective and an explicit mathematical formula for setting these deterrence values. The instructions then give them a discussion of the punishment objective but no explicit formula for setting punishment values. Finally, the instructions give them guidance with respect to setting the punitive damages level based on their deterrence and punishment answers, and these instructions serve to bound the punitive damages amount by restricting it to be a value between the deterrence value and the punishment value.

These instructions raise a number of interesting issues with respect to jury performance that have yet to be addressed by previous research. Can and will juries successfully implement this formula in carrying out the punitive damages assessment task? The setting of punitive damages for deterrence and the determination of the overall damages amount involve tasks in which there is an explicit way of determining whether juries are right or wrong in their efforts. To what extent will juries be able to handle the mathematical task correctly? The punishment objective is more open-ended and less amenable to an explicit test of whether juries are behaving knowledgeably. Nevertheless, one can ascertain whether juries are responsive to the character of the behavior of the defendant and the other details of the case in setting the punishment amount, which is what one would expect if juries are behaving rationally.

If instructions are to be effective, then possibly extraneous aspects of the case should not impede jurors' ability to carry out the instructions. A phenomenon that was found to be influential in chapter 4 was that of anchoring effects in which plaintiffs' attorneys presented jurors with a dollar anchor that contaminated the deliberation process. If in fact jurors adhere to the explicit mathematical formula specified in exhibit 9.1, then that should greatly reduce the influence of anchoring effects and similar phenomena that would lead to the kinds of random punitive damages awards that might otherwise be observed. This hypothesis will be explored as an additional test of the efficacy of the instructions.

III. Study Design
A. Materials and Procedures

The effect of the instructions was tested using a sample of jury-eligible adults who considered a legal case using these instructions. Each respondent considered one of five different scenarios involving the disposal of twelve drums of dangerous chemicals by an industrial chemical research firm. The nature of my experimental design was to present different subgroups of the sample with different scenarios and to compare the responses across the different experimental treatments. In each instance respondents applied the Polinsky-Shavell formula. By altering the characteristics of the scenario presented to the respondent, it is possible to assess the incremental effect of different aspects of the case on the performance of the jury instructions. Moreover, in every instance it will also be possible to develop tests that ascertain whether in fact the respondents adhered to the Polinsky-Shavell formula. The text of the five different scenarios appears in the exhibit 9.2.

In addition to the scenarios in which respondents considered the Polinsky-Shavell formula, the experiment also included a sixth scenario for a group of sixty-nine respondents who considered a case in which there was no such formula presented. These respondents had the more standard punitive damages formula guidance and considered a case that was identical to those considered by the Polinsky-Shavell formula sample except for a somewhat different damages amount. However, by rescaling

Table 9.1. Experimental Design for Punitive Damages Toxic
Waste–Dumping Scenarios

Scenario	Probability of Detection	Character of Dumping	Anchoring Information
1	.25	Not stealthy	None
2	.01	Not stealthy	None
3	.01	Stealthy midnight dumping	None
4	.01	Stealthy midnight dumping	Plaintiff's attorney requests minimum penalty of $25 million, ideally $50 million
5	.01	Stealthy midnight dumping	Similar case in news with $50 million award reduced on appeal to $25 million

the damages amount, it is possible to make a direct comparison of the results, as these scenarios were otherwise identical.[6]

Table 9.1 summarizes the experimental structure that was used. In scenario 1 there is a 0.25 probability that the illegal dumping will be discovered by the EPA inspector. The company was in fact caught and fined $100,000 to cover the additional water-treatment costs. The respondents then had to determine the appropriate value of punitive damages. The other scenarios varied the character of the dumping and the probability of detection but not the damages amount.

Summary of Experiment

Description: Each subject read one variation of an environmental accident case summary and instructions and was then asked to choose a punitive damages award against the defendant. There were five variations involving manipulation of three factors: (1) the probability that the defendant's tortious behavior would be detected; (2) whether the defendant was deliberately stealthy in his behavior; and (3) whether or not a suggested award magnitude was included in the scenario.
Number of subjects: 353 jury-eligible citizens.
Location: Austin, Texas.
Decisions: Individual survey.
Stimuli: Written case summary and instructions.

By its very nature, the experimental design that I have constructed focuses on differences across the scenarios rather than the absolute levels

6. In particular, to achieve the rescaling, one simply multiplies the results for the conventional damages findings by a factor of five.

of responses. As a consequence, factors that are common to each of the scenarios will tend to net out when making the comparisons. In each instance people considered the scenarios as individuals, not as groups. They also did not participate in an actual trial. However, these and other elements are common across all scenarios. The distinctive nature of the experiment is that by comparing the effects across different experimental treatments, it is possible to isolate whether there is in fact any responsiveness to the key aspects of the experimental design that are pertinent to assessing how individuals will apply the Polinsky-Shavell instructions.

The imperfect enforcement in scenario 1 did not arise from any stealth on the part of the manager responsible for the dumping. Rather, the survey indicated: "The manager knew that there was a 25% chance that the EPA inspector was going to be visiting the plant next week, and that if he did, the dumping would be discovered." Thus, in this scenario there is no attempt on the part of the shift manager to take an action that would decrease the probability of being caught, so that the 25% chance of being caught could be viewed as an exogenous probability. For this scenario there was no anchoring information given by the plaintiff's attorney or from any other source.

With scenario 1 as with the other scenarios, it is possible to determine whether the respondents applied the implications of the Polinsky-Shavell instructions properly. In particular, is the deterrence value calculated accurately, and is the overall punitive damages amount some value that is bounded by the deterrence value and the punishment value?

Scenario 2 is in some ways identical to scenario 1, as the probability of detection below 1.0 arises from exogenous factors rather than the stealth of the dumping company. For scenario 2 the probability of detection is 1%. Based on the reciprocal probability rule for setting punitive damages, the appropriate level of punitive damages with a 0.25 probability of detection is 3 times the value of the damages inflicted, and for a 0.01 probability of detection, it is 99 times as great.[7] Thus, if the respondents were perfectly rational, then the deterrence value of punitive damages for scenario 2 should be 33 times as great as the assessed deterrence value of damages for scenario 1. It should be noted that the 0.25 probability of detection for scenario 1 lies between two probabilities in the punitive damages table appearing in exhibit 9.1, which gives the appropriate value of

7. Overall damages including compensatory damages should be 4 times as great as the loss with a 0.25 probability of detection and 100 times as great with a 0.01 probability.

damages if the probability of detection is 70% or 80%. Applying these values leads to a potential damages range from $233,000 to $400,000, whereas with a .01 probability of detection the appropriate damages amount for deterrence is $9.9 million. If one treats as correct any damages value in this range for scenario 1, then the appropriate ratio of damages for scenario 2 to that of scenario 1 should be in the range of 24.8 to 42.4 if respondents are applying the deterrence table properly.

In scenario 3 there is the same probability of detection as in scenario 2, but the scenario is altered so that the reason why there is a low probability of being caught is that the dumping firm engages in a stealthy midnight dumping to avoid detection. In particular, the chemical manager took the following precautions to avoid being detected: "To prevent being caught, his crew loaded the chemical drums onto unmarked trucks and dumped the chemicals in a rural stream at 3:00 A.M. The manager believed that this 'midnight dumping' would reduce the risk of getting caught to $\frac{1}{100}$. Thus, there is a 99% chance of escaping any penalty. He decided that it was worth the gamble because it was the fastest way to get rid of the chemicals and it was dangerous to keep the chemicals."

Giving respondents information regarding the stealthiness of the activity that led to the imperfect enforcement has two potential ramifications. First, if respondents do not apply the deterrence damages formula in situations in which the low probability of detection does not arise from stealthy behavior on the part of the company, then indicating that the dumping arose from evasive behavior may increase the credibility of the deterrence approach. Indicating that the imperfect enforcement comes from evasive behavior may help overcome some of the reluctance to embrace the optimal deterrence approach, as was found in chapter 8. The second ramification of stealthy behavior is that it makes the parties more appropriate targets for a high punishment value for punitive damages. In this example we now have a shift manager who undertakes the deceitful act and who might be responsive to financial penalties levied on the company so that punitive damages in this instance may cause defendants to penalize their "*blameworthy employees* who engaged in reprehensible behavior," as the punishment instructions in exhibit 9.1 indicate. By comparing the results for scenario 3 with scenario 2, it is possible to determine whether these two influences are operative.

The fourth scenario has the identical fact situation to scenario 3, except that there is an additional complication regarding a plaintiff's attorney's request for a damages amount. In particular, the attorney suggests that the appropriate penalty would be $50 million and that the minimum penalty should be $25 million. Will such dollar values serve as anchors that influence jury thinking? Based on the Polinsky-Shavell formula, calculating the deterrence value of punitive damages is a strictly mathematical exercise that should be independent of such anchoring effects. Similarly, the total punitive damages amount should lie between the deterrence values and the punishment values irrespective of such anchoring. However, potentially the punishment value itself could be influenced, and it may also be the case that juries do not properly respond to the jury instructions, but instead are influenced by anchoring effects. Anchoring biases are a well-documented phenomenon in the literature, but past studies have not considered the efficacy of jury instructions that narrowly constrain jurors to behave in a way that should eliminate anchoring effects. By comparing the results for scenario 4 with scenario 3, it will be possible to assess whether anchoring does in fact have an influence.

The final scenario 5 explores the influence of a different source that might produce anchoring. Rather than hearing the pleas of a plaintiff's attorney regarding appropriate damages levels, suppose that jurors have in fact read about penalties levied in similar cases elsewhere. Such information is frequently available to jurors, especially with respect to products for which there is a national line of litigation. How does this information affect the setting of punitive damages?

In scenario 5 juries receive information that they have read in a newspaper article describing a similar case in which the jury awarded punitive damages of $50 million, but this amount was reduced on appeal to $25 million. As with the anchoring results in scenario 4, the question is whether this anchoring information based on publicity will alter the results when compared to scenario 3, which does not include any anchoring information. Moreover, there is an additional comparison of interest, which is whether anchoring information based on media coverage is more or less influential than the anchoring information arising from the pleas by the plaintiff's attorney. Thus, the comparison of the results of scenario 5 with scenario 4 will be of interest as well.

B. Participants

The participants in this study consisted of 353 adult respondents, all of whom were jury-eligible citizens in the Austin, Texas, area. A marketing research firm contacted these respondents by phone and brought them to a central location in July 2000. Each respondent was paid $40 to complete a survey that was approximately thirty minutes in length. The average age was forty-one years. The sample included a good mix by gender (59% female) and race (13% black, 20% Hispanic, and 5% other non-white races). The respondent education levels were concentrated among high school graduates and those who have had at least some college.

Each participant recruited for my study was told that they would participate in an opinion study. Before considering the toxic-dumping case in the Polinsky-Shavell punitive damages instructions, respondents also were given general instructions regarding their role in considering the case as well as a general instruction that would provide the standard type of legal rationale for punitive damages.

The overall structure of the survey consequently established a strong sense of the legal context that a typical juror will face in a real-world situation. Respondents were very much aware that they should treat the legal situation as if they were members of a jury. Moreover, they received a general background regarding the legal basis for punitive damages. They then considered the specific toxic-dumping case scenario and, based on the Polinsky-Shavell punitive damages instructions, established damages levels pertinent to the case.

IV. Results

How well did the respondents perform in carrying out the Polinsky-Shavell punitive damages instructions? The answer to this question depends on a variety of tests and comparisons involving the different scenarios.

Table 9.2 summarizes the overall statistics pertaining to the accuracy

Table 9.2. Accuracy of Deterrence Responses

	Percentage of Respondents			
Survey Version	Missing Responses	Deterrence Value Correct	Final Award in Range	Final Award in Range and Deterrence Correct
1	9	20	73	19
2	6	11	79	11
3	4	21	75	18
4	7	7	76	6
5	9	14	78	14
Total	7	15	76	14

of the deterrence responses in terms of whether the respondents could successfully apply the mathematical formula in part A of the instructions. The statistics there pertain to the results for each of the versions of the survey as well as for the overall findings. The first column of statistics indicates the percentage of the sample for which responses were missing. A value of zero would not be considered missing, but overall about 7% of the sample simply drew a blank in terms of being able to solve the problem. Many simply put a question mark by the answer for calculating the deterrence amount or made some rough but unsuccessful attempts to begin a numerical calculation. The subsequent analysis in section VI will indicate that these respondents were not random, but in fact were concentrated among the groups whom one might expect to have some difficulty in carrying out the numerical calculations required. While the Polinsky-Shavell instructions generated a significant number of missing values that averaged 7% across all five of the experimental treatments, an additional case scenario in which respondents received conventional punitive damages instructions but not the Polinsky-Shavell formula had no missing values among the sixty-nine respondents. Thus, a general lack of attention to the survey task within the context of my experiment does not appear to be the explanation for the missing values that were observed when respondents were asked to carry out the tasks outlined in the Polinsky-Shavell instructions.

The next column of statistics in table 9.2 pertains to those who calculated the deterrence value correctly. For survey 1, all responses between 233,000 (probability of escaping liability of 70%) and 400,000 (probability of escaping liability of 80%) were treated as correct. The overall average value of correct responses is 15% for all five scenarios, as this amount ranges from 7% for scenario 4 to 21% for scenario 3. Thus, only a small minority of the respondents could handle the key deterrence value calculation correctly.

Several differences are noteworthy. First, the introduction of stealthy behavior in scenario 3 as opposed to scenario 2 almost doubles the frequency with which respondents assessed the correct value of punitive damages, which is $9.9 million based on the fact scenario. Stealthy behavior apparently increases the willingness of respondents to apply the deterrence damages formula.[8] The second noteworthy comparison is

8. The percentage of respondents with correct deterrence values is significantly different between scenarios 2 and 3 at the 89% level, two-tailed test, thus falling short of the usual standards of significance.

that the percentage of correct answers equal to 7% for scenario 4 is sub-stantially below that for the equivalent scenario 3, where the only differ-ence is that scenario 4 included an anchoring plea for a penalty by the plaintiff's attorney.[9] This anchoring plea led to the lowest percentage of correct calculations of punitive damages for deterrence for any of the scenarios in the table. In this situation in which there was a potential an-choring, respondents in effect ignored the mathematical table in assess-ing punitive damages. The anchoring effect of the media coverage of a related punitive damages case in scenario 5 also decreased the accuracy of respondents' application of the formula when compared to the results in the parallel scenario 3, but to a lesser extent than did the plaintiff's at-torney anchoring effect in scenario 4.

The fourth column of statistics in table 9.2 pertains to whether the final award is in the appropriate range as dictated by the punitive dam-ages instructions. In particular, the instructions specifically indicate that the punitive damages amount should be between the deterrence value and the punishment value. Roughly three-fourths of the sample gave re-sponses that satisfied this requirement. Overall, 76% of the respondents gave a final punitive damages amount that was in the appropriate range, as this task is a relatively minor mathematical stumbling block when com-pared to the initial calculation of the deterrence value based on the re-ciprocal of the probability of detection.

The overall test for mathematical correctness is whether respondents calculated the deterrence value correctly and whether their final answer was also in the appropriate range. As the final column of statistics in table 9.2 indicates, virtually all respondents who calculated the deter-rence value correctly also gave a final punitive damages value that was in the correct range. Overall, 14% of the sample satisfied both of these math-ematical tests. The low value was that only 6% of the respondents with the anchoring scenario 4 met these requirements, as the effect of the an-chor swamped the respondents in their efforts to apply the instructions.

How did the punishment and deterrence values compare? The key pair of results for testing the influence of stealthy behavior is the differ-ence between scenario 2 in which the employees were not stealthy and the otherwise identical scenario 3 in which there is stealthy midnight dumping. While 3% more respondents had punishment values exceeding

9. The percentage of respondents with correct deterrence values is significantly different between scenarios 3 and 4 at the 95% level, two-tailed test.

deterrence values for scenario 3 as compared to scenario 2, an almost identical 4% of the respondents were more likely to have deterrence values exceeding punishment values. The main change is the decrease in the number of respondents giving equal values for both deterrence and punishment. Thus, there seems to be no apparent effect of stealthy employee behavior on the relative degree of punishment assessed by respondents, which is not what one would expect if respondents were following the punitive damages instructions.

Given the explicit nature of the jury instructions in exhibit 9.1, the actual level of damages assessed by respondents is of interest as well. Table 9.3 presents the distribution of damages values for each of the components of the damages calculation. Panel A of table 9.3 presents the deterrence values for the survey versions.

For survey 1, the correct value of damages is $300,000, but values of $233,000 to $400,000 are permissible since the probability of escaping liability lies in a range of values in the deterrence calculation table in exhibit 9.1. The median response of $355,500 is quite plausible, but the mean value is roughly an order of magnitude greater than is appropriate because of the influence of the high damages assessments.

For survey 2 and in all subsequent surveys in which the probability of detection is 1%, the correct deterrence value based on exhibit 9.1 is $9.9 million. Comparison of surveys 1 and 2 provides a direct test of whether respondents were sufficiently sensitive to the change in the probability of detection, which decreases from 25% for survey 1 to 1% in survey 2, leading to an optimal deterrence amount in survey 2 that is 33 times greater than in survey 1, or a range of 24.8 to 42.4 times greater given the range of guidance provided by the values in the table in exhibit 9.1. Notwithstanding the major difference in the probability of detection, the actual deterrence values assessed are only slightly different for these two survey versions. The median response in survey 2 is $500,000, which is only 1.4 times as great as the median response in survey 1, whereas it should have been much more than an order of magnitude greater. Similarly, the mean response is only 1.3 times as great, which also indicates a substantial insensitivity to the probability of detection. Quite simply, respondents were ignoring the guidance of the deterrence table and were not taking into account the differing value of the detection probability when setting the optimal deterrence amount.

The results for survey 3 indicate a higher median value, but a mean value that is almost the same as survey 2. For survey 3, I report two sets

Table 9.3. Distribution of Damages Values

Survey Version	Median	Mean
Panel A: Deterrence Value		
1	355,500	2,904,242
2	500,000	3,772,735
3 (full)	900,000	3,827,285
3 (trimmed)	900,000	3,737,981
4	25,000,000	34,079,231
5	9,900,000	20,132,381
Panel B: Punishment Value		
1	300,000	5,613,678
2	300,000	1,416,485
3 (full)	500,000	145,854,864
3 (trimmed)	500,000	2,411,553
4	25,000,000	29,186,615
5	10,000,000	16,371,905
Panel C: Final Punitive Damages Award		
1	475,000	5,717,022
2	500,000	3,521,074
3 (full)	800,000	146,610,261
3 (trimmed)	800,000	3,178,059
4	26,000,000	34,844,000
5	12,650,000	22,295,476

Note: The trimmed sample excludes one respondent who assessed a $9.9 billion value for the punishment amount and the final punitive damages award.

of results. One set of results reports findings for the full sample of respondents. The second set of results omits one respondent who assessed $9.9 billion for both the punishment value and the final punitive damages award. This person is trimmed to eliminate the effect of this outlier on the punishment and deterrence values. The deterrence value responses for survey 3 are greater than those for survey 2 in terms of the median response, as the presence of stealthy behavior increases the deterrence value levied. However, based on the punitive damages formula, it should have no influence. Perhaps the character of the behavior leading to the low probability of detection increases respondents' willingness to apply the formula.

The anchoring effect in survey 4 proves to be dominant. The plaintiff's attorney gave respondents a minimum award level of $25 million and a desired award of $50 million. This information increased the median assessed deterrence value to $25 million and the mean value to $34 million. Respondents, in effect, abandoned the constraints imposed by the deterrence value table and based their judgments largely on the anchoring influence.

Matters are less bleak for the results for survey 5 in which there is media information. The deterrence value for the median respondent equals the correct deterrence value that should be assessed given the jury instructions. The influence of these media anchors consequently serves to boost the deterrence values levied so that the median respondent is at the correct value, although the mean damages assessed amount of $20 million is over double the correct deterrence value because of the influence of the media anchor information.

The punishment values levied by respondents in panel B of table 9.3 follow a pattern quite similar to those for the deterrence values. It is noteworthy that the introduction of stealthy behavior for survey 3 had only a very small effect on the median punishment value assessed. For the punishment values, the dominant influence that is apparent was the strong influence of the two anchoring scenarios. As with the deterrence values, the median damages value assessed for survey 4 is $25 million, which is the minimum value that the plaintiff's attorney recommended as being acceptable.

The final punitive damages awards levied by respondents have median values that closely parallel the punishment values and the deterrence values. However, in three of the five survey versions, the final punitive damages award has a median value that lies outside of the median value range of the deterrence and punishment values, which is inconsistent with the general guidance given to setting punitive damages awards. The mean punitive damages awards are much greater. The highest value is for survey 3 for the full sample of respondents to that scenario, as one respondent levied a $9.9 billion punitive damages award. This individual also answered the deterrence question correctly and had a final punitive damages award that was between the deterrence value and the punishment value, so that it does not appear to be an error by the respondent, but rather a sense that the punishment value should be greatly boosted above the deterrence amounts.

Although the effect of the Polinsky-Shavell instructions may vary depending on the particular case context, the general influence in this particular instance appears to be to decrease the assessed value of punitive damages awards for scenarios in which there is no anchoring effect. The final punitive damages awards are $800,000 or less for surveys 1, 2, and 3, which are lower than the amounts that were found in a sixth version of the survey in which respondents did not consider the Polinsky-Shavell punitive damages instructions but instead relied on more standard guidance.[10]

A graphic illustration of the influence of the anchoring effects in surveys 4 and 5 is to examine the number of respondents who gave the anchoring amounts as their deterrence values. One percent of respondents for surveys 1 through 3 assessed a $25 million deterrence award, 4% assessed a deterrence value between $25 million and $50 million, and no respondents assessed a $50 million deterrence value. For survey 4 in which there is a plaintiff's attorney anchor, 20% assessed a $25 million deterrence value, 12% assessed a $50 million deterrence amount, and 17% assessed a value between these two extremes. Similar kinds of influences are apparent for the punishment value for scenario 4, except that there is a shift of respondents from the anchoring amount of $50 million to some value between $25 million and $50 million when assessing punishment. The final award amount for survey 4 is much more highly concentrated in the range between $25 million and $50 million than the previous responses.

Similar but much less dramatic anchoring effects are apparent for survey 5 in which there is a media coverage anchor. Another notable difference is that no respondents assessed a punishment value between $25 million and $50 million, as there is a greater concentration at the two

10. More specifically, for a $20,000 damages value, respondents assessed punitive damages amounts of $1 million. If the damages value had been $100,000 as in the scenarios in this experiment and responses were scaled proportionately, the assessed punitive damages value would be $5 million. However, even the median assessed damages amount without such a proportional adjustment exceeds the assessed punitive damages using the Polinsky-Shavell formula for scenarios 1, 2, and 3.

endpoint values. The final punitive damages levied often were $25 million or more, but the extent of the effect is not as great as for survey 4. The media coverage manipulation continues to have less dramatic influence than does the plea from the plaintiff's attorney.

How did the respondents arrive at their final punitive damages figure? Based on the instructions given to them, the number should be between the two component punitive damages values. Thus, one can formulate what respondents did as being some kind of weighted average of their two responses, where these weights should sum to 1.0.

To test for these relationships, table 9.4 reports the regression results in which the final punitive damages amount is regressed on the two component values—the deterrence value and the punishment value. No constant term is included in the regression because on a theoretical basis there should be no such value, as the damages amount should be zero if both the deterrence value and the punishment value are also zero. The empirical estimates that included a constant term also indicated effects that were not statistically significant at the usual levels in every instance, and the coefficients on the remaining variables were not sensitive to the inclusion of a constant term. Whereas a coefficient of 0.5 on the deterrence value and the punishment value would indicate equal weighting of these two components, in every instance the punishment value has a greater weight.[11] The weight on the punishment value ranges from 0.7 for survey 1 to a high of 2.4 for survey 2, with an average across all surveys of 0.8. The deterrence value, which is purportedly the more important value from the standpoint of the Polinsky-Shavell framework, consistently receives a lower weight than does the punishment value and in the case of survey 2 plays no statistically significant role whatsoever in influencing the final damages value. These results indicate that the mathematical calculations that produced the first step of the punitive damages calculation, the deterrence value, were not in fact regarded as the most salient contributor to the respondents' assessment of punitive damages. Rather, it was the more nebulously characterized punishment value that proved to be most instrumental in setting the punitive damages awards.

A second observation is that respondents did not simply form some kind of weighted average of the two punitive damages values. Rather,

---

11. More specifically, based on the pertinent F tests, one can always reject the hypothesis that the deterrence coefficient and punishment coefficient are identical.

Table 9.4. Relation of Final Damages and Damages Components

	Regression Results for Final Damages Coefficient[a] (Standard Error)					
	All Surveys	Survey 1	Survey 2	Survey 3	Survey 4	Survey 5
Deterrence	0.359*	0.263*	−0.018	0.296*	0.302*	0.544*
Value	(0.021)	(0.129)	(0.144)	(0.084)	(0.031)	(0.036)
Punishment	0.821*	0.728*	2.350*	0.780*	0.845*	0.730*
Value	(0.029)	(0.085)	(0.405)	(0.122)	(0.044)	(0.053)
R^2	0.886	.746	.341	0.762	.934	.957

[a] The constant terms were never statistically significant and are consequently suppressed. The coefficients for the other variables are almost identical with and without a constant term. Estimates for survey 3 are for trimmed sample excluding one outlier.

* Indicates coefficients are statistically significant at the 95% confidence level, two-tailed test.

in every instance the weights sum to a value of more than 1.0, with an average across all survey versions of 1.17. There is consequently a tendency to not treat the deterrence values and punishment values as simple components of a weighted average when setting the overall punitive damages level. Rather, respondents engaged in a much more explosive punitive damages calculation that boosts the overall level of punitive damages above what would result from any simple weighting scheme.

V. Results for Synthetic Juries

Although individual responses may not always be correct, it could be that juries would perform much more successfully. The approach that I will take here will be to construct synthetic juries based on the individual responses. I will then analyze the median responses of these synthetic juries, which is generally believed to be indicative of likely jury behavior. The evidence in chapters 2 and 3 indicates that actual experimental juries lead to more extreme results than one would expect based on the synthetic-jury analyses. One might hypothesize that this movement to extreme results may be less in this instance. These particular jury instructions involve a specific mathematical formula for which there is a right answer for the optimal deterrence portion of punitive damages. The different character of the task suggested by these instructions consequently could lead to more consensus around the correct value than qualitative instructions for which there is no right or wrong answer.

The procedure used was to construct twelve-person juries by drawing a sample of twelve individuals at random with replacement from the sample set. For each survey version, a total of a thousand synthetic juries were constructed, thus providing a very large sample to enable one to make fairly precise judgments regarding the likely performance of such juries. In situations in which the sixth- and seventh-ranked jurors have differing damages amounts to any of the questions, the midpoint value of their responses served as the median value.

The first question to be addressed is whether the synthetic juries are more successful in correctly applying the deterrence value calculations. As it turns out, whether they are or not depends on whether the median respondent on an individual basis applied the formula correctly. For survey 1, 74% of the juries gave a correct answer to the punitive damages deterrence value, as did 27% of the juries for survey 5. In each instance the median individual response to the deterrence question reported in table 9.3 was in the correct range. Somewhat strikingly, for the other three survey versions, no more than 2% of any of these juries gave correct values for the deterrence questions. In these instances the median respondent on an individual basis was not close to the correct deterrence value. For surveys 2 and 3, the individual responses reported in table 9.3 were at least an order of magnitude too low, and for the anchoring survey 4, the median deterrence value was more than twice as great as the correct answer. Thus, in terms of jury performance, the general implication is that, overall, juries could perform more successfully if the median juror applies the deterrence formula correctly, but if the median juror errs considerably, then the jury as a whole will not perform satisfactorily.

VI. Demographic Differences

How well a set of jury instructions performs in enabling jurors to make punitive damages judgments depends not only on their average implications for a sample, but also on whether all segments of society can comprehend the instructions and make reliable judgments. Thus, a key issue is whether there is widespread ability to apply the instructions or whether there are narrowly defined segments of the population who do not comprehend these instructions.

Based on the previous results, the principal test for the accuracy of responses is whether the respondent calculated the deterrence value correctly in setting the base punitive damages amount dictated by the jury

Table 9.5. Demographic Differences in the Accuracy of Responses

	Deterrence Value Correct	Deterrence Value Incorrect or Missing	Deterrence Value Incorrect
Age	38.60	41.84	41.91
Female	0.44	0.62*	0.61*
White	0.85	0.60*	0.61*
Black	0.06	0.14	0.14
Hispanic	0.06	0.22*	0.21*
Other nonwhite races	0.04	0.05	0.04
High school	0.02	0.15*	0.15*
Some college	0.19	0.35*	0.35*
College grad	0.56	0.33*	0.34*
Professional degree	0.23	0.16	0.16
Smoker	0.15	0.16	0.15
Seatbelt user	0.90	0.90	0.90

*Designates values significantly different from the value-correct column, 95% confidence interval, two-tailed test.

instructions in exhibit 9.1. Table 9.5 provides a breakdown of the sample characteristics of those respondents who answered the deterrence value correctly, those who got the deterrence value incorrect or had missing data, and a final column that indicates incorrect responses. As is evident, the demographic profile of the incorrect and missing group is almost identical to those who simply got the answer incorrect, so that for simplicity I will focus on the incorrect or missing column and compare that to those who answered the question correctly.

Respondent age does not appear to be a particularly influential characteristic. There is no significant age difference in whether respondents answered the question correctly.

Gender, however, does appear to be more influential. Whereas 44% of the sample answering the question correctly were women, 62% of those giving incorrect or missing answers were female. This result may be reflective of a gender difference in mathematical skills, but it also may be indicative of a greater reluctance by female respondents to surrender their punitive damages judgment to a mathematical formula.

Two of the racial differences proved to be significant. Overall, 85% of the respondents who answered the deterrence value correctly were white, as compared to 60–61% who had incorrect or missing values. The opposing pattern is displayed by the Hispanic respondents, who constituted 6% of the correct respondents and 22% of the incorrect respondents. A similar but less dramatic pattern is exhibited by the black respondents.[12]

Educational levels proved to be pivotal. Only 2% of the sample giving correct answers had high school educations or less, as compared to 15% with incorrect answers. Respondents with some college also experienced particular difficulties in successfully completing the deterrence question. The main outlier in terms of overall performance was college graduates, who constituted 56% of those with correct answers and 33% of those with incorrect or missing answers. Respondents with professional degrees also tended to perform disproportionately well, though the differences are not significant across the different columns.

Although college graduates and those with professional degrees often did the survey in a manner that followed the Polinsky-Shavell instructions, a considerable portion of this group did not carry out these instructions. As the statistics in the final column of table 9.5 indicate, 50% of those who did not give correct deterrence values according to the Polinsky-Shavell formula either were college graduates or professionals. Given the fact that this formula only required simple multiplication, it would be difficult to make the case that these individuals were unable to carry out the basic arithmetic. A more compelling explanation is that many respondents were simply unwilling to carry out these instructions. This unwillingness is consistent with the similar reluctance to apply this approach on the part of University of Chicago Law School students, reported in chapter 8, who also did not find the reciprocal probability rule for setting punitive damages to be a sensible approach.

Attitudes toward risk taking more generally do not appear to be consequential. Neither smoking status nor use of seat belts influenced whether respondents answered the questions correctly.

VII. Conclusion

Can providing jurors with a detailed rationale and mathematical formula for setting punitive damages solve the problem of random and highly variable punitive damages awards? The experimental results re-

12. The difference for the black respondents fell just shy of statistical significance at the 95% confidence level, two-tailed test. The sample of black respondents was, however, small.

ported here are not promising. Few respondents were able to make the key calculation pertaining to the optimal deterrence value for punishment. A much greater percentage carried out the second mathematical task of setting a total award value between the punishment value and the deterrence value, but even this straightforward exercise posed difficulties for a significant segment of the population. Respondents also were not sensitive to the probability of detection, which is the key parameter of importance in the law and economics perspective on punitive damages. Perhaps most troubling is that these difficulties are not random, but are highly concentrated among particular demographic groups, specifically minorities and the less well educated.

The character of the experimental evidence demonstrates that people did not carry out the Polinsky-Shavell instructions in setting punitive damages. The experiment did not distinguish whether people were unable to implement these instructions or were unwilling to follow these instructions. There was clearly a significant minority of the population who found the basic multiplication tasks required too difficult. However, the substantial portion of college-educated and professional respondents who did not assess punitive damages levels consistent with the Polinsky-Shavell approach suggests that there is also a substantial problem in motivating individuals to apply the formula. This reluctance is consistent with other evidence on University of Chicago Law School students, indicating that people simply do not find this approach a compelling or reasonable way to assess punitive damages amounts.

Matters, of course, may be somewhat different in actual jury contexts if this formula were ever adopted. In practice, jurors might take the task more seriously and attend to the instructions to a greater extent in an actual case situation. However, seeking refuge in explanations that lie outside of any feasible experimental structure ignores the major strength of the experimental design. My study made it possible to distinguish the incremental effect across different aspects of the design, such as the probability of detection. Other features of the case and the experimental context were the same across all respondents. What these results demonstrate is that changes in the character of the cases simply do not have the kinds of effects on individual judgments that would be predicted if people followed the Polinsky-Shavell instructions.

Cases in the real world will not be abstractions but will include a wide variety of other kinds of information not included in the scenarios tested here. An example of this kind of information that was incorporated in the study design consisted of anchoring influences in terms of appeals by a plaintiff's attorney and media coverage of a related case. The character of the jury instructions should lead respondents to ignore such anchoring biases when setting the value of punitive damages for purposes of deterrence. However, this was not the case, as this supposedly extraneous information swamped the influence of the quite explicit jury instructions. Respondents in effect cast aside the formal guidance once presented with some other damages value anchor that they could use in setting the damages amount.

When going from individual performance to group performance, the driving factor is the performance of the median juror. In situations in which the median juror had sound judgment and was able to properly interpret the punitive damages instructions, the jury performance was quite good—even much better than would be expected based on the small minority of individual respondents who got the correct answer. However, if the median juror had a deterrence value assessment that was substantially off the mark, then the performance of group decision making in our synthetic-jury analysis was much worse than what would be expected based on the individual results. This kind of magnification of effects may be enhanced even more within the context of actual group deliberations, as previous experimental research suggests.

These results do not imply that one can never devise jury instructions that will put punitive damages on sound footing. However, they do highlight the challenging character of this task. Many respondents are simply reluctant or unable to carry out even the most basic mathematical calculations. Moreover, they appear quite willing to abandon the jury instructions when they have other rationales for setting punitive damages that they find to be either more convenient or more compelling. The neglect of the Polinsky-Shavell jury instructions by my large sample of jury-eligible citizens is consistent with the performance of juries more generally.

Exhibit 9.1

In considering the imposition of punitive damages on the defendant, you should determine three dollar amounts: (A) an amount to accomplish deterrence; (B) an amount to accomplish punishment; (C) a final amount—your punitive damages award—between your answers for A and B.

A. *Deterrence*

1. Punitive damages fulfill the deterrence objective to the extent that they deliver a message and warning to the defendant and to other similarly situated firms to take appropriate steps to prevent harm in the future. But punitive damages will not fulfill the deterrence objective if they cause firms to take wasteful steps to prevent harm, if they cause the prices of products and services to rise excessively, or if they cause firms to withdraw socially valuable products or services from the market.

2. To achieve the deterrence objective, your principal task is to estimate the likelihood that the defendant might have escaped having to pay for the harm for which it should be responsible. Thus, for example, if the harm was noticeable and likely to lead to a lawsuit, your estimate of the likelihood of escaping liability would be relatively low. But if the harm might not have been attributed to the defendant, or if the defendant tried to conceal its harmful conduct, your estimate of the likelihood of escaping liability would be relatively high.

3. You should use the table below to determine the punitive damages multiplier that corresponds to your estimated probability of escaping liability. Then multiply the compensatory damages amount by your punitive damages multiplier. The resulting number is the *base punitive damages amount.*

Probability of Escaping Liability (%)	Punitive Damages Multiplier
0	0.00
10	0.11
20	0.25
30	0.43
40	0.67
50	1.00
60	1.50
70	2.33
80	4.00
90	9.00
99	99.00

4. The base punitive damages amount should not be adjusted because of any of the following considerations:
a) reprehensibility of the defendant's conduct;
b) net worth, revenues, or profits of the defendant;
c) potential harm, that is, the harm that might have been caused by the defendant's conduct;
d) gain or profit that the defendant might have obtained from its harmful conduct;

e) litigation costs borne by the plaintiff;

f) components of harm that you did not include in compensatory damages;

g) whether the harm included personal injury.

What amount do you believe the base punitive damages amount should be?

B. Punishment

1. Punitive damages fulfill the punishment objective to the extent that they cause defendants to penalize their *blameworthy employees* who engaged in reprehensible behavior.
2. In considering punishment, you should keep in mind that the defendant's payment of compensatory damages already may lead to the punishment of blameworthy employees to some extent.
3. In considering how well the imposition of punitive damages will fulfill the punishment objective, you should also bear the following in mind:

   a) the extent to which you believe blameworthy employees can be identified and penalized by the defendant. The easier this identification is, the higher should be the level of punitive damages.

   b) the extent to which you believe that innocent parties will suffer as a result of the imposition of punitive damages on the defendant; such parties might include shareholders as well as customers, who may have to pay higher prices for the defendant's products or services. The more likely it is that innocent parties will be punished, the lower should be the level of punitive damages.
4. In the light of these considerations, you should determine the amount of punitive damages that you believe will accomplish proper punishment.

What amount of punitive damages do you believe the punishment amount be?

C. Determination of Punitive Damages

Punitive damages should be an amount between the amount that you found appropriate for the purpose of deterrence and the amount that you found appropriate for the purpose of punishment. If you attach greater importance to the deterrence objective, punitive damages should be closer to the amount that you found best to promote deterrence. If you attach greater importance to the punishment objective, punitive damages should be closer to the amount that you found best to promote punishment.

Using your estimates of the base punitive damages amount, the punishment amount, and your assessment of the company's behavior, what do you believe the punitive damages amount should be? Please write the amount of punitive damages you believe is appropriate in the blank below.

_____

Exhibit 9.2

Scenario 1

The *Toxic Chemical Research Institute* develops new chemicals for industrial uses. As part of its operations, it generates concentrated amounts of highly toxic chemical wastes. Usually, a waste disposal company removes the waste to a safe landfill set aside for that purpose. However, due to extremely adverse weather conditions, the landfill is temporarily closed. The company has 12 steel drums of dangerous chemicals that it is eager to remove from the plant before a major production run for its most important customer. There is no legal way to dispose of the chemicals quickly. The company decided instead to violate U.S. government rules for safe disposal of dangerous chemicals.

The shift manager, worried about the accumulating chemicals, decided that the easiest way to get rid of the chemicals would be to dump them in the stream behind the plant. The manager knew that there was a 25% chance that the EPA inspector was going to be visiting the plant next week, and that if he did the dumping would be discovered. Thus, there was also a 75% chance of not getting caught. Despite the risk of getting caught, he told his crew that it was worth the gamble because it was the easiest way to get rid of the chemicals, and it was dangerous to keep the chemicals.

An EPA inspector did identify the spill and determined that *Toxic Chemical Research Institute* was responsible for it. No health hazard to humans occurred, but there was $100,000 in cost to the city due to additional water treatment costs. EPA fined the company $100,000 to cover these costs. The company paid this $100,000 amount.

The city is now seeking punitive damages to punish the company's behavior. Your task is to determine the amount of punitive damages to levy, if you believe punitive damages are warranted. Below are the guidelines for determining these amounts, provided as part of the judge's instructions.

Scenario 2

The *Toxic Chemical Research Institute* develops new chemicals for industrial uses. As part of its operations, it generates concentrated amounts of highly toxic chemical wastes. Usually, a waste disposal company removes the waste to a safe landfill set aside for that purpose. However, due to extremely adverse weather conditions, the landfill is temporarily closed. The company has 12 steel drums of dangerous chemicals that it is eager to remove from the plant before a major production run for its most important customer. There is no legal way to dispose of the chemicals quickly. The company decided instead to violate U.S. government rules for safe disposal of dangerous chemicals.

The shift manager, worried about the accumulating chemicals, decided that the easiest way to get rid of the chemicals would be to dump them in the stream behind the plant. The manager knew that there was a 1% chance that the EPA inspector would be visiting the plant next week, and that if he did the dumping would be discovered. His best estimate is that there was only a 1% chance of being inspected, caught and penalized. Thus, there was a 99% chance of escaping any penalty. Despite the risk of getting caught, he told his crew that it was worth the gamble because it was the easiest way to get rid of the chemicals, and it was dangerous to keep the chemicals.

An EPA inspector did identify the spill and determined that *Toxic Chemical Research Institute* was responsible for it. No health hazard to humans occurred, but there was $100,000 in cost to the city due to additional water treatment costs. EPA fined the company $100,000 to cover these costs. The company paid this $100,000 amount.

The city is now seeking punitive damages to punish the company's behavior. Your task is to determine the amount of punitive damages to levy, if you believe punitive damages are warranted. Below are the guidelines for determining these amounts, provided as part of the judge's instructions.

Scenario 3

The *Toxic Chemical Research Institute* develops new chemicals for industrial uses. As part of its operations, it generates concentrated amounts of highly toxic chemical wastes. Usually, a waste disposal company removes the waste to a safe landfill set aside for that purpose. However, due to extremely adverse weather conditions, the landfill is temporarily closed. The company has 12 steel drums of dangerous chemicals that it is eager to remove from the plant before a major production run for its most important customer. There is no legal way to dispose of the chemicals quickly. The company decided instead to violate U.S. government rules for safe disposal of dangerous chemicals.

The shift manager, worried about the accumulating chemicals, knew that if he dumped the chemicals nearby that his company would definitely be caught and punished. To prevent being caught, his crew loaded the chemical drums onto unmarked trucks and dumped the chemicals in a rural stream at 3 A.M. The manager believed that this "midnight dumping" would reduce the risk of getting caught to $\frac{1}{100}$. Thus, there is a 99% chance of escaping any penalty. He decided that it was worth the gamble because it was the fastest way to get rid of the chemicals, and it was dangerous to keep the chemicals.

An EPA inspector did identify the spill and determined that *Toxic Chemical Research Institute* was responsible for it. No health hazard to humans occurred, but there was $100,000 in cost to the city due to additional water treatment costs. EPA fined the company $100,000 to cover these costs. The company paid this $100,000 amount.

The city is now seeking punitive damages to punish the company's behavior.

Your task is to determine the amount of punitive damages to levy, if you believe punitive damages are warranted. Below are the guidelines for determining these amounts, provided as part of the judge's instructions.

Scenario 4

The *Toxic Chemical Research Institute* develops new chemicals for industrial uses. As part of its operations, it generates concentrated amounts of highly toxic chemical wastes. Usually, a waste disposal company removes the waste to a safe landfill set aside for that purpose. However, due to extremely adverse weather conditions, the landfill is temporarily closed. The company has 12 steel drums of dangerous chemicals that it is eager to remove from the plant before a major production run for its most important customer. There is no legal way to dispose of the chemicals quickly. The company decided instead to violate U.S. government rules for safe disposal of dangerous chemicals.

The shift manager, worried about the accumulating chemicals, knew that if he dumped the chemicals nearby that his company would definitely be caught and punished. To prevent being caught, his crew loaded the chemical drums onto unmarked trucks and dumped the chemicals in a rural stream at 3 A.M. The manager believed that this "midnight dumping" would reduce the risk of getting caught to $\frac{1}{100}$. Thus, there is a 99% chance of escaping any penalty. He decided that it was worth the gamble because it was the fastest way to get rid of the chemicals, and it was dangerous to keep the chemicals.

An EPA inspector did identify the spill and determined that *Toxic Chemical Research Institute* was responsible for it. No health hazard to humans occurred, but there was $100,000 in cost to the city due to additional water treatment costs. EPA fined the company $100,000 to cover these costs. The company paid this $100,000 amount.

The city is now seeking punitive damages to punish the company's behavior. Your task is to determine the amount of punitive damages to levy, if you believe punitive damages are warranted. In his closing statement, the plaintiff's attorney made the following arguments: "Your job as jurors is to impose a penalty which will make this corporation, and others, conduct their business in a way which protects the defenseless citizens of Texas who have no other way of getting the company to be responsible. This is your job. A penalty against this company has to be one that they will notice. It would not destroy this company or even cause them long-term financial harm to impose a penalty on them of $50 million, about 20% of their net worth, or about two and one-half times their annual profit. Certainly a minimum penalty should be one year's profit, about $25 million, so the range you may want to consider is between $25 million, about one year's profit, and $50 million. I don't think that anything less than $25 million would have much effect as far as deterring them and getting them to be more careful in their operations."

Below are the guidelines for determining these amounts, provided as part of the judge's instructions.

Scenario 5

The *Toxic Chemical Research Institute* develops new chemicals for industrial uses. As part of its operations, it generates concentrated amounts of highly toxic chemical wastes. Usually, a waste disposal company removes the waste to a safe landfill, set aside for that purpose. However, due to extremely adverse weather conditions the landfill is temporarily closed. The company has 12 steel drums of dangerous chemicals that it is eager to remove from the plant before a major production run for its most important customer. There is no legal way to dispose of the chemicals quickly. The company decided instead to violate U.S. government rules for safe disposal of dangerous chemicals.

The shift manager, worried about the accumulating chemicals, knew that if he dumped the chemicals nearby that his company would definitely be caught and punished. To prevent being caught, his crew loaded the chemical drums onto unmarked trucks and dumped the chemicals in a rural stream at 3 A.M. The manager believed that this "midnight dumping" would reduce the risk of getting caught to $1/100$. Thus, there is a 99% chance of escaping any penalty. He decided that it was worth the gamble because it was the fastest way to get rid of the chemicals, and it was dangerous to keep the chemicals.

An EPA inspector did identify the spill and determined that *Toxic Chemical Research Institute* was responsible for it. No health hazard to humans occurred, but there was $100,000 in cost to the city due to additional water treatment costs. EPA fined the company $100,000 to cover these costs. The company paid this $100,000 amount.

The city is now seeking punitive damages to punish the company's behavior. Your task is to determine the amount of punitive damages to levy, if you believe punitive damages are warranted. Before being placed on the jury, you read about a similar case that took place in California. A jury there fined the company $50 million in punitive damages. However, the company appealed, claiming the award was excessive. The punitive damages amount was reduced to $25 million by the appeals court in California. The company claimed that this amount was still too high and that it would continue to fight the award in court.

Below are the guidelines for determining these amounts, provided as part of the judge's instructions.

10

Judging Risk and Recklessness

W. Kip Viscusi

I. Introduction

A substantial literature has documented the difficulties affecting choices under uncertainty. Risk beliefs may be biased, and subsequent decisions may be in error as well. These errors are usually not random, but instead follow many quite systematic patterns. By analyzing the pattern in such biases and heuristics, it becomes possible to predict how people will tend to err in other risk decisions.[1]

These errors are not restricted to people's private decisions. Evidence in the preceding chapters suggests that jurors have substantial difficulty in thinking about accident cases as well. Determination of liability and assessments of damages each may be fraught with error. Moreover, these biases are not random and in some cases reflect patterns of behavior that have been established in the literature more generally.

Risk judgments of various kinds are central to jurors' implementation of legal rules. Applying negligence criteria requires that jurors assess the adequacy of risk-cost trade-offs. Similarly, risk-utility tests, assessments of the adequacy of a product design, and similar matters all require that jurors be able to make sensible judgments once presented with appropriate risk evidence. Assessments of whether the defendant's conduct led to willful and reckless imposition of risks on others and consequently merit punitive damages likewise require that jurors be able to perceive

1. See, e.g., the prospect theory model of Daniel Kahneman and Amos Tversky, "Prospect Theory: An Analysis of Decision under Risk," 47 *Econometrica* 263 (1979). A normative Bayesian approach that predicts many of the anomalies that are incorporated into the prospect theory framework is reported in W. Kip Viscusi, "Prospective Reference Theory: Towards an Explanation of the Paradoxes," 2 *J. Risk & Uncertainty* 235 (1989); and W. Kip Viscusi, *Rational Risk Policy* (1998). See Christine Jolls et al., "A Behavioral Approach to Law and Economics," 50 *Stan. L. Rev.* 1471 (1998), for a discussion of how many of these anomalies link to legal contexts.

the magnitude of the risk, determine how corporations and other defendants should have responded in that context, and evaluate the extent of the shortfall in the level of precautionary behavior.

Making risk judgments lies at the heart of punitive damages criteria. Consider, for example, some of the guidance provided by the jury instructions from *Jardel Co., Inc. v. Hughes,* Del. Supr., 523 A.2d 518 (1987), which were discussed in chapter 5. In assessing whether a company was reckless or displayed callous disregard for the rights of others, jurors must consider four factors, each of which involves explicit risk judgments:

> First, a defendant must be subjectively conscious of a particular grave danger or risk of harm, and the danger or risk must be a foreseeable and probable effect of the conduct. Second, the particular danger or risk of which the defendant was subjectively conscious must in fact have eventuated. Third, a defendant must have disregarded the risk in deciding how to act. Fourth, a defendant's conduct in ignoring the danger or risk must have involved a gross deviation from the level of care which an ordinary person would use, having due regard to all the circumstances.

Whether jurors can make such judgments in a reliable manner hinges quite explicitly on how they think about risk, particularly within the context of the kinds of situations encountered in litigation.

To explore such issues, this chapter will use an original sample of almost five hundred jury-eligible citizens. Each of these participants considered a detailed series of questions regarding risk beliefs, willingness to bear risks, and a wide variety of risk judgments that parallel those arising in courtroom situations. Moreover, since many of the cases considered punitive damages, they also received general instructions regarding the awarding of punitive damages that covered the principal justifications for punitive damages in jury instructions:

> Several of the questions deal with punitive damages for safety decisions. As you may recall, courts may award punitive damages for conduct that is reckless. A company is reckless if it is conscious of a grave danger or risk of harm, it evaluated the danger, it disregarded the risk when deciding how to act, and its conduct involved a gross deviation from the level of care an ordinary person would use. In the punitive damages cases discussed below, courts will separately award compensatory damages to meet the income losses associated with the accident.

Several tests of the rationality of juror behavior are possible. First, do jurors perform well with respect to legal norms, such as legal rules for negligence doctrines? Second, do jurors perform well in objective-risk decision terms—for example, are their risk beliefs accurate? Chapter 11 compares the performance of jurors to that of judges facing similar scenarios. This commonality will make it possible to assess whether jurors or judges are better able to deal with the types of risk judgments that arise in tort liability contexts.

II. Background and Hypotheses

The organization of this chapter is around several behavioral hypotheses that have been identified in the literature as well as in related studies in this volume. First, people often are unable to make sensible trade-offs between risk and cost. That result is an underlying theme of the railroad accident analysis in chapter 6 and corporate risk-analysis scenarios in chapter 7. If people are in fact unable to make sound cost-benefit judgments, it will have profound ramifications for their interpretation of legal rules. Section III considers whether jurors will in fact implicitly do cost-benefit balancing. Our hypothesis is that if individuals are in fact incapable of making such risk-balancing decisions, they will be predisposed to awarding punitive damages in a much greater series of circumstances than is warranted.

The hypothesis considered in section V stems from the substantial literature on how people deal with risk ambiguity and uncertainty more generally. In particular, suppose that the behavior by the defendant led to a particular damages amount, but at the time of the accident it was not known whether the damage would have been worse than the amount actually observed or less severe. There is a well-documented bias of people placing excessive emphasis on the worst-case scenario in accident contexts. In situations in which information is revealed to the public about potential risks, it is the worst-case scenario that receives the greatest attention rather than the mean estimate of the risk. Indeed, this tendency is so great that many government policies likewise have institutionalized this bias of emphasizing the worst-case outcome as opposed to what is expected to happen.[2] A working hypothesis is that when jurors likewise are confronted with a situation in which the accident could have been worse, then they too will place excessive weight on worst-case possibilities rather than on the actual damages amounts that have been observed.

The final set of hypotheses to be examined derives from the literature

2. For further discussion, see W. Kip Viscusi, *Rational Risk Policy* (1998).

on risk belief and risk valuation. Studies in the literature indicate that people tend to overestimate low-probability events, such as those likely to be encountered in accident contexts. Here we present detailed data based on individual responses to explore whether our sample of jury-eligible citizens is subject to the same kinds of error. As part of this analysis of risk beliefs and attitudes toward risk, this chapter examines whether there is evidence of a *zero-risk mentality*. Evidence in chapter 6 indicates that people often state that we should be uncompromising in our risk-management efforts. As a result, we would predict that people often may not be willing to make finite trade-offs between risk and cost even when doing so is an implicit decision that we make daily as part of our lives.

III. Experiment 1: Risk-Cost Trade-offs

How well do people fare when given the task of assessing whether a corporation has made an appropriate judgment in its efforts to balance risk and cost?[3] Such balancing is implicit in the Learned Hand rule for making negligence judgments. This criterion is also the same as efficiency-oriented economists would recommend, which is that one should adopt safety measures provided that the benefits exceed the costs.

A. Participants

The participants in the jury sample consisted of 493 jury-eligible adults who were recruited by a Phoenix, Arizona, survey firm.[4] Respondents took the survey, which lasted approximately thirty minutes, and were compensated for their participation. The sample included a diverse adult population group. The sample averaged forty-five years of age, with at least some college education. Females were overrepresented, but seat belt use and smoking rates were comparable to national estimates.

A. Materials and Procedure

In this experiment, respondents considered a scenario involving an airplane repair situation. Unlike the scenarios in chapter 7, there is no

---

3. See Richard Posner, *Economic Analysis of Law* (3rd ed., 1986); and A. Mitchell Polinsky, *An Introduction to Law and Economics* (2nd ed., 1989), for reviews of these doctrines and their linkage to the original Learned Hand formula. These principles are elaborated for the risk context in W. Kip Viscusi, "The Social Costs of Punitive Damages against Corporations in Environmental and Safety Torts," 87 *Geo. L.J.* 285 (1998).

4. Sample size may be a few subjects less for some questions due to nonresponses.

corporate risk analysis. Each person considered only one scenario, but a total of four different scenarios were tested across different subsamples. There is some cost of repair and associated expected benefits from the repair for each of the scenarios. The cost of the repair remains unchanged across the scenarios, as do the expected benefits. However, the scale of the losses increases and the probability of an accident diminishes to keep the expected benefits of making the repair constant. Do juror judgments incorporate such changes that leave expected benefits unchanged? The parameters of the problem are such that the $2,000 cost of the repair always exceeds the $1,500 value of the expected benefits so that the repair decision never passes a cost-benefit test. Thus, the firm should not be found negligent, much less be punished by a punitive damages award.

Summary of Experiment

Description: Each subject read one version of an airplane defect story. There were four versions, including (1) two combinations of probability that there would be property damage and its magnitude if the defect were not repaired, and (2) two combinations of probability that there would be deaths and their number if the defect were not repaired. In each case the subject was first asked if the company should repair the defect, and then if the company should be liable for punitive damages if they did not repair it and an accident occurred.

Number of subjects: 493 jury-eligible citizens.

Location: Phoenix, Arizona.

Decisions: Individual survey.

Stimuli: Written case summary and instructions.

Large-loss/low-probability events create potential problems for decision making. The intent of these manipulations is to see whether increasing the size of the stakes dominates jurors' thinking even when the probability of an accident diminishes proportionately. If jurors are not sensitive to the proportional drop in the probability that occurs for the scenarios when the size of the stakes increases, then that will suggest that firms operating in contexts in which the stakes are great will be severely disadvantaged. Even if companies' safety behavior has resulted in a very low probability of an accident, jurors may focus on the magnitude of the stakes involved rather than the expected damages, that is, the probability of damage multiplied by the size of the loss.

The jury-eligible citizens considered one of four different scenarios, where their first task was to determine whether they would have ordered a repair, had it been their decision. The decision to repair the plane is not, however, identical to finding that the firm was liable on account of negligence. Respondents might favor making a repair but would not hold the firm liable. This question is intended to engage respondents in the repair task and to begin thinking about how they would make the risk-cost trade-offs. Each scenario was a variant of the initial scenario given below:

> You are CEO of Rocky Mountain Airlines. The cargo door on a plane does not operate properly. Fixing it costs $2,000. If it is not fixed, there is absolutely no safety risk. Very reliable engineering estimates indicate that there is only a $\frac{1}{10}$ chance that there will be a total loss to your company of $15,000 due to materials damage to cargo over the life of the plane. Thus, there is a 90% chance that there will be no damage whatsoever. Your company has no insurance but will be liable for the cost of this damage.

Respondents were then asked whether they should repair the plane, and if the plane is not repaired and there is damage, should there be punitive damages? The other scenarios raised the losses to $1.5 million, $150 million (29 deaths valued at a $5 million figure that reflects the full social value of life), and $1.5 billion (290 deaths valued at $5 million each) and decreased the probabilities of an accident to 1/1,000 (for $1.5 million in damages), 1/100,000 (for $150 million in damages), and 1/1,000,000 (for $1.5 billion in damages).

IV. Results: Experiment 1

Most respondents favored repairing the plane in all instances shown in table 10.1. The percentages of the mock-juror sample favoring repairs are 87% to 88% in the two property damage scenarios and 93% to 96% in the two fatality scenarios.

After considering the repair decision, the respondents were then told that the company chose not to repair the plane and that the projected damage did in fact occur. The jury-eligible citizens were then asked whether punitive damages would apply in this instance. The percentage of respondents awarding punitive damages was 74% to 78% for the two property damage scenarios and 95% to 96% for the two personal injury scenarios for which total damages are greater. In every case there is an extremely large percentage of jury-eligible citizens awarding punitive damages. This result is particularly striking since the firm is not even negligent, much less guilty of reckless conduct warranting a punitive award. The punitive damages awards become more frequent as the stakes rise, as the significance tests reported at the bottom of table 10.1 indicate.

Table 10.1. Relation of Jurors' Opinions on Repairing Airplane Defect to Whether Punitive Damages Should Apply If an Accident Occurs

Panel A: Property Damage Low—$15,000; Risk Probability 1/10

	Repair Plane	Don't Repair Plane	Total
Punitives apply	75 (65.2%)	10 (8.6%)	85 (73.9%)
Punitives don't apply	26 (22.6%)	4 (3.5%)	30 (26.1%)
Total	101 (87.8%)	14 (12.2%)	115 (100%)

Panel B: Property Damage High—$1.5 Million; Risk Probability 1/1,000

	Repair Plane	Don't Repair Plane	Total
Punitives apply	105 (73.4%)	7 (4.0%)	112 (78.3%)
Punitives don't apply	19 (13.3%)	12 (8.4%)	31 (21.7%)
Total	124 (86.7%)	19 (13.3%)	143 (100%)

Panel C: Personal Injury—29 Deaths for $150 Million; Risk Probability 1/100,000

	Repair Plane	Don't Repair Plane	Total
Punitives apply	110 (92.4%)	4 (3.4%)	114 (95.8%)
Punitives don't apply	4 (3.4%)	1 (0.8%)	5 (4.2%)
Total	114 (95.8%)	5 (4.2%)	119 (100%)

Panel D: Personal Injury—290 Deaths for $1.5 Billion; Risk Probability 1/1,000,000

	Repair Plane	Don't Repair Plane	Total
Punitives apply	50 (89.3%)	3 (5.4%)	53 (94.6%)
Punitives don't apply	2 (3.6%)	1 (1.8%)	3 (5.3%)
Total	52 (92.9%)	4 (8.9%)	56 (100%)

Panel E: Overall Results

	Repair Plane	Don't Repair Plane	Total
Punitives apply	340 (78.5%)	24 (5.5%)	364 (84.1%)
Punitives don't apply	51 (11.8%)	18 (4.2%)	69 (15.9%)
Total	391 (90.3%)	42 (9.7%)	433 (100%)

Note: Percentages might not sum across rows and columns due to rounding error.
t-statistics:

Repair Plane:	Award Punitives:
A vs. B: 0.340	A vs. B: 0.955
C vs. D: 0.936	C vs. D: 0.354
(A + B) vs. (C + D): 2.782*	(A + B) vs. (C + D): 5.569*

*Significant at 99% confidence level, two-tailed test.

V. Experiment 2: Setting Damages When Losses Are Uncertain

Tort liability situations involve many uncertainties. It is rare that we know in advance that an accident will occur. Moreover, if an accident does occur, the amount of the damage may vary. Dealing with the role of possible loss variance creates potential hurdles for juror judgments. If jurors have ambiguity aversion and anchor their views on the worst-case scenario rather than the actual damages amount, the damages levied will be too high.

Suppose that an accident could generate damages that could have either a high value or a low value. Thus, there will be damages, but there is a lottery on the damages level. What should be the accident award? The legal principles in situations of financial loss are well established. Compensating the accident victim for the amount of the loss provides an optimal level of insurance of the harm. Damages equal to the size of the loss will also create efficient levels of deterrence if we assume away complications such as detectability problems. Thus, paying off damages equal to the high-loss amount when the loss is high and the low-loss amount when the loss is low will generate efficient insurance and deterrence. While there is no other optimal insurance amount, it is possible to create efficient deterrence by always setting damages equal to the expected loss. However, such a penalty will not provide optimal insurance, and for it to provide efficient deterrence, damages must always be paid when there is a damages lottery, even if the low damages amount is zero. However, these cases will not appear in court. If, instead, damages are always set to equal the worst-case scenario, they will provide excessive insurance for the low-loss cases and excessive deterrence. Thus, I will take damages equal to the loss as the normative reference point for compensatory damages awards.

To explore the influence of uncertainty regarding the damages amount, respondents considered an oil well blowout situation in which there was a lottery on damages. Some respondents received the scenario in which the lottery outcome was a low level of losses, while others considered a scenario in which the losses were high. The scenario was as follows:

> Acme Oil Company has been found that it did not meet the legal standards for safe operation of its wells. Consequently, it is liable for an oil well blowout that caused $10 million in property damage and no personal injury. The company in many respects was unfortunate in that such blowouts have a 90% chance of no damage and a 10% chance of $10 million in damages. What damages award would you select?

The counterpart scenario also had $10 million in damages actually occurring, but the company was fortunate in that the damages could have

Table 10.2. Jurors' Awards in Oil Well Blowout Trial

Damages Awarded (in millions)	Number of Responses	Percent of Sample
$0	22	4.5
$5	65	13.3
$10	129	26.3
$30	179	36.5
$75	47	9.6
$100	48	9.8

Note: Median award $30 million; Geometric mean award $21.43 million.

t-test on arithmetic means: $t = 4.7942$, which is significant at the 99% confidence level.

been worse—$100 million. Do the respondents focus on what might have been, or do they assess damages properly based on the actual outcome? Focusing on what might have been would be a form of ambiguity aversion or alarmist response to risk that has been identified as an influence in other risk contexts for probabilities.[5] In particular, people often focus on the worst-case scenario in terms of the level of the risk probability when the probability is uncertain. Here the uncertainty is with respect to uncertainty involving the size of the loss. Risk aversion should presumably not be influential because there is no indication that the losses are borne privately and concentrated among a small group.

VI. Results: Experiment 2

Table 10.2 summarizes the damages amounts levied by the sample of jury-eligible citizens. The results in table 10.2 reflect an enormous variation in the assessed damages amount. Even though the actual damages were only $10 million, only 26% of the respondents assessed this damages value. Thirty-seven percent of the sample awarded $30 million in damages. Roughly one-fifth of the sample awarded damages under $10 million, with a similar percentage awarding damages over $30 million. The median award level of $30 million and the geometric mean award level of $21.4 million each greatly exceed the actual damages amount.

5. See W. Kip Viscusi, *Rational Risk Policy* (1998), for a review of this evidence.

The distribution of the responses depends on which scenario the respondent received. In the case in which the firm was fortunate in that the accident did not cause more damage than it actually did, jury-eligible respondents who deviated from the $10 million damages amount in setting awards tended to award levels in excess of $10 million. In contrast, when the company was unfortunate in that the $10 million damages amount could have been zero, there is a greater propensity of the subjects to award damages below the $10 million damages level.

The results for the jury-eligible citizens indicate that the frequency of departures from the $10 million award amount do reflect the expected pattern given the character of how the lottery might have turned out. In situations in which the company was fortunate in that there was a 90% chance of experiencing damages greater than $10 million, over half the sample awarded a damages amount exceeding $10 million, and 14% of the sample awarded damages below $10 million. For the unfortunate case in which the company had a 90% chance of having no damages, but did in fact experience $10 million in damages, 22% of the sample awarded damages below $10 million, and 44% of the sample awarded damages in excess of $10 million. However, there is much greater clustering of these awards above $10 million in the $30 million range rather than the damages amounts of $75 million and $100 million, which were selected much more often in the fortunate-case scenario.

The existence of a damages lottery often leads jurors to assess damages in excess of the actual damages amount, irrespective of whether there was a chance of greater or smaller damages. Damages awards on average will be too great because of the excessive focus on the worst-case scenario. However, this tendency to award damages exceeding the actual amount is much greater when there is a chance that the accident could have been worse than it was. The net result is that potential damages variance before the accident leads jurors to award higher penalties than would be warranted based on sound law and economics principles. Jury-eligible citizens anchored their damages assessments on the worst-case scenario even when it did not prevail.

VII. Experiment 3: Risk Beliefs and Risk Trade-offs

What factors might account for the errors of jurors? Could the problem be errors in how people perceive risk, or does the problem stem from errors in the valuation of risk for any given level of risk beliefs?

This section will explore perceptions of mortality risks and personal risk-cost trade-offs.

Consider first how people perceive risk. Risk judgments are central to assessments of recklessness and risk-cost trade-offs. One of the most well-established results in the literature on risk and uncertainty is that people overestimate low-probability events and underestimate larger risks.[6] The first study generating this result was Lichtenstein et al. (1978), who found that for a set of mortality risks, people exhibit the systematic patterns of bias noted above.[7] Here I will run a similar experiment in which jury-eligible citizens rate the total number of fatalities from different causes. Each individual in the sample assessed the total annual deaths associated with twenty-three major sources of mortality using an approach that paralleled that used in the risk-perception studies above.

The survey question that the respondents considered with respect to the mortality risk assessment was the following:

> In 1990, 47,000 people in the United States died in automobile accidents. How many people died from the other causes of death listed below? You are not expected to know any of these answers exactly. Your best estimate will do. Fill in your best estimate in the space.

The respondents then considered twenty-three different causes of death.

VIII. Results: Experiment 2

Figure 10.1 sketches the level of risk beliefs for the sample as a function of the actual risk level.[8] The dashed 45-degree line is the reference point for determining whether perceived and actual risk beliefs are identical. The risk-perception curve is the solid curve. Figure 10.1 demonstrates the established pattern of overperception of small risks and underassessment of large risks, as respondents tend to overassess risks such as botulism, fireworks accidents, and lightning strikes. In contrast, the truly substantial hazards that we face—such as the risks from diabetes, stroke, all forms of cancer, and heart disease—tend to be underestimated.

6. There are, of course, exceptions. See Howard Kunreuther, *Disaster Insurance Protection: Public Policy Lessons* (1978), for evidence that some low risks tend to be ignored.

7. Sarah Lichtenstein et al., "Judged Frequency of Lethal Events," 4 *J. Experimental Psychol.: Hum. Learning and Memory* 551 (1978).

8. These curves were based on estimates of the natural log of perceived risks as a function of a person-specific intercept and both a linear and quadratic term for the natural log of actual deaths.

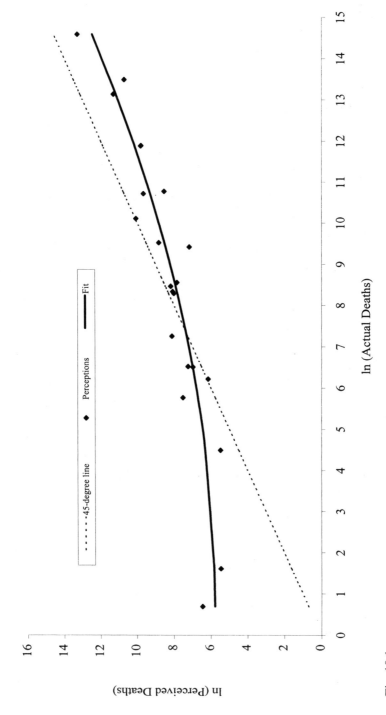

Fig. 10.1.

It is noteworthy that the risk-perception curve for large risks is closer to the 45-degree line than it is for smaller risks. The greatest errors in judgment appear to take place with respect to small-probability events, such as those that are likely to arise in accident contexts. The discontinuity in risk beliefs near zero is also evident from the curve. As risk levels become infinitesimally small, perceived risks remain large. The zero-risk mentality is in part a reflection of how small risks are overestimated, making them seem much worse than zero risk.

A second critical attribute for determining how individuals will make decisions regarding risk is their risk-cost trade-off. The most widely used measure of this type in the economics literature is the implicit value of life. This terminology does not refer to the amount one would pay to avoid certain death. Nor does it pertain to the appropriate level of compensation after a fatality. Rather, it gives individuals' rate of trade-off between small probabilities of death and money. Economists typically base these estimates either on the revealed trade-off in higher wages for a risky job or the lower prices people pay for more hazardous products. Most of these estimates based on wage equations cluster in the range of $3 million to $7 million, with a midpoint value of $5 million.[9]

In order to elicit survey responses that are meaningful, it is essential to create a credible survey context that will in fact elicit the underlying risk-cost trade-off. U.S. Supreme Court Justice Stephen Breyer has suggested that a particularly useful way to think about value-of-life issues in general is to ask people how much they would be willing to pay for a marginally safer car.[10] These personal risk trade-offs could then be used to guide the individual in thinking about the risk trade-off that corporations should strive to achieve. Survey evidence in the literature regarding hypothetical improvements in automobile safety have yielded estimates for the implicit value of life comparable to those that have emerged from wage-job risk studies using actual labor market behavior.[11]

9. For a review of this evidence, see W. Kip Viscusi, "The Value of Risks to Life and Health," 31 *J. Econ. Literature,* 1912 (1993); and W. Kip Viscusi, *Rational Risk Policy* (1998).

10. Stephen Breyer, *Breaking the Vicious Circle: Toward Effective Risk Regulation* (1993).

11. For a review of these studies in comparison to the wage equation literature, see W. Kip Viscusi, "The Value of Risks to Life and Health," 31 *J. Econ. Literature,* 1912 (1993). A recent study of the implicit value of life reflected in used-car purchases, which parallels the case-study approach advocated by Justice Breyer, is that of Mark Dreyfus and W. Kip Viscusi, "Rates of Time Preference and Consumer Valuations of Automobile Safety and Fuel Efficiency," 38 *J.L. & Econ.* 79 (1995).

The specific question that the respondents considered regarding the value of life was the following:

> Suppose you could reduce your annual risk of death in a car crash by 1/10,000. Thus, if there were 10,000 people just like you, there would be one less expected death per year in your group. This risk reduction would cut your annual risk of death in a car crash in half.
>
> How much would you be willing to pay each year either for a safer car or for improved highway safety measures that would cut your motor vehicle risks in half?

Respondents then considered five different dollar ranges as well as the possibility of spending an infinite amount on such a safety improvement, where this was defined as being "all present and future resources." Converting responses to an implicit value-of-life measure is a straightforward exercise. The risk change indicated in the question was a decrease in the probability of death of 1/10,000. For those who gave finite responses, the mean implicit value of life of $5.1 million was quite reasonable and in line with estimates in the literature.

What is disturbing is that almost 10% of the sample—or forty-seven respondents—indicated that they had an infinite value-of-life amount. Such responses indicate a failure to be willing to make such complex risk trade-offs. These respondents fell prey to the zero-risk mentality and are willing to pay any price to achieve safety. Such unbounded commitments to safety are not feasible, given the multiplicity of hazards that we face and the limited resources we have to address them. A belief in the zero-risk approach will make jurors less willing to accept the behavior of corporations that make finite risk trade-offs.

Thus, in addition to the differences found in the accident scenarios, the jury-eligible citizens displayed two classes of systematic errors in dealing with risk more generally. They are likely to believe that low-probability hazards are more dangerous than they are. Moreover, in considering risk contexts, they are susceptible to the zero-risk mentality. Each of these sources of error will make jurors more likely to err in a systematic manner in their liability judgments and damages assessments.

IX. Conclusion

Anomalies in individual behavior regarding risk are not restricted to private decisions. People's participation in juries also involves consideration of risk contexts for cases involving accidents. An important question for assessing the function of our judicial system is how juries in fact approach such decisions and whether their judgments are flawed in a systematic manner.

The results of this study of risk attitudes of jury-eligible citizens suggest that jurors particularly fall short of reasonable standards of behavior. Overall, 74% of jury-eligible citizens favored punitive damages in the small-property-loss airline repair case, even though the company was not even guilty of negligence. When faced with damages resulting from a previous risk lottery, only 26% of jury-eligible citizens awarded damages equal to the loss. The dominant focus instead was on the worst-case scenario that might have prevailed but did not. Moreover, 10% of the jury-eligible citizens indicated they had infinite risk trade-offs. This zero-risk mentality is likely to lead them to be particularly uncompromising when faced with realistic risk-cost trade-offs in accident contexts.

These findings raise the more fundamental issue of whether jurors make risk judgments sensibly when comparing the costs and benefits in risk contexts, determining whether a firm should be liable for an accident, and assessing the appropriate level of damages to be levied. Jurors fall substantially short of what one might hope for in terms of a desired pattern of decisions, particularly in small-probability/large-loss cases. Failure to think sensibly about risk and risk-cost trade-off issues will have ramifications for jurors' ability to make sound assessments regarding the various criteria that come into play in judging whether a company was reckless.

11

Do Judges Do Better?

W. Kip Viscusi

I. Introduction

The shortcomings in individual decisions involving risk influence the responses of social institutions to risk. In a democratic society, governmental action is responsive to citizen preferences. Substantial evidence indicates that the governmental operation of hazardous waste cleanup efforts, pharmaceutical regulation, risk-assessment practices, and a wide variety of other aspects of government risk regulation embody the same types of irrationality that have been identified in the literature dealing with irrationality of choice under uncertainty.[1] Evidence in chapter 10 and earlier chapters indicates that jurors may also be susceptible to biases in risk beliefs and risk decisions, thus contaminating their liability judgments.

Is there any reason to believe that judges will do better? Judges are human and may be prone to the same types of irrationalities as are other people. To what extent do these various forms of irrationality carry over to how they think about risk decisions for legal contexts?

Judges are not a random draw from the population and may not reflect all the usual patterns of error. They should be less prone to the kinds of biases and risk-decision errors exhibited by the populace more generally. In addition to being better educated than the average individual, judges are also experienced observers of risky decisions. After having handled a large series of cases involving accidents and hearing the

1. For a comprehensive perspective on these issues, see W. Kip Viscusi, *Rational Risk Policy* (1998). A detailed analysis of these issues for hazardous waste cleanup efforts appears in James T. Hamilton and W. Kip Viscusi, *Calculating Risks? The Spatial and Political Dimensions of Hazardous Waste Policy* (1999). An exposition of the underlying theory appears in Roger G. Noll and James E. Krier, "Some Implications of Cognitive Psychology for Risk Regulation," 19 *J. Legal Stud.* 747 (1990).

testimony presented by both sides, judges should be much better able to put risk decisions in perspective. Judges are also able to observe the outcome in these cases and whether the decisions are overturned on appeal. Because the appeals process provides a check on judicial errors, observation of this feedback mechanism should enhance judges' ability to make sounder risk decisions over time.

A. Participants

This chapter will examine the responses by a sample of ninety-five state judges to a written survey about risk decisions.[2] Although reliance on the results of a questionnaire may not capture the particular biases that are most influential in actual judicial decisions, it does provide a structured framework for exploring a wider range of issues than can be examined using case data. The judges in the sample were participants in the law and economics programs offered by the University of Kansas Law and Organizational Economics Center. The judges were sent these written surveys before the program began and returned the surveys before participating in the program, where the survey formed the basis for class discussion. The response rate was close to 100%. The sample consisted of program participants in two different sessions, both of which took place in 1997. Although the meetings were in Copper Mountain, Colorado, and Sanibel, Florida, participants in the program were from state courts throughout the country. The participants included many judges from state courts of appeals, state superior courts, and state supreme courts. The experience base of the sample consequently is likely to be greater than that of the average state court judge.

This chapter consists of a series of explorations of the rationality of judges' treatment of risk, each of which will be explored in turn. Most of these issues parallel those considered for juror samples. It begins in section 2 with an examination of the effect of hindsight, focusing on the railroad accident case described in chapter 6. Unlike jurors who did not behave symmetrically in the two situations, judges performed in a much more consistent manner. Section 3 considers the process of handling judicial trade-offs in airline accident cases using the same scenarios as in

2. While ninety-five judges participated in my study, the sample size for completed surveys varied depending on the particular question. For example, ninety-four judges completed the railroad accident section of the survey, and a low value of eighty-four judges assessed the risks of different causes of death.

chapter 10. To what extent do the judges balance risk and cost in a reasonable manner? A source of anomalies explored in section 4 is that risks are often not known with precision. There may be substantial ambiguity pertaining to the degree of hazard or the size of the likely damages. Do judges place greatest emphasis on worst-case possibilities, as did the jurors in chapter 10, or do they avoid these errors by focusing on actual damages levels? Are judges subject to the same degree of biases in accident risk beliefs as are jurors? Section 5 explores biases in risk beliefs involving risks of death. A final issue pertaining to personal risk preferences is the individual's risk trade-off in terms of the value of life, which is the subject of section 6. The fundamental result of these assessments is that while the performance of judges may not always be ideal, it is consistently superior to that of jury-eligible citizens.

Summary of Experiment

Description: Judges were given the same scenarios and questions as jury-eligible subjects in chapter 6 (Looking Backward in Punitive Damages: 20-20 Vision?) and in chapter 10 (Judging Risk and Recklessness), as well as additional questions to test their understanding of risk.

Number of subjects: 94 state judges.

Location: Judges from courts throughout the United States.

Decisions: Individual survey.

Stimuli: Written case summary and instructions.

II. Experiment 1: Hindsight Bias

The courts operate after the fact. In the case of accidents, courts consider situations in which accidents have already occurred as opposed to contexts in which there is a prospective risk of an accident. Given the retrospective nature of judicial proceedings, an important potential source of bias that has been identified in the literature on risk perception is that of *hindsight bias*.[3] Judge Easterbrook characterized the problem as follows: "The *ex post* perspective of litigation exerts a hydraulic force that distorts judgement."[4] After an accident, the potential causes often are much more apparent than they were before the accident occurred. The role of hindsight extends beyond accidents to other domains as well,

---

3. For discussions of hindsight bias, see chapter 6 and Mark Kelman et al., "Decomposing Hindsight Bias," 16 *J. Risk & Uncertainty,* 251 (1998). Also see Jeffrey J. Rachlinski, "A Positive Psychological Theory of Judging in Hindsight," 65 *U. Chi. L. Rev.* 571 (1998); and Christine Jolls et al., "A Behavioral Approach to Law and Economics," 50 *Stan. L. Rev.* 1471 (1998).

4. See his comments in *Carroll v. Otis Elevator,* 896 F.2d (1990).

as is reflected, for example, in the second-guessing of managerial decisions in major sports contests. This section will consider the railroad accident case from chapter 6 in which the respondents must also make the appropriate risk or liability decision as well as assess the risk. The jury-eligible citizens treated the prospective accident decision much differently than the retrospective decision.

A. *The Railroad Accident Case:* Ex Ante *and* Ex Post *Scenarios*

Judges considered extensive case descriptions involving railroad accidents. In the foresight version, a railroad operator was said to be protesting a pending National Transportation Safety Board (NTSB) order to make improvements to a section of the track deemed by the NTSB to be hazardous. The repairs were expensive and would result in a severe economic impact on the community served by the railroad. In twenty years of operations, there had been no accidents on that section of the track. In the hindsight version, the judges were given exactly the same information except they were also told that an accident had occurred causing damages to nearby residents and businesses. The group of judges considering the case after the accident had occurred consequently viewed an *ex post* scenario, where the main decision was whether punitive damages should be awarded. These scenarios are discussed more fully in chapter 6.

This experiment represents a test of hindsight effects. Will judges choose to penalize safety decisions that turn out badly after the fact, even though they would have made the same decision before? Thus, the first experimental manipulation is within judges comparing the results for different experimental treatments. The second experimental test is to compare results for each experimental manipulation between judges and jurors.

B. *Railroad Case Results*

The judges who considered the risk scenario *ex ante* largely supported relief of the NTSB order, as 85.1% did not favor requiring the safety improvements. For the judges considering the *ex post* scenario, 76.6% were sympathetic with the railroad and only 23.4% agreed with punitive damages. The differences in terms of the percentage of judges who were sympathetic to the railroad were not statistically significant ($t = 0.84$).

This behavior contrasts substantially with that observed using the same survey instruments with mock juries reported in chapter 6. For citizen and juror respondents, 33% took an antirailroad position in the foresight case, as compared to 15% for the judges. However, whereas in the hindsight case 67% of the citizens/jurors took an antirailroad position, only 25% of the judges did so. Judges' attitudes change very little across the foresight and hindsight cases, whereas there was a stark increase in citizens/jurors' antirailroad sentiment in the hindsight case.

There is more evidence of hindsight bias in the judges' risk assessments than in their safety and judicial decisions. When asked to assess the risk of a serious accident happening before the line is closed, judges with the *ex ante* scenario assess the risk probability as 0.20, whereas judges with the *ex post* scenario assess the risk as 0.36. The *ex post* risk assessment is consequently almost twice as great as the *ex ante* risk value, where this difference is statistically significant at the 1% level ($t = 3.16$). Judges also considered the risk on a linear grave-danger scale, scaling the risk from zero to nine. Such metrics are not as meaningful as a probability scale and do not have the same quantitative significance, but it is useful to report these results both to show the robustness of the findings and to facilitate comparisons with the literature. Judges with the *ex ante* scenario rated the risk as 2.45, while judges with the *ex post* scenario rated the risk as 4.28. These differences are also significant at the 1% level ($t = 3.76$). Judges' risk assessments seem to be more affected by hindsight bias than are their safety decisions.

Judges also differ less than jurors in how hindsight affects their risk beliefs. Judges' assessed probability of a serious accident roughly doubles from 0.20 to 0.36, as do the risk assessments of mock jurors—from 0.34 to 0.59. Although the absolute increase in probabilities is less for judges than for the jurors—0.16 versus 0.25—the overall character of these results is that judges' risk beliefs are more in line with those of mock jurors than are their overall railroad liability judgments. This pattern suggests that it is how judges interpret legal rules rather than their risk beliefs that primarily accounts for the lesser effect of hindsight bias on their decisions.

A useful test for the reasonableness of the judges' responses is whether they are significantly related to benefit-cost principles, or a negligence test. For the *ex post* scenario, the survey indicated the cost of the damage as well as the repair cost. Coupling this information with the judges' own reported assessed probability of an accident makes it possible to determine whether the cost of the repairs exceed the expected benefit, as indicated by the expected accident costs. For the foresight case, the survey did not indicate the dollar cost of an accident. As a result, I will use the hindsight survey cost value in making the benefit-cost calculations for all scenarios, recognizing that different respondent assessments of the likely costs will affect their benefit-cost calculations in the foresight case.

Table 11.1 divides the entire sample and each of the two survey scenario groups into different benefit-cost ratio quartiles. The *ex post* scenario in which respondents knew the costs is the most informative. Somewhat strikingly, none of the respondents with a benefit-cost ratio below

Table 11.1. Correlation of Implicit Net Benefits and Benefit-Cost Ratios (B/C) with Probability of Ruling against Railroad

B/C Percentile Range	Net Benefit	B/C	Probability of Ruling against Railroad
Ex Post Scenario Only (47 observations)			
00–24	−1.1–0.1	0.52–1.04	0.00
25–50	0.1–6.1	1.04–3.65	0.00
51–74	6.1–9.7	3.65–5.22	0.50
75–100	9.7–18.1	5.22–8.87	0.53
Ex Ante Scenario Only (47 observations)			
00–24	−2.3–0.1	0.00–1.04	0.10
25–50	0.1–0.1	1.04–1.04	0.13
51–74	0.1–2.5	1.04–2.09	0.30
75–100	2.5–20.5	2.09–9.91	0.09
Entire Sample (94 observations)			
00–24	−2.3–0.1	0.00–1.04	0.07
25–50	0.1–2.5	1.04–2.09	0.12
51–74	2.5–7.9	2.09–4.43	0.13
75–100	7.9–20.5	4.43–9.92	0.44

6.1 favored punitive damages. Only when the benefit-cost was 6.1 or greater did respondents become evenly divided between favoring and opposing punitive damages. Negligence alone does not lead judges to favor punitive damages in this instance, but rather there must be a quite substantial departure from benefit-cost norms. For the sample of citizens and mock jurors in chapter 6, no comparable relationship was evident, as their trigger for awarding punitive damages was not correlated with benefit-cost judgments.

The results for the *ex ante* scenario are more mixed, no doubt because these benefit-cost calculations assume a cost figure that may differ from what the respondent assessed. The overall results for the full sample do, however, reflect a rise in antirailroad sentiment with the benefit-cost range, a result due to the strong relationship found in the *ex post* scenario.

Table 11.2 breaks the responses into groups of individuals who are either for or against the railroad. For the *ex post* scenario, the calculated

Table 11.2. Correlation of Railroad Verdict with Implicit Net Benefits and Benefit-Cost Ratios (B/C)

Ex Post Scenario		
Ruling	Mean Net Benefit	Mean B/C Ratio
For Railroad	4.17	2.81
Against Railroad	12.97	6.64

Note: *t*-statistic (for vs. against railroad): 6.39, significant at 99% confidence level for B/C comparison.

Ex Ante Scenario		
Ruling	Mean Net Benefit	Mean B/C Ratio
For Railroad	2.65	2.15
Against Railroad	1.99	1.86

Note: *t*-statistic (for vs. against railroad): 0.40 for B/C comparison.

Entire Sample		
Ruling	Mean Net Benefit	Mean B/C Ratio
For Railroad	3.37	2.46
Against Railroad	8.70	4.78

Note: *t*-statistic (for vs. against railroad): 3.20, significant at 99% confidence level for B/C comparison.

benefit-cost ratio for the antirailroad group is double that of the pro-railroad group, a difference that is statistically significant. However, for the *ex ante* scenario in which respondents lacked the cost data to do a benefit-cost test, the estimated benefit-cost results do not differ significantly across the two groups. In this instance the test reflects whether the perceived accident probabilities affect the railroad attitude, but the results do not control for perceived costs. The strong *ex post* scenario results suggest that when the pertinent economic factors are available, judges do think in an efficiency-oriented manner when making punitive damages judgments.

Judges more than jurors are likely to be consistent in their liability judgments both before and after an accident. Judges consequently are less susceptible to hindsight bias. Moreover, to the extent that judges awarded punitive damages in the retrospective scenario, these judgments were strongly grounded in a divergence between the benefits and costs of railroad repair—an economic test that surely should be at the heart of any recklessness judgment. The overall performance of judges for the railroad case was consequently quite strong, both in absolute and relative terms.

III. Experiment 2: Risk-Cost Trade-offs
A. *The Airline Crash Risk Experiment*

The standard economic prescription for determining an efficient level of safety is whether the benefits of the safety improvement exceed the cost. For continuous changes in safety, the question is whether safety levels have been increased until the marginal benefits just equal the marginal costs. These same kinds of principles form the foundation for law and economics interpretation of negligence rules and ideally should be incorporated in punitive damages judgments as well.[5]

Judges considered one of three survey questions designed to test the degree to which they would apply the principles embodied in this standard negligence test. These cases involved the airline accident scenarios in chapter 10.[6] The cost of the safety improvement in every instance was $2,000. In addition, the expected benefits of the safety improvement, which equal the reduction in the risk probability multiplied by the size

5. For an exposition of these negligence rules in law and economics, see Richard Posner, *Economic Analysis of Law* (3rd ed., 1986); and A. Mitchell Polinsky, *An Introduction to Law and Economics* (2nd ed., 1989); among others.

6. An additional scenario was added for the jury-eligible citizens in chapter 10.

of the loss, equaled $1,500 in every instance. Thus, using a benefit-cost test or applying the negligence rule as cast in law and economics terms would suggest that the safety measure is not efficient and that the firm should not be held liable for the repair.

The three experimental manipulations varied the probability of the accident and the size of the loss but held constant the expected value of the loss that would be prevented by undertaking the $2,000 repair. In the first instance, judges considered a property damage loss of $15,000 coupled with a risk probability of $1/10$ that would be eliminated through the safety repair. The expected loss is consequently $1,500, which is less than the repair cost. The second variant increased the size of the property damage by a factor of 100 to $1.5 million, reducing the probability of loss by a factor of 100 to equal 1/1,000, leaving the expected loss unchanged at $1,500. The third variant increased the size of the loss to $1.5 billion, which included the value of personal injury losses, and accompanied it with a probability of the loss of 1/1,000,000. Thus, this change scaled losses up by a factor of 1,000 and scaled the probability down by a factor of 1,000, leaving the expected loss unchanged. For the personal injury question, the lives lost were valued at $5 million/life and respondents were told that this amount would reflect the full social value of the loss. In every instance the survey indicated that the company had sufficient resources to pay the damages.[7]

An example of one of these questions (the intermediate case) is the following:

> You are CEO of Rocky Mountain Airline. The cargo door on the plane does not operate properly. Fixing it costs $2,000. If it is not fixed, there is absolutely no safety risk. Very reliable engineering estimates indicate that there is only a 1/1,000 chance over the expected life of the plane that there will be a total loss to your company of $1.5 million due to property damage caused by this problem. Thus, there is a 999/1,000 chance that there will be no damage whatsoever. Your company has no insurance but does have sufficient resources to pay these damages.[8]

7. This statement will reduce but perhaps not eliminate the possible influence of risk aversion in affecting some of the responses. Since the loss-size variation primarily affects the company and not the parties injured, negligence rules should be applied in a risk-neutral fashion. Moreover, the $5 million value-of-life figure fully reflects the social loss, and no risk-aversion bonus is warranted from an economic standpoint.

8. It should also be noted that the losses associated with this risk occur over the life of the plane so that including the role of discounting would reduce the discounted expected value of the loss to an amount below $1,500.

Respondents were then asked to circle whether or not the firm should undertake the repair and, second, if the repair is not undertaken and there was $1.5 million in property damages, to indicate whether punitive damages should be awarded.

How one views the scenario depends in part on the test being applied. The CEO of the company should presumably be concerned with profit maximization. The safety measures described involved financial effects that would all be internalized by the firm. Because the safety improvements fail a benefit-cost test, they would not enhance firm profitability. Judges responding as CEOs might, however, impute a loss in the value of the company's reputation in the event of an accident involving personal injury, making them more likely to advocate safety improvements in this instance.

Application of legal rules should not be affected by broadly based reputational effects. If a safety measure does not pass a benefit-cost test, the company should not be found negligent for failing to adopt it. Punitive damages pertain to situations of reckless behavior. To be reckless, not only must the foregone safety measure pass a benefit-cost test, but presumably there should be a wide spread between benefits and costs, a repeated failure by the company to adopt safe practices, or other considerations that make the company truly reckless and not simply negligent. In none of the three scenarios is there any basis for awarding punitive damages. Indeed, by construction the company will never be negligent for failing to adopt the safety improvement.

B. Airline Case Results

Table 11.3 summarizes the responses to the two questions for each of the risk scenarios. In the case of the low property damage amount, 68% of the judges would not undertake the repair, which is consistent with economic efficiency principles. Almost one-third of the sample would undertake the repair even though the cost of the repair was below the expected benefits.

The attitude toward punitive damages in this low-loss case shown in panel A of table 11.3 differs moderately depending on whether repairing the plane to prevent a $15,000 loss is attractive. In each case a minority of the judges believed that punitive damages would apply if the repair was not undertaken and a loss occurred, where the fraction favoring punitive damages is greater for those who chose to repair the plane. What is perhaps most striking is that three of the judges who did not believe

Table 11.3. Relation of Judges' Opinions on Repairing Airplane Defect
to Whether Punitive Damages Should Apply if an Accident Occurs

Panel A: Property Damage Low—$15,000; Risk Probability 1/10			
	Repair Plane	Don't Repair Plane	Total
Punitives apply	5 (11.4%)	3 (6.8%)	8 (18.2%)
Punitives don't apply	9 (20.4%)	27 (61.4%)	36 (81.8%)
Total	14 (31.8%)	30 (68.2%)	44 (100%)

Panel B: Property Damage High—$1.5 Million; Risk Probability 1/1,000			
	Repair Plane	Don't Repair Plane	Total
Punitives apply	7 (24.2%)	1 (3.4%)	8 (27.6%)
Punitives don't apply	7 (24.2%)	14 (48.2%)	21 (72.4%)
Total	14 (48.4%)	15 (51.6%)	29 (100%)

Panel C: Personal Injury—290 Deaths for $1.5 Billion; Risk Probability 1/1,000,000			
	Repair Plane	Don't Repair Plane	Total
Punitives apply	11 (68.8%)	0 (0%)	11 (68.8%)
Punitives don't apply	5 (31.2%)	0 (0%)	5 (31.2%)
Total	16 (100%)	0 (0%)	16 (100%)

Panel D: Overall Results			
	Repair Plane	Don't Repair Plane	Total
Punitives apply	23 (25.8%)	4 (4.5%)	27 (30.3%)
Punitives don't apply	21 (23.6%)	41 (46.1%)	62 (69.7%)
Total	44 (49.4%)	45 (50.6%)	89 (100%)

Note: t-statistics for comparisons of scenario responses:
Decision to repair airplane: Decision to award punitive damages:
Scenario A vs. Scenario B: 1.427   Scenario A vs. Scenario B: 0.943
Scenario B vs. Scenario C: 4.034*   Scenario B vs. Scenario C: 2.854*
Scenario A vs. Scenario C: 5.760*   Scenario A vs. Scenario C: 4.178*
*Significant at 99% confidence level, two-tailed test.

that the plane should be repaired nevertheless would have awarded punitive damages had the plane not been repaired and a loss was suffered. For the entire group, 18% of the judges would award punitive damages, which is not in line with economic efficiency principles since not only are punitive damages not warranted, but based on a negligence test, the repairs should not even be undertaken.

Panel B of table 11.3 indicates how the responses change if the stakes are increased by a factor of 100 and the probability of damages is reduced by a factor of 100. Judges in this instance are almost evenly divided as to whether the plane should be repaired. Respondents who did not indicate that repairing the plane was worthwhile almost unanimously opposed punitive damages, whereas for the respondents who favored repairing the plane, there was an equal division between those who supported punitive damages and those who did not.

The final variation in panel C increases the loss to $1.5 billion, which includes the value of personal injuries, where the survey indicated that this damages amount is intended to reflect the full social cost of the accident. As before, the expected loss is $1,500, but the responses differ quite starkly from those in the previous scenarios. Respondents are now unanimous that the plane should be repaired. Moreover, over two-thirds of the respondents supported punitive damages in this instance. What appears to be most consequential is that in situations involving personal injury, there is a much greater willingness to undertake repairs and impose punitive damages than in situations involving property damage, even though the expected economic losses are the same in each instance. The results in panel C for both the award of punitive damages and repairing the plane differ to a statistically significant degree from the results in panels A and B.

Notwithstanding the weakness in some judges' responses, the performance of judges was more balanced than that of the jury-eligible citizens in chapter 10. The percentages of the mock-juror sample favoring repairs are 87% to 88% in the two property damage scenarios and 93% to 96% in the two fatality scenarios.

When the jurors were asked whether to assess punitive damages after the accident, the percentage of respondents awarding punitive damages was 74% to 78% for the two property damage scenarios and 95% to 96% for the two personal injury scenarios for which total damages are greater. These results are much different than those of judges. Whereas 88% of the jurors favored airplane repair for the panel A case, only 32% of the judges did. Similarly, 74% of the jurors favored punitive damages in that case, as compared to only 18% of the judges. The 74%–18% disparity between jurors and judges in the decision to award punitive damages provides striking evidence that judges exercise more restraint in the awarding of punitive damages. This result is consistent with the frequent overturning or reduction of punitive damages by judges, especially upon appeal. In this low-stakes case, most judges acted in accordance with economic efficiency norms in making their decision and in choosing whether to punish a company whose decision turned out badly, whereas most of the jury-eligible sample failed to do so.

As the size of the loss increases to $1.5 million in panel B of table 11.1, the differences narrow but are still considerable. The repair percentages are 87% for the jurors and 48% for the judges, while the punitive damages percentages are 78% for the jurors and 28% for the judges.

In the situation of personal injury, all the judges would repair the plane, which is comparable to the 96% figure for jurors.[9] Whereas 69% of the judges would award punitive damages, 96% of the jurors would do so. Extreme losses involving personal injury narrow the gap between judges and jurors, but jurors remain much more willing to levy punitive damages.

In terms of the overall responses to the scenarios, judges were evenly divided between repairing and not repairing the plane, even though strict application of economic negligence rules would indicate that not repairing the plane was desirable. Moreover, even though the firm was not negligent in these examples, many judges believe that punitive damages were applicable, particularly when nonmonetary losses are high. Awarding punitive damages when a firm meets a negligence standard is certainly inappropriate, as it indicates a failure to reflect on the underlying benefit-cost trade-offs, particularly when there are large nonmonetary stakes.

IV. Experiment 3: Setting Damages When Losses Are Uncertain

Risks could be ambiguous in terms of the probability or the level of damages. In some cases firms are unlucky in that the damages amount that occurs is much less than the loss that one might have suspected on average, whereas in other instances the firm may have been fortunate in incurring damages amounts less than might be expected on average. Will respondents be guided by what actually occurred, what might have occurred, or some combination of the two? From the standpoint of appropriate incentives, one should set the damages amount based on the actual loss, not on what might have been. Failing to do so is a common error in thinking about punitive damages.[10]

---

9. Judges did not consider the panel C scenario from chapter 10, table 10.1.

10. The importance of thinking about damages in terms of the actual loss rather than potential losses is articulated in A. Mitchell Polinsky and Steven Shavell, "Punitive Damages: An Economic Analysis," 111 *Harv. L. Rev.* 869 (1998).

A. *The Oil Well Blowout Case*

The scenarios were the same as were considered by the jury-eligible citizens in chapter 10. The scenario in which the company was fortunate given the damages lottery it created through its actions was the following:

> Acme Oil Company has been found negligent and liable for an oil well blowout that caused $10 million in property damage and no personal injury. The company in many respects was fortunate in that such blowouts have a 90% chance of $100 million in property damages and a 10% chance of minor damage of $10 million. What damages award amount would you select?

The counterpart scenario in which the company did not fare as well with respect to the damages lottery was the following:

> Acme Oil Company has been found negligent and liable for an oil well blowout that caused $10 million in property damage and no personal injury. The company in many respects was unfortunate in that such blowouts have a 90% chance of no damage and a 10% chance of $10 million in damages. What damages amount would you select?

B. *Oil Well Case Results*

All but five of the judges answered these questions in line with law and economics principles, focusing on the actual damages amount that occurred. Even though the judges were given six damages award categories from which to choose, 92% of them correctly selected $10 million as the damages amount for both cases. Judges' assessment of damages awards consequently does not seem to be affected by risk-ambiguity biases and is quite consistent with what one would do if implementing sound law and economics principles.

Unlike the responses of judges, the results for the jury-eligible citizens reflect an enormous variation in the assessed damages amount. Even though the actual damages were only $10 million, only 26% of the respondents assessed this damages value. In contrast, virtually the entire judges' sample selected $10 million in damages. Thirty-seven percent of the juror sample awarded $30 million in damages. Roughly one-fifth of the sample awarded damages under $10 million, with a similar percentage awarding damages over $30 million. The median award level of $30 million and the geometric mean award level of $21.4 million each greatly exceed the award amount selected by judges.

Whereas judges focused on the actual damages amount, jurors focused instead on worst-case scenarios. The damage that might have occurred, but that did not, drove jurors' thinking. The result is excessive damages and more than can be justified based on efficient deterrence.

V. Experiment 4: Mortality Risk Perceptions

A central ingredient of accident and risk-related cases is the risk component itself. How risk information is processed will color one's overall perception of an accident context. Such perceptional biases may be consequential for judges and their treatment of risk-related issues. Thus, these biases are of interest in their own right as well as in explaining how judges will assess legal issues involving risk, such as judgments of recklessness.

A. Risk Beliefs

Chapter 10 found that jurors exhibited one of the most well-established results in the literature on risk, which is that people systematically overestimate small mortality risks and systematically underestimate large mortality risks. How do judges fare when confronting the same risk-perception task? Assessing judges' performance is instructive because judges are the arbiters of how the legal system treats risk in a wide variety of contexts, including accidents, medical malpractice cases, and products liability cases, as well as cases involving dimly understood health risks, such as breast implants.

The experimental approach followed that presented in chapter 10, as each judge considered a list of the different causes of death for which the judges were asked to assess the total number of deaths. The judges were not given the list of deaths in order of importance and were not told the actual death rate. Rather, the judges received the following information:

> In 1990, 47,000 people died in automobile accidents. How many people died from the other causes of death listed below? Fill in your best estimate in the space.

Respondents then considered each of the causes of death listed in table 11.4, but in a random order.

The principal empirical issue is whether judges' risk beliefs are accurate, are inaccurate but in a random way, or reflect systematic biases. The final bias issue is of greatest concern since it may taint judicial rulings in a particular direction. Random errors are of least concern since one would not expect people to know the exact number of deaths from different

Table 11.4. Actual and Perceived Risks of Death
for Major Sources of Mortality

Cause of death	Actual deaths in 1993	Mean perceived deaths	Geometric mean of perceived deaths
Botulism	2	1,250.7	225.0
Fireworks accident	5	667.4	127.1
Measles	5	1,335.2	231.9
Lightning strikes	89	1,337.6	206.3
Pregnancy (birthing complications)	320	58,082.4	4,850.7
Appendicitis	500	3,080.3	589.4
Accidental electrocution	670	4,811.0	1,076.9
Hepatitis	677	8,574.8	1,789.9
Accidental firearm discharges	1,416	28,844.4	8,675.2
Accidental drowning	3,979	6,491.3	1,964.2
Fire and flames	4,175	11,973.9	3,634.7
Asthma	4,750	14,533.5	2,962.5
Accidental poisoning	5,200	13,535.3	1,909.6
Accidental falls	12,313	9,849.3	2,057.3
Stomach cancer	13,640	42,415.7	14,145.3
Homicide	24,614	48,093.4	21,634.1
Breast cancer	45,000	84,511.9	31,750.0
Diabetes	47,664	61,812.0	12,907.6
Stroke	144,088	132,480.6	44,538.7
Lung cancer	145,000	149,512.0	53,317.2
All forms of cancer	505,322	462,148.8	185,024.8
Heart disease	720,000	518,422.3	169,867.2
All causes	2,148,463	2,993,906.0	1,158,700.0

Note: The number of observations range from 79 to 84 for the different mortality risk groups.

causes. Table 11.4 also reports their associated risk values, where most of these causes of death overlap with categories considered in previous studies. The table lists these causes in order of their importance in terms of the number of deaths associated with the cause in 1993. The total number of deaths for the different causes ranged from two deaths from botulism to over 2 million deaths per year from all causes.[11]

11. The number of respondents to these questions ranged from 79 to 84 because of missing values for some of the survey answers. Respondents who did not answer typically skipped the entire page since it was much more time-consuming than the rest of the survey.

B. Mortality Risks Results

Table 11.4 reports the actual death-risk levels, the mean perceived deaths, and the geometric mean of perceived deaths (the measure most often used in previous studies). The responses by the judges reflect the widely observed pattern of overestimating small risks and underestimating larger risks. In particular, based on the geometric mean values in the final column of table 11.1, judges overestimated all risks in the lower-risk categories, from botulism to accidental firearm discharges. Thereafter, they underestimated all of the larger-risk groups from accidental drowning to all causes of death, with the exception being stomach cancer, which they overestimated by a very small amount. The main difference in the patterns displayed by the mean perceived deaths as opposed to the geometric means is that for the mean values there is a much wider range of death categories for which people overestimated the risk, ranging from botulism to diabetes and including lung cancer as well.

Figure 11.1 presents the estimates based on a regression analysis of the responses. As is indicated, the judges overassessed the small risks, such as botulism and fireworks accidents, and underestimated the larger risks of death, such as stroke and heart disease. It is noteworthy that the extent of the overestimation of the small risks is much greater than the extent of the underestimation for large risks. People tend to have much less information and a smaller sample size on which to base estimates for the very small risks that they face, making these judgments much more imprecise than the risk assessments for the more consequential hazards. Thus, this figure indicates that the nature of the size-related bias in risk beliefs is more than simply a situation of overestimating small risks and underestimating large risks. There is also evidence that the absolute value of the gap between risk beliefs and the true risk levels narrows as one moves to the very high-risk categories. For the truly significant risks, the judges did quite well in terms of the accuracy of the risk assessments.

Figure 11.1 sketches the level of risk beliefs for judges and for chapter 10's sample of jury-eligible citizens, which is the solid curve in the figure. It is noteworthy that the risk-perception curve for judges is closer to the 45-degree line along which perceived risks equal actual risks almost throughout the risk range. Judges have more accurate risk beliefs than do the jury-eligible citizens. The relative discrepancy is particularly great for the large risks, for which the judges have an error in their risk assessments that is approximately half as great as that of the jurors. These

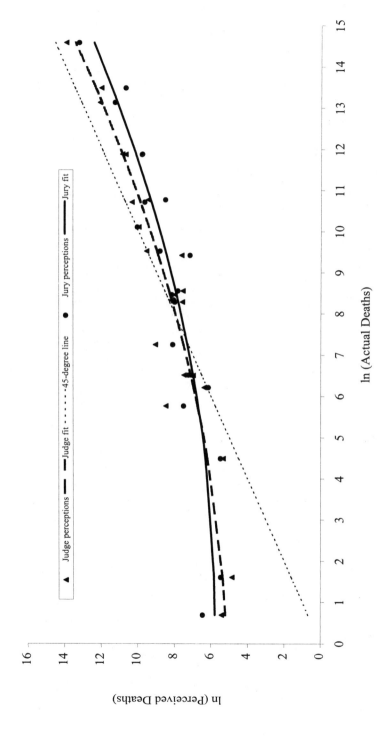

Fig. 11.1.

results suggest that judges are likely to have more accurate risk beliefs than jurors. To the extent that risk beliefs enter assessments of reckless-ness and risk-cost balancing, judges should make more balanced deci-sions, which is what the previous results showed.

VI. Experiment 5: The Value of Life
A. Risk-Cost Trade-offs

A critical variable that may affect judges' assessment of risk situa-tions is their own attitude toward risks to life and health. An extreme at-titude toward risk-cost trade-offs would be reflected in the zero-risk men-tality phenomenon examined in chapters 6 and 10. The most commonly used measure of the individual's implicit value of life is the person's risk-cost trade-off for mortality risks. This amount is not the level of com-pensation required to make one indifferent to certain death. No amount of money may suffice. Rather, it is the risk-cost trade-off rate that is per-tinent when facing small risks of death, or the value of a statistical life. In the usual context in which one is purchasing a product that must be made safer or instituting a government regulation to foster safety, the measure I advocate is society's willingness to pay for the reduction in risk. This value provides the basis for determining what the reference point should be in terms of the level of society's investment in greater safety. This value-of-life measure is now used throughout the U.S. federal govern-ment to value risks to life and health. Although the usual reference point for assessing the implicit value of life is the wage-risk trade-off reflected in workers' job choices, a number of other studies have also examined the trade-off reflected in stated-willingness-to-pay questions.[12] The focus of this section of the survey was to ascertain the personal value of life es-timates for the judges, which in turn will serve as a measure of their will-ingness to bear risk.

In particular, the survey posed the following question framed in terms of the judges' willingness to pay for a reduction in mortality risk:

> Suppose that participating in this course poses a one-time-only risk of death of 1/10,000. Thus, if there were 10,000 judges in this course, there would be one expected death in your group. This risk is the average annual mortality risk faced on the job by the typical U.S. blue-collar

12. For review of this literature, see W. Kip Viscusi, "The Value of Risks to Life and Health," 31 *J. Econ. Literature* 1912 (1993).

worker. Which dollar range best reflects the amount you are willing to pay to eliminate this risk you have taken?

Judges then considered six dollar ranges from zero to $50 to a high range of above $1,000, where the survey also included a final category of "infinite-all present and future resources." Calculating the implicit value of life from these responses is straightforward and indicates what is actually meant by the value-of-life terminology. Suppose, for example, that a judge responded that an amount between $200 and $500 would be appropriate for reducing the mortality risk by 1/10,000. Let us take the midpoint of this range, or $350, as the pertinent value for the respondent. Suppose that there were 10,000 judges with similar responses. Then overall there would be one expected death in this group. It would be possible to raise 10,000 × $350, or $3.5 million, in order to prevent this one statistical death. This amount is the value of life, which is simply the amount people are willing to pay per statistical death averted. Similarly, one can view the value of life in terms of the willingness to pay per unit risk, which is simply $350 divided by 1/10,000, which equals $3.5 million.

B. Value-of-Life Results

Table 11.5 indicates the distribution of the value-of-life estimates for the judges in the sample obtained based on these calculations. The mean value of life for the respondents, excluding the three judges who indicated an infinite value, was $3.6 million. The median response was substantially less.

Overall, these responses seem to be somewhat low, but by no means outside of the range of estimated value-of-life statistics in the literature. Most estimates based on labor market data indicate an implicit value of life on the order of $3 million to $7 million for workers in average-risk jobs and an implicit value of life in the vicinity of $1 million for workers in higher-risk jobs. Thus, the general order of magnitude of the responses seems appropriate. A reason why it is likely that these judges' responses may tend to be a bit low is that hypothetical survey risks will not be as compelling as an actual risk of death. To the extent that the respondents discounted the probability of death and treated it as smaller than is stated in the survey, which is certainly appropriate given their relatively safe lifestyles, then one would tend to get lower willingness-to-pay answers and consequently lower estimates of the implicit value of life based on survey responses.

Table 11.5. Distribution of Implicit Valuations
of Life Elicited from State Judges

Value of life range	Number responding
0–$500,000	42
$500,000–$2,000,000	16
$2,000,000–$5,000,000	12
$5,000,000–$10,000,000	4
Over $10,000,000	14
Infinite	3
Mean	3,551,136
(Standard error of mean)	($564,527)
Median	1,250,000

Note: Values were coded as the midpoint of each range,
using $15 million for the over-$10 million category when calculating the mean. Responses indicating infinite value of life
were omitted from the calculation of the mean and standard
error of the mean. The total sample size was 91 for this survey
question.

The results as they relate to the zero-risk mentality are of particular
interest. Only 3% of the judges indicated an unlimited willingness to pay
for greater safety.[13] What is disturbing is that almost 10% of the juror
sample—or forty-seven respondents—indicated that they had an infinite
value-of-life amount. Such responses indicate a failure to be willing to
make such complex risk trade-offs.

Jurors more than judges fall prey to the zero-risk mentality and are
willing to pay any price to achieve safety. Such unbounded commitments
to safety are not feasible, given the multiplicity of hazards that we face
and the limited resources we have to address them.

VII. Conclusion

Judges are human and may reflect the same kinds of irrationalities
as other individuals. Judges did exhibit the well-established pattern of
overestimating small risks and underestimating large risks, but their risk
assessments for substantial risks were not substantially in error. Moreover, they were less biased than were the beliefs of jurors. Judges' expressed risk-cost trade-offs as reflected in their implicit values of life

13. In addition, 4% of the judges did not respond to the question.

were in line with that of other population groups in terms of the general order of magnitude of the valuation. Moreover, unlike jury-eligible citizens, judges were less likely to fall prey to the zero-risk mentality of stating a belief in an infinite trade-off.

This chapter also examined whether these types of biases affected attitudes in judicial contexts. Jurors' decisions were fraught with error and were predisposed toward excessive awarding of punitive damages. However, judges were much more likely to make decisions based on risk-cost balancing and to make decisions much more in line with standard law and economics prescriptions.

Judges are much less prone to hindsight bias than are jurors in their treatment of corporate safety decisions. Indeed, in making legal judgments, there was little effect of hindsight for judges, as compared to substantial effects for mock jurors. An interesting aspect of the results is that whereas the safety decisions of the judges were not affected by the hindsight bias, there was consistent evidence that the risk assessments were sensitive to whether the judgment was being made *ex ante* or *ex post*. Unlike jurors, judges seem to be better able to put aside potential biases in risk assessments that arise with hindsight and still make sound decisions.

The superior performance of judges is not unexpected. Judges are better educated on average, have more experience in assessing accident situations, and have greater knowledge of legal rules. While these findings alone do not warrant a transfer of greater authority over punitive damages from jurors to judges, in conjunction with the results in other chapters, they do provide a basis for believing that many of the problems we have identified would be ameliorated by such reforms.

Part II

Conclusions

12

Putting It All Together

Reid Hastie

In the previous ten chapters, we have reported the results from twenty empirical studies of jurors and juries making punitive damages decisions. These experimental tests were conducted on thousands of jury-eligible citizens, on hundreds of mock juries, and on a few hundred experienced trial judges asked to render punitive damages verdicts under legally realistic task conditions. These tests provide a detailed picture of the behavior of jurors, juries, and judges making punitive damages decisions. We now review the major empirical findings and extract some essential principles and themes.

The experimental methods employed by these studies have shed new light on the decision processes of jurors and juries. This detailed account has enabled us to identify orderly elements of jury decision making and to distinguish them from those elements that are erratic and unpredictable. Our findings can be separated into three conceptual categories derived from the judgmental functions of the jury. First, there are the reliable and coherent aspects of the judgment process. For example, the lay jury performs the task of assessing the *relative* moral offensiveness of the defendant's conduct reliably. Second, there are systematic biases, some due to fundamental properties of the human mind, others due to culturally based, learned habits. For example, we believe the hindsight effect that makes past events seem more inevitable, and foreseeable, is a universal habit of the healthy, adult human mind. Third, there are aspects of human behavior that seem to be erratic and unpredictable in terms of commonsense intuitions and behavioral science principles. For example, the great variability in dollar awards, for identical descriptions of a defendant's conduct, appears to derive from idiosyncratic and largely unknown differences in jurors' and juries' backgrounds and reactions to the evidence and instructions.

The present empirical findings depict the juror as a decision maker whose good intentions, natural abilities, and adaptive strategies are overwhelmed by the demands of the punitive damages decision task. Consequently, juror decisions are systematic and predictable when judging the relative moral reprehensibility of a defendant's conduct, but decisions concerning the absolute distinction between liable and not liable and assessments of dollar awards are unreliable and unpredictable.

The following summary of major empirical findings is divided into three substantive categories: setting dollar awards, judging recklessness and liability, and reasoning about risk and uncertainty, corresponding to the major subsections in part 1 of this volume. We conclude our review with a summary of what we discovered about the performance of judges making similar decisions.

I. Setting Dollar Awards

The present empirical studies of all stages of the punitive damages decision show that the major locus of unreliability and disorder in punitive damages decisions is in jurors' assessments of an appropriate dollar award (see chapters 2, 3, and 4). Although jurors cannot render the prior decisions concerning liability with perfect reliability (remember that cases that ultimately go to trial have been selected by the pretrial negotiation process to be among the most difficult to decide), the dollar-award-setting process seems to be distinctively unpredictable. One of the virtues of experimental tests is that the method affords the assessment of direct measures of the variability of respondents' reactions to exactly the same case. In our studies we focused on the interjuror consensus on moral reprehensibility and intent-to-punish judgments, then on dollar awards. At the beginning of the jurors' decision process, moral reprehensibility judgments seem orderly and reliable. But later in the process, dollar awards for identical cases are variable and unpredictable, even when comparing jurors whose initial sense of outrage and intent to punish were similar. How can we understand the unreliability of the dollar-award assessment process?

Jurors are instructed that the purposes of a punitive damages award are to punish and deter the defendant's misconduct. They are told the amount of punitive damages necessary to *punish* a defendant is the penalty that effectively expresses disapproval of conduct that society condemns. The amount of punitive damages that is necessary to *deter* a defendant (and others) is the amount of money that will induce a defendant (and others) not to repeat the wrongful conduct. Jurors are told nothing about typical awards in comparable cases, and they are given no help on the complex question of how to infer the punitive impact or deterrent efficacy of a dollar sanction. Compounding the problem created by lack of guidance, popular media reports of civil awards provide an inaccurate picture of the relevant statistics.[1] Compared to the analogous instructions and evidence presented on the issue of compensatory damages or in criminal sentencing, including capital punishment, the punitive damages judgment is vastly underconstrained by instructions or by relevant experience. (Of course, criminal sentencing is usually conducted by an experienced judge and often further constrained by the use of sentencing schedules and guidelines, designed to solve exactly the problems of variability, capriciousness, and unpredictability.) This difficulty is revealed in dollar-award variability of several orders of magnitude across jurors for identical punitive damages cases. Perhaps the most surprising result is that jury deliberation does not serve to damp the variability, but rather to amplify it.

A. Award-Setting Strategies

In the study reported in chapter 2, we describe the award-setting process as a translation from one metric, an intent-to-punish scale, to another, a dollar-award scale. The data shows that there is considerable comparative agreement among individual jurors across cases on the intent-to-punish scale. The ordering of cases by rated outrage and intent to punish is highly consistent when different jurors rated a common set of cases, implying that there is fundamental agreement on what constitutes bad and worse conduct. These judgments are consistent with everyday conceptions of bad conduct: malicious, deliberately injurious actions are judged to be the most reprehensible, followed by deliberate, callously reckless actions, and then careless or negligent actions.

Support for the claim that dollar awards are erratic has accumulated in research based on analyses of archival award statistics demonstrating

1. Daniel S. Bailis and Robert J. MacCoun, "Estimating Liability Risks with the Media as Your Guide: A Content Analysis of Media Coverage of Tort Litigation," 20 *Law & Hum. Behav.* 419 (1996); Stephen Daniels and Joanne Martin, "Myth and Reality in Punitive Damages," 75 *Minn. L. R.* 1 (1990); Marc Galanter, "Real World Torts: An Antidote to Anecdote," 55 *Md. L. Rev.* 1093 (1996); Steven Garber and Anthony G. Bower, "Newspaper Coverage of Automotive Product Liability Verdicts," 33 *Law & Hum. Behav.* 93 (1999).

the unpredictability of jury punitive damages awards in actual court-rooms. Our reading of this controversial literature is that jury verdicts are highly variable for similar cases, especially across jurisdictions.[2] Of course, these studies can support only tentative conclusions, because no two legal cases are identical. (Although it is tempting to cite some "natural experiments," such as the discrepant verdicts in two Alabama cases involving refurbished BMW automobiles; see discussion in the introduction to this volume.) Thus, the experimental studies described in chapters 2 and 3 are especially informative, because they provide demonstrations of this variability under controlled conditions, where different mock jurors were presented with exactly the same cases. In several experiments on award setting, huge amounts of variability in dollar awards were observed across jurors judging identical cases presented under identical conditions. For example, consider the case receiving the median juror and jury award from the set of fifteen studied (*Hughes v. Jardel,* in which a shopping mall employee sued the mall owners for damages after she was assaulted on the premises) (see table 3.2). The jurors' median dollar award was $500,000 and the 10th percentile of all the awards was $30,000 compared to the 90th percentile of $3.25 million. Thus, the difference between the 10th percentile award and the 90th percentile award is more than $3 million. The research reported in chapter 4, from an independent study, demonstrates a dollar-award range of from $0 to $4.5 billion for the same case—again, presented under fixed conditions, with realistic jury instructions. Apparently, even the *identically* situated, much less the merely similarly situated, cannot expect to be treated similarly under the punitive damages regime.

This massive variability is the rule and not an exception. This variability, also observed in actual cases, means that there is great uncertainty about what punitive consequences will follow in many important risk-management situations. Of course, as uncertainty about the outcomes of a dispute-resolution institution increases, so do the rates at which cases go to trial, resulting in expensive settlements to avoid uncertain trials, which can stifle innovation and produce other economic inefficiencies.[3]

2. Cf., Theodore Eisenberg et al., "The Predictability of Punitive Damages," 26 *J. Legal Stud.* 623 (1997); and A. Mitchell Polinsky, "Are Punitive Damages Really Insignificant, Predictable, and Rational? (Response to Theodore Eisenberg et al., same issue at 623)," 26 *J. Legal Stud.* 663 (1997).

3. Cf., George L. Priest and Benjamin Klein, "The Selection of Disputes for Litigation," 13 *J. Legal Stud.* 1 (1984); Samuel R. Gross and Kent D. Syverud, "Getting to No: A Study of Settlement Negotiations and the Selection of Cases for Trial," 90 *Mich. L. Rev.* 319 (1991); and

B. Damping versus Amplifying the Variability in Dollar Awards

A common assumption is that jury deliberation will exert a moderating influence on individual juror assessments and reduce variability in the distribution of dollar awards. However, the principal finding of the present tests of jury influence on punitive damages awards was that deliberation *increased both the size and the variability* of awards (chapter 3). For example, in the case *(Hughes)* that received the median award levels in this study, the median dollar *jury* award was $1 million and the 10th percentile of all dollar awards was $200,000, compared to the 90th percentile of $20 million. Thus, for juries, the range between the 90th percentile and the 10th percentile was almost $20 million. The same range calculated on *individual juror* awards for this case was about $3 million. Again, this enormous variability is typical in jury as well as juror awards; and the variability was consistently larger for juries than for their individual members across all judged cases.

Furthermore, an inflation of dollar awards was the result; using the median (middle) juror award as a standard, low- and high-median juries concluded with larger awards. For every one of the fifteen cases studied, deliberating juries produced higher dollar awards than predicted from their members' individual predeliberation awards. This *severity shift* is reflected in many statistics: 83% of the nonzero-award jury results were higher than the median of their members' awards; 27% of the jury (group) awards were at the top of or outside the range of their member juror (individual) awards; and the average jury award was ranked 5.1 on a 1 to 7 scale defined by the highest and lowest member award ranks (4.0 is the middle rank on a seven-point scale; the jury is inserted into the rank ordering of its six members). This result is not an anomaly; similar results are reported in dollar compensatory damages awards by Diamond and Casper.[4]

With reference to group effects on the dollar awards, a simple center-of-gravity or averaging rule does not apply, as there was a consistent tendency for juries to shift to higher dollar awards and for awards to become

---

Robert D. Cooter and Daniel L. Rubinfeld, "Economic Analysis of Legal Disputes and Their Resolution," 27 *J. Econ. Literature* 1067 (1989).

4. Shari S. Diamond and Jonathan D. Casper, "Blindfolding the Jury to Verdict Consequences: Damages, Experts, and the Civil Jury," 26 *Law & Soc'y Rev.* 513, 553 (1992), especially at 553 ff. concerning inflation effects of the deliberation process.

more variable across juries than across jurors. Observations of the social deliberation process suggest that it is easier for jurors to argue for a
higher dollar award in deliberation (after making a liable "punish" decision), than to argue for a lower award (chapter 3). Thus, the tendency for
juries to shift to more severe dollar awards may be partly explained by
the momentum created by discussion preceding the "punish" result of
the first stage of deliberation.

C. Anchor Effects on Dollar Awards

Our hypothesis is that an individual juror's reexpression of an intent
to punish in terms of a dollar-award scale is best described by an *anchor-
and-adjust strategy*. Such a strategy includes five cognitive substages:
(1) selection of a salient value as a starting-point *anchor;* (2) inference
from that anchor value to a numerical dollar award; (3) search for additional relevant information; (4) adjustment of the initial value in light
of the new information; and (5) a decision to stop adjusting and to conclude with the current value. Anchor-and-adjust judgments typically exhibit an underadjustment or "conservative bias" with reference to the
initial anchor value.[5] This means that the initial anchor exerts a large,
sometimes arbitrary influence on the final judgment (what has sometimes been called a "first impression" or "primacy effect" in other judgment situations[6]). This description applies to both the individual juror
assessment strategy and to the group jury consensus process.

In the context of a punitive damages judgment, the anchor-and-adjust
translation process is unreliable in at least two regards: First, since there
are no generally accepted theories of deterrence and punishment that
might provide normatively sound standards for dollar-award amounts,
there is little guidance and great variability in individual jurors' selections of initial anchor values. Second, with no numerical reference points,
scale-transformation rules, and an unbounded scale, the adjustment process is also variable both within and across individuals (in chapter 2 we
refer to this second condition as *scaling without a modulus,* following a
technical usage in traditional psychological research). So, the consensus

5. Amos Tversky and Daniel Kahneman, "Judgment under Uncertainty: Heuristics and
Biases," 185 *Science* 1124 (1974); Timothy D. Wilson et al., "A New Look at Anchoring Effects:
Basic Anchoring and Its Antecedents," 125 *J. Experimental Psychol.: Gen.* 387 (1996).
6. Michelle C. Anderson and Robert J. MacCoun, "Goal Conflict in Juror Assessments of
Compensatory and Punitive Damages," 23 *Law & Hum. Behav.* 313 (1999).

in judgments of outrage and intent to punish is shattered by the disorderly translation-into-dollars stage of the award-setting process.

The first step when a juror translates intent to punish into a dollar award involves choosing an anchor value. Unfortunately, this is a mysterious and erratic process.[7] Jurors in major cases have said that they rely on many surprising values. For example, in a recent $4.9 billion verdict against General Motors, jurors told reporters that they relied on the annual advertising budget of the corporation as the anchor value for their dollar award.[8] In the present studies, mock jurors' explanations of their dollar awards revealed a great diversity of anchor-value choices for a single fact situation: $1 million per plaintiff, $25,000 per "defendant's error," "one-half of the defendant corporation's annual profits," among numerous others. But there was no obvious rationale for most values and

7. In addition to the erratic, uncertain character of the anchor-value selection process, there is empirical evidence of some systematic problems with the award-setting process. For example, when jurors must set more than one award, they are instructed to decide on each award, one at a time, independently from one another. But although the instructions are clear about the functions of the punitive damages award, jurors may illegitimately use the punitive awards as a form of compensation. In the studies reported in chapter 4, approximately 25% of the respondents indicated they intended their punitive award to serve as additional compensation. Anderson and MacCoun also report that jurors are prone to conflate the two amounts (id.).

Additional evidence from the present research program, outside of the studies reported here, illustrates the fragile nature of the dollar-award assessment process. When jurors are asked to consider identical cases in isolation or in comparison with another case from a different category, their awards change. In a study conducted by Daniel Kahneman et al., "Predictably Incoherent Judgments: Comparing Cases from Different Categories" (2000) (unpublished manuscript, Department of Management, University of Texas, Austin), the damages awards assigned to a sample of personal injury cases averaged $1 million when the cases were judged in isolation. But the dollar awards for the same cases more than doubled (to an average award of $2.25 million) when they were judged after an award was assessed for an unrelated financial loss case. This contrast effect of context is especially remarkable when we consider the semantic and moral implications of the absolute-dollar response scale: We do not want our punitive sanctions for one defendant to be contingent on the momentary context of other wholly independent cases. This kind of context dependency of an "intendedly absolute" dollar scale violates principles of rational choice and, combined with the possibility of arbitrary context effects, is a violation of the goal of equitable legal procedures. Christopher K. Hsee et al., "Preference Reversals between Joint and Separate Evaluations of Options: A Review and Theoretical Analysis," 125 *Psychol. Bull.* 576 (1999); Mark Kelman et al., "Context-Dependence in Legal Decision Making," 25 *J. Legal Stud.* 287 (1996). Furthermore, when events at trial do not provide a deliberately controlled context, jurors' memories will still provide a context of remembered cases. Unfortunately, these memories are systematically biased by the selective media reportage of civil awards. Bailis and MacCoun, *supra* note 1, at 419; Garber and Bower, *supra* note 1, at 93.

8. Ann W. O'Neill et al., "G.M. Ordered to Pay $4.9 Billion in Crash Verdict Liability," *L.A. Times,* July 10, 1999, at A1.

no mention of the deterrence or punishment clauses from the judges' instructions on the law. When a justification was presented, it was usually stated as simply a desire to "send a message" to the defendant or to "hurt" the harmdoer (chapter 4). If there is a modal anchor-selection habit, it is to rely on some function of the compensatory damages value, though this mode represents the reasoning of no more than a quarter of the mock jurors. But, again, it is difficult to discern a systematic pattern in the "noisy" signals from the final dollar-award numbers.

Ironically, caps on damages awards may function to increase some award amounts because they also can serve as anchors: Hinsz and Indahl, Robbennolt and Studebaker, and Babcock and Pogarsky all found that awards increased in size and in variability when award caps were presented in the instructions to the jurors.[9] The studies reported in chapter 7 demonstrate that the value-of-a-statistical-life figure used in a defendant corporation's cost-benefit analysis was relied on by some jurors in wrongful death cases. Ironically, in such instances companies who spent more on safety received higher punitive awards.

The studies reported in chapter 4 also explore the impact of plaintiffs' attorneys' attempts to manipulate jurors' anchor values by suggesting numbers to the jury in their closing arguments. The judges' instruction that these attorneys' arguments are not evidence appeared to be ineffectual. Plaintiffs requested either a low award anchor ("So the range you may want to consider is between $15 million and about half a year's profit, $50 million"—ranges were used because this is a common rhetorical expression used by plaintiffs' attorneys) or a high award anchor ("So the range you may want to consider is between $50 million and about a year's profit, $150 million"). This one sentence, in a nonevidentiary portion of the trial, more than doubled the median awards in the high-anchor conditions. Similar effects were observed in the studies reported in chapter 9, in which a plaintiff's attorney's request and a newspaper article about a completely independent case overwhelmed explicit instructions on how to calculate a dollar award. In addition to demonstrating the power of salient judgment anchors, this phenomenon illustrates how

9. Verlin B. Hinsz and Kristin E. Indahl, "Assimilation to Anchors for Damage Awards in a Mock Civil Trial," 25 *J. Applied Soc. Psychol.* 991 (1995); Jennifer K. Robbennolt and Christina A. Studebaker, "Anchoring in the Courtroom: The Effects of Caps on Punitive Damages," 23 *Law & Hum. Behav.* 353 (1999); Linda Babcock and Greg Pogarsky, "Damage Caps and Settlement: A Behavioral Approach," 28 *J. Legal Stud.* 341 (1999).

small events at trial (e.g., a one-sentence, nonevidentiary remark) can contribute to variability in the labile award-setting process.

The research reported in chapter 4 also shows that jurors were consistently partial to local plaintiffs. *With identical evidence and financial conditions,* the median awards were $35 million higher for local plaintiffs (an increase of over 200%), compared to the awards for geographically and economically remote plaintiffs. (Across *all* experimental conditions, the increase was $4.2 million in one study and $25 million in the second study.) Here, jurors' self-reports on their award-setting strategies were not informative, but our interpretation would be that the sympathetic bias toward local plaintiffs probably exerts its influence on the anchor-selection stage of the judgment process. A similar manipulation of the defendant's status had a smaller but statistically nonsignificant effect on dollar awards. Contrary to the motive of economic self-interest for wealth redistribution, there was no effect of the defendant company's location.

D. Reasoning about Punishment, Deterrence, and Incapacitation

Jurors are told that their dollar awards should reflect the degree to which they want to punish and deter the defendant's conduct. But the concepts of proper punishment and effective deterrence are not clear-cut in everyday or even in legal settings. Millennia of analysis have produced little expert consensus on proper punishment and how to achieve it in criminal contexts, and especially in civil contexts. It is no wonder that despite their conscientious efforts, civil jurors are confused and often in disagreement with one another.

Evidence that jurors do not think coherently about deterrence is presented in chapter 5. Mock jurors were asked to recall and explain the relevance of the issues of punishment and deterrence as presented to them in their jury instructions. Recall of these instructions was disconcertingly low, usually at average rates below 10%. Among those few who did give a principled justification for a dollar award, the most common reason given was to "send a message to the corporate boardroom." Not a single juror, out of the hundreds queried, stated an interpretable relationship between their intent to punish and the specific dollar amount chosen. The only jurors who expressed a coherent theory of punishment and awards were those who indicated that they wanted to incapacitate the defendant. A small percentage of mock jurors explained their awards by noting that they wanted to "put the company out of business for good," and they usually chose award values related to the defendant company's net worth: "I picked $1,060,000,000 because that was the company's net worth in the financial statements we were given."

Most legal evaluations of appropriate penalties are dependent on historical precedents, presuming that an acceptable punishment is one that is consistent with common practice. A controversial but influential jurisprudential theory is based on principles of economic self-interest and the efficient allocation of societal resources.[10] Polinsky and Shavell summarize the implications of the current law and economics literature on punitive damages.[11] They conclude that the major justification for punitive damages, beyond compensatory damages, is based on deterrence, which, in turn, should depend solely on the probability that the defendant's wrongful conduct is detected and punished. The principle is that effective deterrence must ensure full payment of all costs, including compensation for the harm caused. Thus, as probability of detection decreases, the amount paid by those held liable must increase to compensate for those who did not have to pay. For example, if the wrongful action is detected and punished only one time out of ten, the one who is caught must pay ten times the cost of the harm, that is, ten times the compensatory damages.[12]

The study described in chapter 8 investigates people's reactions to justifications for dollar awards on the basis of the theory of efficient deterrence. Twentyfold changes in the probability that the (unquestionably) wrongful act would be detected (from 1 chance in 100 to 1 chance in 5) had no effects on mock jurors' dollar awards. Contrary to the logic of optimal deterrence, they apparently felt that probability of detection was irrelevant to dollar-award amounts.

Chapter 9 reports a study of jurors' acceptance and ability to apply exactly these principles. Polinsky and Shavell propose model punitive damages instructions, based on their theory of efficient deterrence.[13] The efficacy of these instructions was tested by telling jurors to apply them to

    10. Cf., A. Mitchell Polinsky, *An Introduction to Law and Economics* (2nd ed., 1989); and William M. Landes and Richard A. Posner, *The Economic Structure of Tort Law* 160–63 (1987).
    11. A. Mitchell Polinsky and Steven Shavell, "Punitive Damages: An Economic Analysis," 111 *Harv. L. Rev.* 869 (1998).
    12. *Id.*
    13. *Id.*

assess dollar awards in five case scenarios. The results show that with very explicit instructions, including a table to aid numerical calculations, barely 20% of mock jurors could perform the calculation correctly. Another group given the same instructions but also presented with an award amount suggested by the plaintiff's lawyer performed even more poorly. Only 10% of them did the calculation correctly; the vast majority were drawn to the attorney's suggestion. Just as in the study reported in chapter 8, most of these experimental participants ignored the probability of detection.

II. Judging Recklessness and Liability

Several of the experiments probed the processes in juror and jury decisions about the liability of a defendant for punitive damages. In the study reported in chapter 5, two-thirds of the individual jurors and deliberating juries found the defendants liable for punitive damages in four actual cases that trial judges and appellate courts decided did not warrant such liability. Further measurements indicated that most jurors and juries spent little time considering the legal principles on which they were instructed to base their judgments. What accounts for the jurors' and juries' deviation from judicial judgments and apparent neglect of instructions on the law?

Jurors are instructed that they may award punitive damages only if they find that the defendant's conduct was malicious or manifested reckless or callous disregard for the rights of others.[14] The issue of malice rarely arises in the accidental injury cases (products liability and environmental damages) that are the focus of the present research program. We are primarily concerned with judgments of recklessness, the most common issue in jury punitive damages decisions. The essence of the legal concept of recklessness is that an actor has *consciously* considered taking an action, concluded that there is significant danger of harm to another person(s), and then has chosen to take that action anyway, rather than a safer alternative. The judge's instructions on punitive damages require an affirmative response to all of four questions to conclude the defendant is liable: First, was the defendant subjectively conscious of a particular grave danger or risk of harm, and was the danger or risk

14. W. Page Keeton and William Lloyd Prosser, *Prosser and Keeton on the Law of Torts* (5th ed., 1984); Ronald W. Eades and Graham Douthwaite, *Jury Instructions on Damages in Tort Actions* (3rd ed., 1993).

a foreseeable and probable effect of the defendant's conduct? Second, did the particular danger or risk of which the defendant was subjectively conscious occur? Third, did the defendant disregard the risk in deciding how to act? Fourth, did the defendant's conduct in ignoring the danger or risk involve a gross deviation from the level of care that an ordinary person would use, having due regard to all the circumstances?

Since jurors and juries do not appear to comprehend or apply the legal definitions and instructions concerning recklessness (see discussion below), we must turn to the commonsense or folk psychology of blame. Behavioral research on attributions of responsibility for accidents, especially when there is considerable *ex ante* uncertainty that an accident will occur, leads us to expect jurors will exhibit two general commonsense biases when judging past mental states of the defendant. First, it is a fundamental human habit to constantly update the current knowledge we have about important situations; cognitive psychologists call this maintaining a current "situation model." When we move to a new physical location, we update our "mental model of the situation" and do not bump into objects as we navigate through our environment; when a significant event occurs (an election, a sports event, an accident), we "update" our knowledge about that situation and no longer entertain alternative "counterfactual" outcomes. This habit prepares us to make effective decisions about our future actions in a changing world. However, an inevitable byproduct of this adaptive habit is that events in the past seem more comprehensible than they were before they occurred. One implication is that *ex post* judgments of liability, by jurors or by judges, attribute more *ex ante* foreknowledge to another person than is reasonable. In short, a juror is prone to a *hindsight bias* when judging what the defendant could have and should have been able to foresee when taking an action that resulted in harm to the plaintiff (see results and discussion in chapter 6).

Second, there is a tendency to rely on *everyday intuitions* about what is proper rather than on the law, especially when the legal principles are unfamiliar and sometimes even incomprehensible to the juror. In order to explain the high rates of jury-judge disagreements in certain kinds of trials, Kalven and Zeisel, in their classic study *The American Jury* (1966),[15] identify conditions under which jurors were "liberated" to fol-

---

15. Harry Kalven Jr. and Hans Zeisel, *The American Jury* (Thomas Callahan and Philip Ennis collabs., 1966).

low their nonlegal intuitions and sympathies.[16] Our data showing jurors' inattention to and poor comprehension of the judge's instructions support this conclusion (see chapter 5 and the discussion below). The difficult punitive damages instructions, composed of unfamiliar and confusing terminology, motivate jurors to rely on their intuitions, emotional reactions, and sympathy for the parties, rather than the law.

A. Adherence to Instructions on the Law

A fundamental question, especially for appellate evaluations of due process, concerns the extent to which jurors adhere to the trial judge's instructions on the law. Do jurors pay attention to the instructions, comprehend them correctly, and then apply the instructions conscientiously as they make decisions? Our empirical studies demonstrate that jury instructions do not play a governing role in jurors' decisions concerning liability for punitive damages. The empirical findings (reported in chapter 5) demonstrate the low level of comprehension, recall, and application of the judge's instructions by both jurors and juries.[17]

Jurors' memories for the instructions on deciding liability, measured only minutes after they rendered their verdicts, were poor, with median levels of prompted recall lower than 20% correct. There was a weak correlation between instruction recall and verdicts: The better the juror's recall, the more likely he or she was to agree with judges' rulings on the cases judged. Another indicator was present in jurors' verbal self-reports about their decision processes. Even when asked specifically about each component of the larger decision, only one out of twenty mock jurors claimed to have considered the full set of legally required elements.[18] These results suggest that jury instructions are mostly ignored in jurors' decisions about punitive damages.

16. For similar arguments see Norman J. Finkel, *Commonsense Justice: Jurors' Notions of the Law* (1995); and Paul H. Robinson and John M. Darley, *Justice, Liability, and Blame: Community Views and the Criminal Law* (1995).

17. For completeness, we note that Neil Vidmar has criticized some aspects of the study reported in chapter 5. Neil Vidmar, "Juries Don't Make Legal Decisions! And Other Problems: A Critique of Hastie et al. on Punitive Damages," 23 *Law and Hum. Behav.* 705 (1999). His comments are directed at nonempirical issues concerning our interpretations of findings and their implications for legal procedures, and we provide a detailed rebuttal of his criticisms in Reid Hastie, David A. Schkade, and John W. Payne, "Reply to Vidmar," 23 *Law and Hum. Behav.* 715 (1999).

18. Reid Hastie, "The Role of 'Stories' in Civil Jury Judgments," 32 *U. Mich. J.L. Reform* 227 (1999).

The American jury is often defended with the argument that group deliberation is an effective remedy for the weaknesses and biases of individual reasoning and judgment. Perhaps group deliberations are more conscientious, especially with reference to adherencc to the jury instructions from the judge. Chapter 5 reports on 121 mock juries deciding the question of liability for punitive damages in four different fact situations. Detailed content analyses of their deliberations reveals that juries were barely more conscientious than jurors. When deliberation contents were scored for thoroughness of coverage of the five legal criteria that were presented in their jury instructions as essential to conclude punitive damages were warranted, the modal jury discussed fewer than half of the issues. Notably, the more thoroughly a jury discussed the instructions, the more likely it was to reach the same verdict that trial and appellate courts had reached for the original cases. But although more thorough consideration of the relevant law increased the probability of reaching the legally correct verdict, most juries were not highly conscientious. Juries' low level of attention is illustrated by the fact that not a single one of the 121 deliberating juries received a perfect thoroughness score, by both mentioning and discussing each of the essential elements from the jury instructions on liability for punitive damages.

One important discovery from the present studies of the jury deliberation process is that the group process recapitulates the two-stage outrage model for the individual juror decision process introduced in chapter 2. The jury decision, like the juror decision, is a two-stage sequence: First, a dichotomous punish/not-punish decision; second, if the first stage concludes with "punish," an award-assessment process (chapters 2 and 3). The liability decision can be described as a proportionality group decision scheme: The probability of a verdict is predicted by the proportion of members of the jury who begin deliberation favoring that verdict (chapter 5). But, perhaps reflecting the asymmetry in the plaintiff's preponderance-of-the-evidence burden of proof, there is a slight advantage to the defendant over and above the proportional prediction rule. So, a majority of member jurors in favor of the defendant is somewhat likelier to prevail than the same-sized majority in favor of the plaintiff.

B. Shared Intent to Punish

If jurors are not following their instructions on the law, how are they making punitive damages decisions? Findings reported in chapter 2 and 3 indicate that there is substantial agreement such that the *ordering* of jurors' outrage and intent-to-punish judgments is consistent with the spirit of the law and with common sense. Jurors' judgments depend on the outrageousness of the defendant's conduct, and especially inferences about the defendant's state of mind. Deliberate intent to harm the plaintiff (malice) is judged to be most egregious; callous disregard of an obvious potential for injury to the plaintiff or gross negligence is next; and finally, a truly unintended and unforeseeable accidental injury. Fact situations that vary along this continuum produce a predictable ordering of ratings of attributed causality, responsibility, and blamability.[19]

Empirical tests summarized in chapters 2 and 3 show that jurors' reactions of *outrage* and their corresponding *intentions to punish* are ordered according to this continuum and that there is substantial between-juror consensus on the ordering. This high degree of agreement is reflected in high correlations between the average judgments of different groups of jurors (e.g., by gender, ethnic background, income, age) across the twenty-eight cases, for judgments of outrage and intent to punish (averaging over +.90). Similar results were obtained in a separate study with fifteen case scenarios (chapter 3). This high degree of consensus implies that both the fact-finding process and moral evaluation judgments are reliable and similar across jurors.[20] However, consensus does not demonstrate that jurors follow the law. The high degree of disagreement with legal authorities, reported in chapter 5, suggests that jurors and judges rely on different standards, at least when they must make an *absolute* discrimination between liable and not liable.

Thus, we observe high rates of *disagreement* among jurors and between jurors and judges on the answer to the question "Do you find the defendant liable for punitive damages?" for individual cases (reported in chapter 5), at the same time we observe high levels of *agreement* on the ordering of cases with reference to the reprehensibility of the defendants'

---

19. E.g., Anderson and MacCoun, *supra* note 6; Corinne Cather et al., "Plaintiff Injury and Defendant Reprehensibility: Implications for Compensatory and Punitive Damage Awards," 20 *Law & Hum. Behav.* 189 (1996); Neal Feigenson, *Legal Blame: How Jurors Think and Talk about Accidents* (2000); Frank D. Fincham and Joseph M. Jaspars, "Attribution of Responsibility: From Man the Scientist to Man as Lawyer," 13 *Adv. Experimental Soc. Psychol.* 81 (1980); Valerie P. Hans, *Business on Trial: The Civil Jury and Corporate Responsibility* (2000); Marylie Karlovac and John M. Darley, "Attribution of Responsibility for Accidents—A Negligence Law Analogy," 6 *Soc. Cognition* 287 (1988); and Jennifer K. Robbennolt, "Punitive Damage Decision Making: The Decisions of Citizens and Trial Court Judges," Social Science Research Network (December 11, 2000), at http://papers.ssrn.com (*Law & Hum. Behav.* forthcoming 2001).

20. Hastie, *supra* note 18.

conduct. Our interpretation is that common sense and legal instructions converge on principles that are used to make *relative* judgments of degree of reprehensibility. But the complex multiple-element instructions on the *absolute* threshold for liability are both unfamiliar and ineffective. In other words, we believe that disagreements on the *absolute* liability judgment represent a failure of legal instructions to provide sufficient guidance to produce consensus, while the *relative* moral reprehensibility judgment is both intuitively and legally simpler. Judges may differ from jurors both because they are more capable of comprehending and applying the unfamiliar (to a layperson) legal instructions, and because they exhibit smaller hindsight biases and less confusion when reasoning about uncertainty (see discussion of chapter 11 below). And, of course, judges have much more experience with related cases and their outcomes, which also serve to calibrate their decision thresholds for new cases.

C. Hindsight Effects

Previous studies of *ex post* evaluations of *ex ante* judgments in many domains (medical, engineering, political, sports, legal) demonstrate that people are likely, in hindsight, to believe that they and others should have known and would have known that a past event was likely to occur. The situation for a juror judging punitive damages is especially prone to hindsight biases because it depends so heavily on inferences about the defendant's past state of mind. This phenomenon was demonstrated with experimental manipulations described in chapter 6 (see also chapter 10 and the discussion below concerning misperceptions of risk). One group of experimental jurors was asked to make *ex ante,* foresight predictions, and another group to make *ex post,* hindsight postdictions (chapter 6). These experiments showed that jurors were overconfident that they "would have known" *ex ante* that an accident was going to occur, and they generalized from their own (unreasonable) overconfidence to denigrate the judgments of others (the defendant or other decision makers) who did or might have permitted the actions that resulted in an accident. Furthermore, the jurors inferred from their hindsightful conclusion that the defendant had failed to take reasonable precautions and had exhibited a gross deviation from reasonable care. In a railroad accident case, *ex ante* two-thirds of the experimental jurors approved of the request to allow the railroad to continue operations, but *ex post* (jurors given exactly the same description but also told that an accident had occurred) two-thirds judged that the railroad's behavior was reckless and that the railroad was liable for punitive damages.

These findings, in the context of a punitive damages decision, are parallel to the results of dozens of analogous studies, including some high-fidelity mock-juror studies of the judgment of negligence.[21] Indeed, Rachlinski has interpreted recent changes in the legal medical malpractice decision as evidence for the law's acknowledgment that even carefully instructed fact finders will be susceptible to hindsight biases.[22] He concludes that the legal test for malpractice changed partly to prevent the hindsight bias that would be likely to occur in such cases (from a "should have known" test to a "customary standard of care" test).

D. Identification with the Parties

Many observers suspect that jurors, contrary to their instructions, react to the personal characteristics and reputations of parties involved in trials. In the context of punitive damages, commentators have suggested that juries may intend to redistribute wealth from "haves" to (especially local or similarly situated) "have-nots." We tested these notions by conducting experiments in which the relationships between the jurors and the parties were manipulated (reported in chapter 4); specifically we varied the geographical proximity and economic relationships between the jurors, the lead plaintiff, and the defendant. In the context of identical fact patterns, the defendant was depicted as local or remote; similarly, the plaintiff was also depicted as local or remote. In our tests more jurors decided in favor of a geographically local plaintiff versus a remote plaintiff in all experimental conditions (chapter 4). However, contrary to the motive of economic self-interest for wealth redistribution, there was no reliable effect of the defendant company's location.

III. Reasoning about Risk and Uncertainty

While there is substantial consensus among jurors about the relative reprehensibility of harmful actions, there are systematic biases in reasoning about uncertain risky events that undermine the acceptability

---

21. Kim A. Kamin and Jeffrey J. Rachlinski, "Ex Post ≠ Ex Ante: Determining Liability in Hindsight," 19 *L. & Hum Behav.* 89 (1995). For a review of hindsight effects in many other judgments, see Scott A. Hawkins and Reid Hastie, "Hindsight: Biased Judgments of Past Events after the Outcomes Are Known," 107 *Psychol. Bull.* 311 (1990).

22. Jeffrey J. Rachlinski, "A Positive Psychological Theory of Judging in Hindsight," 65 *U. Chi. L. Rev.* 571 (1998).

of those judgments. We summarize these empirical observations under three category headings: zero-risk mentality, an irrational expectation that all risks can be reduced to zero; incorrect and undiscriminating reactions to cost-benefit analyses; and incoherent reasoning about uncertain events.

The ability to reason effectively about responsibility for past events and about risk-cost trade-offs is especially difficult when the relevant events are uncertain and unpredictable. Human beings do not seem to be naturally endowed with a capacity to reason consistently about uncertain events.[23] This tendency to be irrational and to violate the principles of probability theory is especially apparent in judgments of the probability of occurrence of unfamiliar, unique, low-probability events—exactly the situation that is presented to jurors in punitive damages cases.[24] These failings of human reason have many ramifications in judgments like those required by punitive damages decisions. For example, an accurate assessment of the prior likelihoods that various hazardous events will occur is an essential basis from which to judge the carelessness or recklessness with which an individual or a corporation conducts its business. But it is virtually a cliché in the field of risk analysis and risk communication that citizens are afraid of the wrong hazards, and that overreaction is the modal response to unfamiliar, low-probability threats.[25] If a juror assesses the apparent *ex ante* risks of an inherently hazardous enterprise (e.g., the transport of toxic chemicals) as being much higher than they truly are, then that juror will be biased to conclude that an unlucky accident is the result of reckless disregard by the person or organization that made the unavoidable risk-management decision. Similarly, if a juror's attention is drawn to worst-case possibilities, rather than to actual outcomes, his or her assessment of damages will be biased toward larger values. As we have seen (chapter 10), jurors exhibit these biases in reasoning about once-uncertain events, and they are susceptible to hindsight errors as well.

23. Tversky and Kahneman, *supra* note 5, at 1124.

24. Gerd Gigerenzer and Ulrich Hoffrage, "How to Improve Bayesian Reasoning without Instruction—Frequency Formats," 102 *Psychol. Rev.* 684 (1995); Amos Tversky and Daniel Kahneman, "Extensional versus Intuitive Reasoning: The Conjunction Fallacy in Probability Judgment," 90 *Psychol. Rev.* 293 (1983).

25. Barry Glassner, *The Culture of Fear: Why Americans Are Afraid of the Wrong Things* (1999); Paul Slovic, "Perception of Risk," 236 *Science* 280 (1987); Aaron B. Wildavsky, *But Is It True? A Citizen's Guide to Environmental Health and Safety Issues* (1995).

The nature of the legal fact-finding process focuses attention on the instant case, inducing a "tunnel vision" that foregrounds a single, inevitably tragic event in dramatic relief, but obscures related nontragic outcomes from view. Even if there are large numbers of beneficiaries of an innovation (many lives saved or much discomfort prevented by a new drug, a new automobile safety device that protects many but injures a few), a jury is likely to undervalue the benefits side of the ratio. The jurors' attention is captured by the victims who suffered costs of the innovation. Juries also are unlikely to consider the global cost-benefit social welfare bottom line. Faced with a door latch that has resulted in an injury from a side collision, they do not consider the benefits of the same device in rear-end collisions, nor do they consider the economic consequences for the company of installing a safety device to prevent low-probability-of-occurrence injuries on millions of automobiles.[26] Instead, reasoning that "but for an inexpensive part in *this* particular automobile, *this* unique tragedy could have been averted."[27] The emphasis on fact finding *in the instant case* prevents juries from taking an actuarially realistic view of the social costs and benefits of the defendant's conduct. Furthermore, the decisions that are alleged to be reckless in many personal injury and environmental damage torts, especially those with corporate defendants, are made at a distance from the victims. Thus, plaintiffs usually are cast in the role of unwitting victims, whose fate was determined by the actions of a remote, faceless, and uncaring corporation.[28]

There is a universal need for security across human societies and an abhorrence of risks, especially of uncertain hazards.[29] The extreme manifestation of this attitude is known as the *zero-risk mentality,* and it is expressed in a general belief that conscientious defendants should have been able to avoid all adverse consequences of their conduct by taking enough precautions. The zero-risk mentality is linked to a tendency to ignore the actual costs of precautionary measures and to a myopia about

---

26. Cf., Stephen G. Breyer, *Breaking the Vicious Circle: Toward Effective Risk Regulation* (1993).

27. E.g., *Carrol v. Otis Elevator,* 896 F.2d 210, 215 (7th Cir. 1990) (Easterbrook, F., concurring); Andrew Pollack, "$4.9 Billion Jury Verdict in G.M. Fuel Tank Case," *N.Y. Times,* July 10, 1999, at A7; and Andrew Pollack, "Paper Trail Haunts G.M. after It Loses Injury Suit," *N.Y. Times,* July 12, 1999, at A12.

28. Hans, *supra* note 19.

29. Mary Douglas, *Risk and Blame: Essays in Cultural Theory* (1992); Slovic, *supra* note 25; Aaron B. Wildavsky, *Searching for Safety* (1988).

the risk-cost trade-offs inherent in the deployment of limited protective resources. Modern views on technological and natural hazards assume that increased investments in safety in one domain inevitably mean increased risks in another domain where resources have not been deployed.[30] Even experts must exercise "professional self-control" to recognize the systematic trade-offs that are inherent and unavoidable in all consequential risky decisions. There is always a limited amount of resources to spend on risk management; protection or insurance against one hazard inevitably means exposure to other hazards.

A. Zero-Risk Mentality

As reported in chapter 6, we observed that more than 60% of citizen-respondents in our surveys and experiments exhibited a zero-risk mentality by endorsing the statement "If everyone tries as hard as they can, the risk of environmental damage from industrial accidents like train derailments, oil spills, and toxic waste problems can be reduced to zero." The rated strength of this belief was correlated at a moderate level ($+.20$) with hindsight judgments of the probability that an accident would occur.

B. Reactions to Cost-Benefit Analysis Evidence

The results reported in chapter 7 show that when jurors knew a corporation had conducted a risk analysis, relevant to an accident, the punitive damages award was greater than if no such analysis had been conducted. That study compared identical fact situations that existed when an automobile accident occurred. Several groups of jurors each received a different statement of information describing the manufacturer's cost-benefit analysis: whether or not a cost-benefit analysis had been conducted by the company, the technical quality of the analysis, and the assumed value of a "statistical life" used in the calculations. Results reveal that evidence of any kind of corporate risk analysis was a "red flag" that increased the rate of verdicts against the defendant and the magnitude of the dollar damages awards. When the cost-benefit analysis used a high, government-endorsed value-of-life amount (implying the company was willing to spend more on safety), punitive damages liability rates and

---

30. Breyer, *supra* note 26; Guido Calabresi and Philip Bobbitt, *Tragic Choices* (1978); Kenneth R. Hammond, *Human Judgment and Social Policy: Irreducible Uncertainty, Inevitable Error, Unavoidable Injustice* (1996); W. Kip Viscusi, *Fatal Tradeoffs: Public and Private Responsibilities for Risk* (1992).

dollar awards were even higher. Thus, evidence of the defendant's use of the most responsible state-of-the-art technical analysis elicited a negative, punitive reaction from the jurors.

Past comparative research on juror reactions to different kinds of defendants has concluded that identical factual circumstances are likelier to lead to a liability verdict if the defendant is a corporation rather than a nonprofit organization or a private individual. A common interpretation of this difference is that it is due to the belief that a corporation will have more resources that could be devoted to anticipating the possible harmful consequences of a new product or a new design.[31] Thus, corporations are held to a higher "reasonable corporation" standard of care than the ordinary private citizen.

Today corporations often conduct cost-benefit analyses or some other form of technical risk-utility projection (the most publicized examples come from the automobile and pharmaceuticals industries), and such analyses are required by law as a precondition for actions by many governmental agencies. These policies and analytic methods result from the recognition that it is not possible to simply "Just say 'No'" to accidents. Safety is a matter of trading off risks and precautions against costs. Consumers tacitly acknowledge this trade-off when they risk their lives by driving imperfect vehicles at high speeds, rather than paying the costs in money and time for fatality-free traffic systems or when they engage in risky but enjoyable sports like downhill skiing. Cost-benefit analyses provide a formal projection of potential problems with a new or current design, as well as an estimate of the cost to reduce the associated risks. A typical bottom line in such a report is stated in numbers summarizing projected risks and costs: social costs such as potential injuries, pollution, and other hazards versus costs of design and production changes to reduce the risks. Such analysis is essential to making rational choices leading to an optimal balance of risk and cost. However, the study reported in chapter 7 and some recent verdicts (e.g., the Ford Pinto case[32]

31. Hans, *supra* note 19; Richard O. Lempert, "Juries, Hindsight, and Punitive Damage Awards: Failures of a Social Science Case for Change. (Response to Reid Hastie and W. Kip Viscusi, 40 *Ariz. L. Rev.* 901 [1998])," 48 *DePaul L. Rev.* 867 (1999); Robert J. MacCoun, "Differential Treatment of Corporate Defendants by Juries: An Examination of the 'Deep Pockets' Hypothesis," 30 *L. & Soc. Rev.* 121 (1996).

32. Mark Dowie, "Pinto Madness," 2 *Mother Jones,* Sept.–Oct. 1977, at 18; and Gary T. Schwartz, "The Myth of the Ford Pinto Case," 43 *Rutgers L. Rev.* 1013 (1991).

and the Chevrolet Malibu case[33]) indicate that evidence of corporate risk analysis is especially influential in jury decision processes.

Mock jurors' reactions to cost-benefit analyses also provide another example of unexpected anchor effects. When a nonstandard low value of life ($800,000) was used in the cost-benefit analysis, awards were *lower* than when the defendant companies used a higher, government-recommended value ($3 million per statistical life lost)—a value that implied corporate willingness to spend *more* on safety (chapter 7). This means that when the risk analysis expressed a higher degree of corporate conscience, the jurors imposed a greater punishment. Our interpretation is that this difference results from the jurors' habit of anchoring on salient numbers, in this case the value-of-a-statistical-life figure, irrespective of the meaningful implications of the number.

C. Reasoning about Low-Probability Events

Chapter 10 reports several experimental tests of jurors' ability to reason about uncertainty in the context of the sorts of risk-cost trade-offs often under dispute in punitive damages lawsuits. Many behavioral experiments and surveys have already demonstrated that most people exhibit confusion and systematic biases when reasoning about risks to themselves; especially low-probability-of-occurrence, high-consequence events like those that are the focus of dispute in punitive damages cases.[34] What happens when they attempt to reason about risks to others? One of the most basic risk judgments concerns direct estimates of causes of death: How many people die each year in this country as a result of accidents with fireworks? From the consequences of lung cancer? Jury-eligible citizens show the typical pattern of overestimating small-probability fatalities (e.g., in a typical year five people die from fireworks-related accidents, but the average estimate was over six thousand deaths). This bias in risk perception is correlated with implicit estimates of value of life. The respondents were asked to indicate how much they would be willing to pay to reduce risk of death in traffic accidents. The implied value of a life saved could be calculated from their responses. Citizens who had an exaggerated response to small risks also placed the highest value on lives saved. One instructive statistic is that more than 10% of

33. Pollack, *supra* note 27.
34. See also Baruch Fischhoff et al., *Acceptable Risk* (1981); and Slovic, *supra* note 25.

the respondents placed an *infinite value* on life, which can be interpreted as a most extreme expression of the zero-risk mentality.

In a hypothetical safety-hazard problem, jury-eligible citizens were asked if an airline company should pay to repair a cargo door that could cause a modest accident with a low probability (e.g., ". . . there is a $\frac{1}{10}$ probability that there will be a loss to your company of $15,000"). Four experimental scenarios were constructed, designed so that the expected cost of repair always exceeded the expected loss due to an accident (according to the classic Learned Hand formula, these are all situations in which the decision *not* to repair the door is rational and, therefore, should *not* be deemed negligent).[35] The respondents recommended repair 87% to 96% of the time across scenarios and favored punitive damages in 74% to 96% of the experimental scenarios after they were told the accident had occurred. If the Learned Hand standard had been applied, the potential defendant should not have been even negligent; these judgments exhibit a clear overreaction to accidental consequences.

Jurors' misconceptions and inconsistencies when reasoning about uncertain events have been established in a variety of judgment tasks.[36] But, in the context of the punitive damages judgment, where the focus is on retrospectively judging the prudence or recklessness of a defendant's conduct, the consequences of incoherent reasoning converge in producing an antidefendant tendency in the ultimate judgments of responsibility. Misperceptions about risks and hazards that make accidents seem more likely than their actuarial probabilities of occurrence also make it more likely that someone who failed to anticipate an accident will be judged reckless: if the event is deemed likely to occur, failure to anticipate its occurrence will seem more careless, more reckless, and more blamable. Most jurors violate principles of rational risk-cost trade-off reasoning, for example, by recommending excessive precautionary repairs. They also endorse and unrealistically expect that "zero risk" is achievable. Such judgments violate generally accepted principles of social welfare. Jurors tend toward harsh evaluations of conduct by defendants who apply safety policies that may not even be legally negligent. Again, jurors' inability to deal with uncertainty in balancing costs and benefits leads to an antidefendant bias.

35. *United States v. Carroll Towing Co.*, 159 F.2d 169 (2d Cir. 1947) at 173.
36. E.g., Daniel Kahneman et al., eds., *Judgment under Uncertainty: Heuristics and Biases* (1982).

IV. Judges versus Juries

If we are critical of the jury's performance when deciding on puni-tive damages, it is important to ask: What is the alternative to a jury? One obvious legal alternative is a bench trial where the judge serves as primary fact finder and decision maker.[37] What do we know about the performance of judges making punitive damages decisions under con-ditions where direct comparisons to the jury are possible? Robbennolt studied the impact of case factors such as amount of actual and potential damage and defendant's wealth on compensatory and punitive damages dollar awards by jury-eligible citizens and by a sample of state and fed-eral district court judges.[38] She concludes that "the decision making of judges and jurors with regard to damage awards, particularly punitive damage awards, are quite similar." In chapter 11 judges and jurors are compared on further tests of quality of reasoning about uncertain events and on tests of susceptibility to hindsight effects in legal judgments.

A. Risk Management: Reasoning about Uncertainty

Several experimental tests reported in chapter 11 compare judges' and jurors' decisions on identical cases and risk perception and risk-management scenarios. In summary, judges showed most of the same biases as jurors, but to a lesser degree. With reference to risk, fatality-rate estimates by judges were approximately one and a half to twice as accurate as jury-eligible citizens, especially for low-probability, high-consequence risks. Estimates of the implicit value of life by judges were consistent with valuations by other population groups in their general order of magnitude; but jury-eligible citizens were approximately three times as likely as judges to put an infinite value on life. We interpret this finding as evidence that judges are less likely to exhibit the impractical, if not simply irrational, zero-risk mentality.

In a hypothetical airplane cargo door safety-hazard problem, jurors opted for punitive damages at rates ranging from 74% to 96%, although the problems were constructed with cost of repair and probability of accident values so that expected cost of repair always exceeded the

37. Thomas Koenig and Michael Rustad, "The Quiet Revolution Revisited: An Empirical Study of the Impact of State Tort Reform of Punitive Damages in Products Liability," 16 *Just. Sys. J.* 21 (1993); Robbennolt, *supra* note 19; Lisa M. Sharkey, "Judge or Jury: Who Should As-sess Punitive Damages?" 64 *U. Cin. L. Rev.* 1089 (1996).

38. Robbennolt, *supra* note 19.

expected loss due to an accident. For these same problems judges favored punitive damages at much lower rates ranging from 18% to 69% across the experimental scenarios. Given that the potential defendant was not even negligent, judges' answers were much more defensible for these scenarios.[39]

In the tests reported in chapter 11, judges as well as jury-eligible citizens judged scenarios in which $10 million in property damage occurred following an oil well blowout. These studies experimentally varied the amount of potential property damage that could have occurred (but did *not*) from $10 million to $100 million. Mock jurors' punitive damages dollar awards were affected by the hypothetical, counterfactual figures; with the median award of $30 million in the "might-have-been $100 million" scenario (vs. $10 million in the control scenario). But judges' awards were not affected by the "might-have-been $100 million" manipulation, and median awards for $10 million harm were $10 million in damages. Judges' awards are consistent with principles of award setting based on current economic theories of deterrence and efficiency.

B. Hindsight

Consistent with judges' superior performance answering risk-estimate and cost-benefit problems, chapter 11 reports that judges showed smaller hindsight effects than did citizen mock jurors in the context of a punitive damages decision.

The superior performance of judges making judgments under uncertainty and judgments of liability for punitive damages can probably be attributed to expertise and experience with similar situations, although we have not conducted a thorough exploration of the individual personal characteristics that predict performance. (Lempert disagrees and speculates that political or social class factors might be the true causes of the judges' superior performance.[40])

39. Cf., "The Learned Hand Formula" from *United States v. Carroll Towing Co.*, 159 F.2d 169 (2d Cir. 1947).

40. Professor Lempert criticized many aspects of Hastie and Viscusi's (1998) comparative analysis of judge versus juror decision making. We emphatically disagree with his commentary and have written a reply in Reid Hastie and W. Kip Viscusi, "Juries, Hindsight, and Punitive Damages: A Reply to Lempert," under review (2001). For present purposes we would merely note that Lempert appears to agree with our conclusions, although not our methods or interpretations. He writes: "None of this means that jurors do not exhibit hindsight bias. Given the seeming ubiquity of this bias in human decision making, it is likely that they do." Lempert, *supra* note 31, at 881.

V. Summary of Empirical Findings

When punitive damages decisions are studied at the juror and the jury level, the cognitive and social processes, and many of their outcomes, appear to be comprehensible. Many of the patterns of behavior they exhibit make sense in terms of current scientific theories of behavioral decision making, and most of the behavioral phenomena observed in the present studies are analogous to behaviors that have been observed in the nonlegal decisions. Still, no one could have predicted, in advance of our research, exactly what we have discovered about the cognitive, emotional, and social processes involved in punitive damages decisions. Furthermore, our conclusion that most of the substages of the overall decision process are understandable and often predictable will seem surprising given the variability observed in dispositions of cases and in broad distributions of dollar awards reported in studies of archival verdict statistics. We conclude that most of the unpredictability in the final awards results from identifiable aspects of the decision task—especially from the manner in which juries are instructed to measure wrongfulness, by expressing the judgment on a dollar metric scale.

The major empirical findings describing individual juror punitive damages decisions include the following:

1. For the most part, jurors do not attend carefully to or remember much from the trial judge's instructions on liability for punitive damages. In those instances when jurors do conscientiously heed their instructions, they are likelier to conclude that the defendant is not liable (chapter 5).
2. Jurors' comparative assessments of the wrongfulness of defendants' actions and their relative intentions to punish defendants are consistent with commonsense and legal conceptions of blameworthiness (chapter 2).
3. When absolute, liable/not-liable decisions are rendered for representative cases, there is considerable disagreement among jurors and between jurors and legal authorities (trial and appellate judges) on which cases warrant the consideration of punitive damages. We attribute this disagreement to the difficulty of the cases that go to trial because they could not be settled; to the lack of clear guidance provided by traditional instructions on punitive damages; and to jurors' tendency to rely on intuitive notions of reprehensibility, rather

than the instructions they receive on the law from the judge. A small amount of the disagreement with judges is probably due to differences between jurors and judges in the magnitude of hindsight biases, to their relative skills in reasoning about the uncertainty associated with accidental events (see #15, below), and especially to their greater knowledge of similar legal cases and their outcomes (chapter 5).

4. Jurors exhibit large hindsight effects, projecting their *ex post* knowledge of outcomes onto their assessments of the defendant's *ex ante* state of knowledge before the harmful outcome had occurred (chapter 6).

5. People err in systematic ways when making judgments under uncertainty. For example, they frequently overestimate the risk of low-probability accidents, producing exaggerated blame for unlikely accidents and incoherence in their judgments under uncertainty (chapter 10).

6. Knowledge that a defendant has performed a cost-benefit analysis increases jurors' judgments of the defendant's punitive damages liability. Furthermore, juror awards are greater against companies that use a higher value of life in their analysis, even though it implies their willingness to spend more on safety. Apparently jurors lock on to the larger dollar figure as an anchor (see #8, below), not grasping its significance (chapter 7).

7. Jurors' dollar awards are less reliable and less predictable than their relative judgments of wrongfulness. For example, jurors are predictable and consistent when expressing themselves on bounded scales of outrage and intention to punish the defendant (chapter 2).

8. Lacking guidance on how to arrive at an award amount, jurors are drawn to numerical anchors. These anchors may come from the attorneys' arguments or from evidence about the defendant's financial status. The selection of anchor values and any adjustments from them are erratic and unpredictable (chapter 4).

9. Jurors give higher awards to geographically local, familiar plaintiffs than to remote, unfamiliar plaintiffs. But they do not exhibit a reliable bias against out-of-town defendants (chapter 4).

10. Laypersons and (economically sophisticated) law students reject the theory of optimal economic deterrence that is based on the probability of detection; they ignore that probability in setting the award amount. Jurors rarely cite any comprehensible principle of

deterrence or retribution to justify their dollar awards. Even when carefully instructed on the probability-of-detection optimal deterrence principle and given a calculational algorithm, jurors apply the formula unreliably and are easily distracted by irrelevant, but salient numerical values (chapters 8 and 9).

11. Jury verdicts on punitive damages liability are well predicted by the individual predeliberation verdicts of their members, in contrast with their decisions on dollar awards, which change significantly following deliberation (see #14, below) (chapter 5).

12. Neither jurors nor juries rely conscientiously on the punitive damages instructions. However, the few juries that do discuss more of the legally required elements in their deliberations are likelier to agree with trial and appellate judges on the verdict (just as individual jurors who cited more elements were also likelier to reach the approved verdict) (chapter 5).

13. The liability decision is well described by a proportionality group decision rule: The probability that a jury will conclude in favor of the plaintiff or the defendant is predicted by the proportion of jurors who favor that party at the start of deliberation. But there is one minor qualification to the strict proportionality rule: Jury decisions exhibit a slight bias toward the defendant. A precise comparison between the propensities of equal-sized majorities for the defense and for the plaintiff demonstrates that the defense majority is slightly more likely to win (chapters 3 and 5).

14. Jury deliberation tends to increase dollar-award amounts over the predeliberation judgments of individual members, a phenomenon we label the *severity shift*. The severity shift results in both larger and more variable awards at the group jury level, as compared to the individual juror level of analysis (chapter 3).

15. Judges exhibit the same habits as jurors when reasoning under uncertainty, although they are more sensitive to details of the cases being judged; more coherent in their reasoning about probabilities, gains, and losses; and more accurate than jurors. Most notably, their judgments about low-probability events, their valuation of lives, and their susceptibility to hindsight effects are more accurate and more internally consistent than the analogous responses of jurors. We attribute the better performance by judges, compared to jurors, to the judges' higher levels of relevant education and greater experience with relevant legal judgments under uncertainty (chapter 11).

VI. Comments and Conclusions

The punitive damages decision is a mixture of orderly, predictable components and understandable but unpredictable elements. Jurors' evaluations of wrongfulness show considerable consensus across individuals, for example, in the ordering of cases by judgments of outrage evoked by the defendant's conduct and in jurors' intentions to punish. Much of this order derives from jurors' shared assumptions concerning morality and proper conduct—assumptions that are expressed in the legal ordering of improper conduct from malicious to careless actions. Even if jurors and juries pay little heed to their instructions on the law, their culturally inculcated intuitions are likely to be consistent with legal doctrine.

Problems arise when jurors must make absolute judgments. These absolute threshold decisions are not rendered consistently across jurors, but there are some systematic, shared biases. For example, punitive damages decisions exhibit a powerful hindsight effect such that actions and situations judged to be *not* negligent and *not* reckless in foresight are viewed as blameworthy in hindsight. The large hindsight bias produces inferences of foreknowledge when none could plausibly have existed. Jurors also exhibit well-known biases when they make judgments under uncertainty, especially when they are asked to estimate or reason about small probabilities. The common "regressive" tendency to overestimate small frequencies and probabilities and to underestimate larger values was observed in jurors' and judges' judgments. Jurors' reactions to particular kinds of evidence such as testimony about corporate risk analyses and information about party identities are also systematic, but not rational or fair.

The most mysterious part of the punitive damages decision concerns the manner in which jurors translate their judgments of egregiousness or intentions to punish into a dollar-award number. An anchor-and-adjust judgment strategy is the common assessment process followed by most jurors as they translate their intentions to punish into a dollar metric. The anchor-and-adjust judgment process is one of the most common mechanisms of everyday estimation and judgment.[41] Such a strategy is a reasonable solution to the problem of translating one metric (intention to punish) into another, dollar penalties, *if* it is applied conscientiously

---

41. Kahneman et al., *supra* note 36.

and reliably. However, with little background or guidance about a method to assess punitive damages, the particular anchors selected and the application of principles of retribution and deterrence to adjust the dollar amount are erratic and unpredictable cognitive processes. Thus, the "noise" added to judgments at this stage in the decision process breaks down most of the original consensus in evaluations of outrage and intent to punish the defendant's actions. We have indicated the difficulty of this translation judgment with the label *scaling without a modulus.* The difficulty of reliably expressing moral evaluations or attitudes on dollar metrics, and the resulting incoherence and unpredictability in the valuations, has been observed before in applications such as the contingent valuation of public goods[42] and in anomalies in preferences and pricing of casino gambles and other commodities.[43]

We have also demonstrated that salient numbers, such as a plaintiff's request for a specific dollar amount, have a dramatic impact on the jurors' awards. But the selection of such an anchor value, its relationship to intent to punish, and the adjustment process are unpredictable, even in our controlled experimental situations. Of course, the process and its result will be even more difficult to understand in a realistically complex trial, where many more candidate anchor numbers are likely to be salient to the jurors.

Compounding the difficulty in setting awards is the instruction to make retribution and deterrence the primary considerations in choosing a dollar value. Both of these concepts are multifaceted and vague, and there is little consensus among experts, much less among jurors, on what they mean or on how to apply them to factual situations. Furthermore, there was little evidence that jurors attempted to apply these concepts in their self-reports of their judgment processes. Perhaps the only clear example of an attempt to reason about these difficult concepts occurred when a juror had decided that the defendant should be "put out of business," and then relied on financial records to infer a dollar award that would be sure to bankrupt that corporation. (Of course, this award is

---

42. E.g., Daniel Kahneman et al., "Economic Preferences or Attitude Expressions? An Analysis of Dollar Responses to Public Issues," 19 *J. Risk & Uncertainty* 203 (1999); and John W. Payne et al., "Measuring Constructed Preferences: Towards a Building Code," 19 *J. Risk & Uncertainty* 243 (1999).

43. E.g., David M. Grether and Charles R. Plott, "Economic Theory of Choice and the Preference Reversal Phenomenon," 69 *Am. Econ. Rev.* 623 (1979); Paul Slovic, "The Construction of Preference," 50 *Am. Psychologist* 364 (1995); and Amos Tversky et al., "Contingent Weighting in Judgment and Choice," 95 *Psychol. Rev.* 371 (1988).

motivated by the goal of "incapacitation," rather than deterrence.) Jurors also rejected the inverse probability-of-detection deterrence principle, the most widely accepted rule for calculating punitive damages, based on optimal deterrence theory from economics. And even when jurors were carefully instructed on a numerical algorithm to calculate award amounts, only a small fraction correctly made the calculation. But the fundamental problem is that no one, anywhere, ever has applied either retribution or deterrence to provide a defensible translation from a summary moral evaluation to a precise dollar award.

The jury deliberation process is to some degree comprehensible and susceptible to quantitative modeling. A proportionality group decision rule principle describes the transformation of individual liability judgments into the group verdict on liability.[44] But deliberation on the dollar award amplifies, rather than damps, the variability across individual jurors' dollar awards. And there is a systematic severity shift such that, on average, juries assess higher dollar awards than their members. In this case, group deliberation increases the unreliability and unpredictability of the result.

Throughout the present research, we have been impressed by the serious and energetic manner in which citizens performed the difficult legal judgment tasks that are demanded by the punitive damages decision. The many systematic patterns of behavior that we observed are convincing evidence of the jurors' conscientiousness. Nonetheless, the legally required decision tasks often seemed to exceed their individual and social capacities. The decision task is not well defined by the jury instructions; jurors are not provided with the necessary background information or experiences to make reliable judgments; and inherent cognitive limitations interfered with their performance of the specific judgments prescribed by our punitive damages system. Jurors' good intentions and high levels of motivation were thwarted by the inherent complexity of the legal decision task and by the lack of clear instructions or other effective guidance. The result is a decision process that is unreliable, erratic, and unpredictable.

44. James H. Davis, "Group Decision and Social Interaction—A Theory of Social Decision Schemes," 80 *Psychol. Rev.* 97 (1973).

13

What Should Be Done?

Cass R. Sunstein

We have seen that jurors face many problems in trying to generate a sensible system of punitive damages awards. This is not because people are irrational, inattentive, or stupid. It is because the tasks involved are extremely complex. Even the most sensible and informed of jurors is likely to run into problems, simply because of predictable features of human cognition. A major consequence is that many awards are arbitrary. Some awards are undoubtedly too high, indeed far too high. Some awards are undoubtedly too low, indeed far too low. What should be done about the situation?

We emphasize two possibilities here. First, judges should take a firmer role in overseeing jury awards. In such a system the judge would, among other things, measure the jury's award against other awards in similar cases, so as to ensure against extreme outliers—the most serious source of inconsistency and randomness. This would be a modest change from the current system. In an ideal world, judges would decrease awards that are indefensibly high and increase awards that are indefensibly low. The result would be to promote the rationality of the system and to decrease the overall level of unpredictability.

Second, serious consideration should be given to moving away from the jury and toward a system of civil fines, perhaps through a *damages schedule* of the sort that has been used in many areas of the law, including workers' compensation and environmental violations. This would be a more dramatic and radical shift, but it might be the best route for the future, on the ground that if properly devised, a damages schedule would overcome problems in the current system without compromising democratic or other goals. In fact, a large movement in modern law has been toward ensuring social judgments by administrators rather than juries.[1] For punitive damages, a shift in this direction would be fully consistent with many of the most important developments in twentieth-century law.

It is clear that even in the face of our findings, the question of punitive damages reform is not easy to answer in the abstract, above all because people disagree about the purpose of punitive damages awards. If the purpose of such awards is retribution—to impose a certain level of suffering on a defendant—the analysis would be different than if the purpose of such awards is to deter (optimally) future misconduct. Jury instructions typically run the two goals together; but we have seen that the goal of retribution does not march hand-in-hand with the goal of deterrence. For the moment the key point is that many people, including many lawyers and judges, are unsure about economic analysis of the deterrence issue, and any reform proposal that builds on economics will be controversial. But what we have found here should be far less controversial: Whatever one's views about the purpose of punitive damages awards, juries face extremely serious problems in producing sensible and coherent outcomes.

I. Legal Background

The question of punitive damages reform has acquired special salience in light of recent developments within the federal courts. In the landmark case of *BMW v. Gore,*[2] the Supreme Court struck down a punitive damages award as "excessive" and therefore as violative of the due process clause of the United States Constitution. In the *BMW* case, the plaintiff contended that BMW had allowed its cars to be repainted, without giving notice to purchasers of that fact. Gore had been awarded $4,000 in compensatory damages; the jury also awarded him $4 million (reduced to $2 million by the Alabama Supreme Court) in punitive damages. In ruling that this award violated the Constitution, the majority of the Supreme Court emphasized that it seemed grossly disproportionate and therefore excessive. The Court found it important that the $2 million award had no relationship to the compensatory award and to other penalties, recognized by the legal system, for acts of this sort.

For our purposes, a separate opinion by Justice Stephen Breyer is of

1. See Price V. Fishback and Shawn E. Kantor, *A Prelude to the Welfare State: The Origins of Workers' Compensation* (2000).

2. 116 S. Ct. 1589 (1996).

particular interest. To Justice Breyer, the most serious problem with the award in the *BMW* case was that it violated the rule of law. In his view, it did so because the jury was not given instructions that would limit its discretion and ensure some predictability for plaintiffs and defendants alike. Justice Breyer's basic concern was that with respect to punitive damages, the legal system provided practically unlimited discretion in the selection of civil punishments.

BMW has spurred new thinking about how to limit jury discretion in awarding punitive damages. Many litigants, faced with what they see as indefensibly high awards, have urged that the due process clause forbids the jury's judgment in their case. Courts are puzzled about how to respond to these challenges, because *BMW v. Gore* leaves many questions open. Decisions of lower courts are in disarray, despite a Supreme Court decision calling for careful appellate review of constitutional challenges to punitive awards.[3] And even when the Constitution is not at issue, *BMW* exerts an influence on judges: Courts asked to set aside jury judgments on unconstitutional grounds might, and do, avoid the constitutional question by announcing that the jury could not reasonably impose the award that it chose.

BMW v. Gore has also helped spur a flurry of activity in federal and state legislatures.[4] Perhaps Congress, or state government, should take action to limit jury discretion, error, or bias. In fact, many states have taken significant steps in this direction, by creating caps on awards, by separating the liability judgment and the punitive judgment, and by strengthening judicial review of jury practices. In the next decade there is little doubt that efforts of this kind will receive increasing attention.

This book is mostly descriptive, and we will not attempt, in this space, to give a full discussion of possible judicial and legislative reforms. Our more modest goal is to make some observations about how our findings might bear on that question—above all, through an exploration of the

3. *Cooper Industries v. Leatherman Tool Group*, 121 S. Ct. 1678 (2001). For the disarray, see, e.g., *Romano v. U-Haul Int'l.*, 233 F.3d 655 (1st Cir. 2000) (upholding a $285,000 award for civil rights violation); *Shaw v. Titan Corp.*, 1998 U.S. App. LEXIS 10080 (4th Cir. 1998) (upholding a $400,000 award for discriminatory discharge); *Rubinstein v. Administrators*, 218 F.3d 392 (5th Cir. 1998) ($75,000 award for religious discrimination found excessive); *EEOC v. HBE Corp.*, 135 F.3d 543 (8th Cir. 1998) ($4.8 million for racial discrimination and retaliatory discharge is excessive); *Deffenbaugh-Williams v. Wal-Mart Stores*, 156 F.3d 581 (5th Cir. 1998) ($100,000 for racially motivated termination is excessive).

4. For an overview, see "Developments in the Law—The Paths of Civil Litigation," 113 *Harv. L. Rev.* 1752 (2000).

modest reform of strengthened judicial review and the less-modest reform of a new system of civil fines.

II. Experiments and Real Juries

Ours have been experimental studies. In some instances our "juries" consisted of individuals who were given brief narrative descriptions of cases. In some experiments juries did not hear adversary arguments on both sides. A natural question, then, is whether the problems we observe would be eliminated or reduced in the real world of litigation.

There is good reason to think that the problems are not much reduced, if they are reduced at all. As we saw in chapter 3, deliberating juries actually produce more, not less, in the way of unpredictability. The fact that lawyers on both sides can typically exclude certain jurors may possibly reduce the degree of variance in real-world awards, at least if lawyers can anticipate which people will have unusual views that might press juries in unusual directions. On the other hand, variations in the quality of the lawyers, as well as the ability (or inability) of the plaintiff and defendant to hire first-rate counsel, are likely to increase the degree of randomness that we have identified. A well-funded plaintiff with a first-rate team of lawyers is likely to obtain a higher award than a poorly funded plaintiff represented by a solo practitioner, and our studies will not pick up any such effect. To this extent, our studies understate the variance shown in the real world.

Perhaps the most important difference between some (not all) of our studies and the real world is that the latter contains two usual anchors: plaintiff's demand and the jury's own prior determination of compensatory damages. As we saw in chapter 4, the plaintiff's demand is likely to have considerable importance; in general, the more you ask for, the more you get. There is real-world as well as experimental evidence of an anchoring effect from the compensatory award;[5] that award appears to stabilize the punitive award, at least to some degree, by providing a number to which jurors can refer. Indeed the anchoring effect of the compensatory award provides the basis for the widespread claim, made by some on the basis of real-world data, that unpredictability in punitive damages awards may not be an especially serious problem. In an important and influential paper, Theodore Eisenberg and his colleagues claim to have

5. See Theodore Eisenberg et al., "The Predictability of Punitive Damages," 26 *J. Legal Stud.* 623 (1997).

found, on the basis of a study of three thousand trials from seventy-five counties, that punitive awards are indeed predictable.[6]

If Eisenberg and his colleagues are correct, the problem of erratic awards is overstated. But we believe that the real-world data do not support their conclusion.[7] About one-third of the cases in their sample were routine automobile tort cases, and only about 17% were in the more volatile areas of products liability, medical malpractice, and toxic substance liability. Various summary statistics, such as punitive damages frequency or level, do not say a great deal about the sorts of cases that we have been emphasizing in this book.

For purposes of assessing predictability, the first issue is whether punitive damages will be awarded at all. Punitive damages awards seem to vary wildly in the cases studied by Eisenberg et al., with the percentage of plaintiffs' victories with punitive damages awards ranging from 0% to 27% by county. The sources of this variability are unclear; we do not know whether plaintiffs are simply bringing weaker cases in some places than in others, or whether randomness is at work. Support for the latter conclusion comes from the fact that the statistical model used by Eisenberg et al. explains only 12% of the variation in the probability of a punitive damages award. Even that estimate overstates how much liability defendants can anticipate, because in their model one of the explanatory variables is the value of the compensatory award, which is not known before the fact.

What about the level of awards? A close look at award levels reveals that they offer little predictive guidance to either plaintiffs or defendants. In Eisenberg et al., the claim that awards are predictable depends on assuming that there is going to be a nonzero punitive damages award. But whether there will be a punitive damages award is itself hard to predict. The key trial outcome values—the existence and level of the compensatory award—are unknown to the defendant at the time of the risky decision, or to the parties at the beginning of trial, so one needs a model to predict these levels as well before their values can be used to predict punitive awards. Although Eisenberg et al. present no such model, any estimates undoubtedly would involve substantial error.

In addition, it is not easy to foresee the amount of punitive awards

6. See *id.*

7. The following discussion draws heavily on W. Kip Viscusi, "Why There Is No Defense of Punitive Damages," 87 *Geo. L.J.* 381 (1998).

even if we know that there will be a compensatory award. Eisenberg et al. find that the compensatory award explains 46% to 47% of the variation in punitive damages awards, which still leaves the majority of the variation unexplained. But there is a more fundamental problem. The focus of their analysis is not on actual punitive damages awards, but on the *logarithm* of such awards, which is the dependent variable that they attempt to explain. Taking logs of award amounts compresses the extent of the variation in what is of actual concern to defendants and plaintiffs, which is the level of punitive damages, not its log. For defendants, a punitive damages award of $1 million is a thousand times worse than an award of $1,000—but in logs, being faced with the million-dollar award looks only twice as bad (that is, a log value of six versus three). Any transformation of real awards into log awards will naturally shrink much of the extreme variation in the size of punitive damages awards—and the transformation is for that reason misleading.

Indeed, a recent empirical study, based on a larger sample than that used by Eisenberg et al., confirms our finding that punitive awards "are highly variable and unpredictable."[8] The authors do find that compensatory awards, alongside other identifiable factors (such as lawsuit type, firm characteristics, and location of suit), can explain as much as 50% of the variation in punitive awards. But without prior information that there will be a punitive award, "only 1–2 percent of the variation in punitive awards can be explained."[9]

Eisenberg et al. have performed an extremely important service, one consistent with our findings here, in showing the large effect of the compensatory award on the punitive award. Anchors do matter (see chapter 4), and the compensatory award can serve as an anchor. But in terms of actual dollar awards, there remains a great deal of noise in the system, with a number of outlier cases containing inexplicably high awards. Nothing said thus far suggests that the high awards are too high. But when there is a wide range of possible awards, and when differences among them cannot be explained by reference to factors in the case, the legal system is not complying with the aspirations of the rule of law.

There is a further point. To the extent that it exists in any form, predictability comes with a problem of its own: introducing an additional

8. See Jonathan M. Karpoff and John R. Lott Jr., "On the Determinants and Importance of Punitive Damage Awards," 42 *J. L. & Econ.* 527, 571 (1999).
9. *Id.*

layer of arbitrariness, if (as is likely) the anchor is itself arbitrary on normative grounds. There is no reason to think that the plaintiff's demand should carry a great deal of weight in determining the proper award. The compensatory award might seem to be a better anchor, at least if we think that the punitive award should have some relationship to that award. But to the extent that punitive awards seem, often, to be double or triple the compensatory award, is it so clear that the system is not arbitrary? From the standpoint of either retribution or deterrence, the compensatory award should not have this kind of weight. We suspect that juries lacking evident anchors will suffer from the problems we have described, whereas juries resorting to anchors will produce a degree of predictability, but arbitrariness of an important sort, because verdicts amount to a kind of grasping at straws.

III. Predictability, the Rule of Law, and Strengthened Judicial Review

Some proposed reforms attempt to promote rule of law values through, for example, more careful and more specific judicial instructions. In the *BMW* case, Justice Breyer spoke in some detail about the failure of the law sufficiently to discipline jury discretion with clear criteria about the grounds of awards.[10] Thus, a possible response to complaints about arbitrary awards is to increase the specificity of instructions to juries.

Our data strongly support Justice Breyer's general concern, but they point to a source of variability very different from that emphasized by Justice Breyer. Contrary to the common view, the problem does not lie in insufficiently clear instructions to juries. The problem lies instead in various cognitive problems, including anchoring, misunderstanding complex instructions, and the difficulty of measuring attitudes in dollars. For purposes of obtaining the virtues associated with the rule of law, emphasized by Justice Breyer and many others, the solution lies not in clearer (and inevitably detailed) instructions to juries, but in counteracting the arbitrariness and potential for bias that comes from these cognitive problems.

It would therefore be reasonable to react to our studies by suggesting a simple reform: Juries should decide questions of civil *liability,* just as they do questions of criminal liability. But judges should play an exclusive or larger role in selecting the appropriate level of punitive damages—just

10. 116 S. Ct. at 1605–7.

as they do criminal punishment, where judges make the central determination, subject to guidelines laid down in advance. At the very least, judges should feel free to supervise punitive awards with some care, to make sure that they are sensible in light of the various goals of the legal system.

A minimal shift, then, would be to give clear directions to judges to scrutinize the award chosen by the jury, in part by making sure that the award in question is not out of line with other awards in similar cases. Certainly our findings provide strong support for the practice, found in some courts, of reviewing punitive awards to ensure that they are consistent with general outcomes in other cases. Judges need not fear that this practice is undemocratic or antipopulist, for as we have seen, the award of any particular jury may well fail to reflect the community's sentiment on the topic of appropriate dollar awards. A stronger judicial role could also help counteract any problems resulting from anchoring, hindsight bias, or misunderstanding of the jurors' task.

Nothing in this suggestion denies the claim that in some cases a very high punitive award is sensible, perhaps for purposes of retribution, perhaps to ensure greater deterrence. In some cases the defendant should be faced with a high award in part because the relevant harms will not often be detected and punished; perhaps sexual harassment is a case in point. In some cases a high punitive damages award is a good way of producing the right level of caution in risk-averse companies. What we are urging is not that high awards are senseless, but that they should be imposed only for good reasons, not because of arbitrary anchors, hindsight bias, neglect of judicial instructions, or scaling problems.

Of course there is a possible problem with judicial judgments about punitive awards, just as in the case of judicial choice of criminal sentences. In both cases different judges might well reach different conclusions, thus producing arbitrariness. We have seen that judges are not immune to the problems faced by jurors (even if the problems are reduced when judges are involved). Hence there is good reason for guidelines and constraints on judges. Examining comparison cases is a helpful place to start. There are many precedents for this approach. For example, judicially administered damages schedules and scaling through examples have been used successfully in the settlement of mass tort cases.[11] Such ideas have often

11. See Francis E. McGovern, "The Alabama DDT Settlement Fund," 53 *Law & Contemp. Probs.* 61 (1990); Francis E. McGovern, "Resolving Mature Mass Tort Litigation," 69 *B.U. L. Rev.* 659 (1989).

been discussed in the context of pain-and-suffering awards.[12] In a prominent case involving such awards, Judge Amalya Kearse, writing for the Second Circuit, attempted a careful comparison of the case at hand with twelve other cases.[13] Nor has comparison been unavailable in the context of punitive damages, at least in the process of judicial review.[14] In an influential case, the court of appeals for the Ninth Circuit said that a district court should compare other punitive damages cases to "a figure derived from the facts of the case at hand."[15] And comparison of cases is an occasional aspect of appellate review of punitive awards, furnishing a constraint on arbitrariness and inequality.[16]

The Supreme Court has not insisted on this requirement as a matter of constitutional law. In an echo of some early death penalty cases,[17] the Court said that each case might be taken as sui generis, because punitive damages judgments require juries to "make a qualitative assessment based on a host of facts and circumstances unique to the particular case before it. Because no two cases are truly identical, meaningful comparisons of such awards are difficult to make."[18] Thus, the Court said that a comparative approach cannot be a "'test' for assessing the constitutionality of punitive damage awards," even though it would not "rule out the possibility that the fact that an award is significantly larger than those

12. David Baldus et al., "Improving Judicial Oversight of Jury Damages Assessments: A Proposal for the Comparative Additur/Remittur Review of Awards for Nonpecuniary Harms and Punitive Damages," 80 *Iowa L. Rev.* 1109, 1122–225, 1134–37 (1995); Randall R. Bovbjerg et al., "Valuing Life and Limb in Tort: Scheduling 'Pain and Suffering,'" 83 *Nw. U. L. Rev.* 908 (1989).

13. 748 F.2d 740 (2d Cir. 1980).

14. See, e.g., *Bogan v. Stroud,* 958 F.2d 180, 186 (7th Cir. 1992); *Cash v. Beltmann N. Am. Co.,* 800 F.2d 109, 111 n. 3 (7th Cir. 1990); *Estate of Korf v. A. O. Smith,* 917 F.2d 480, 485 (10th Cir. 1990); *Ismail v. Cohen,* 899 F.2d 183, 186 (2d Cir. 1990); *Schultz v. Thomas,* 649 F. Supp. 620, 624–25 (E.D. Wis. 1986); *Sherrod v. Piedmont Aviation,* 516 F. Supp. 46, 56 (E.D. Tenn. 1978).

15. *Morgan v. Woessner,* 997 F.2d 1244, 1257 (9th Cir. 1993).

16. See *Klein v. Grynberg,* 44 F.3d 1497 (10th Cir. 1995); *Stafford v. Puro,* 63 F.3d 1436 (7th Cir. 1995); *Allahar v. Zahora,* 59 F.3d 693 (7th Cir. 1995); *Ross v. Black and Decker, Inc.,* 977 F.2d 1178 (7th Cir. 1992); *Vasbinder v. Scott,* 976 F.2d 118 (2nd Cir. 1992); *Kimzey v. Wal-Mart Stores, Inc.,* 107 F.3d 568 (8th Cir. 1997); *Lee v. Edwards,* 101 F.3d 805 (2nd Cir. 1996); *King v. Macri,* 993 F.2d 294 (2nd Cir. 1993); *Michelson v. Hamada,* 36 Cal. Rptr.2d 343 (Cal. Ct. App. 1994); *Wollersheim v. Church of Scientology,* 6 Cal. Rptr.2d 532 (Cal. Ct. App. 1992); *Baume v. 212 E. 10 N.Y. Bar Ltd.,* 634 N.Y.S.2d 478 (N.Y. App. Div. 1995); *Parkin v. Cornell University, Inc.,* 581 N.Y.S.2d 914 (N.Y. App. Div. 1992).

17. See *Woodson v. North Carolina,* 428 U.S. 280 (1976) (invalidating a mandatory death penalty statute).

18. *TXO Production Corp. v. Alliance Resources,* 509 U.S. 443, 457 (1993).

in apparently similar circumstances" might be relevant to the constitutional issue.[19]

The Court's reluctance to impose a constitutional requirement of comparing cases is understandable in light of the Court's caution about proceeding at the constitutional level in the face of principles of federalism and gaps in the Court's knowledge of the actual world of punitive damages awards. Nothing said here demonstrates that such a requirement would be sensible as a matter of constitutional law. But it is clear that a principal concern with the existing system stems from inadequate constraints on jury discretion, and it is now clear that a serious problem arises from the response mode of dollars and the difficulty of generating predictable dollar amounts. Our findings fortify the wisdom of the occasional appellate practice of comparing punitive damages awards, and they suggest the possibility of a constitutional problem with awards that appear, in practice, to be stabs in the dark. Comparison should become the rule, not the exception. It is therefore reasonable to say that the simplest reform, one broadly in line with current practice, would be to strengthen the hand of reviewing courts in the interest of increasing predictability.

Ideally, judicial review would increase indefensibly low awards and decrease unjustifiably high ones. This option is in fact available in many states, in which courts can engage in both *additur* and *remittitur.* Unfortunately, *additur* is unavailable in the federal courts, on the theory that increased awards would deprive a defendant of its right to a jury trial. But close judicial review of apparently excessive awards would be likely to help in reducing the problems that we have uncovered.

An intriguing recent paper, also by Eisenberg and colleagues,[20] uses archival evidence to compare punitive damages decisions made by judges with those made by juries in actual cases. The authors used data from a later year (1996) for the same set of seventy-five counties examined in the earlier Eisenberg et al. study of predictability. Their striking claim is that decisions made by judges and by juries differ little, either in the rate at which punitive damages are awarded or in the size of awards. The

19. Concurring, Justice Kennedy pointed to the high likelihood of legitimate inconsistency in jury results. Partly this is, in his view, a function of the fact that a jury is empaneled in a single case, not as a permanent body; partly this is a function of the generality of jury instructions (509 U.S. at 472).

20. Theodore Eisenberg, Neil LaFountain, Brian Ostrom, David Rottman, and Martin T. Wells, "Juries, Judges, and Punitive Damages: An Empirical Study," *Cornell L. Rev.* (forthcoming 2002).

authors do note—and it is not a trivial point—that awards by juries are somewhat more erratic than those made by judges.

How does this important evidence bear on our claims here? It would be tempting to urge that because there is a rough aggregate similarity between decisions by judges and juries, it does not matter who makes these decisions. But we think that this conclusion would be premature. In particular, this paper's analysis contains from what the authors acknowledge to be a significant gap—the data set does not provide information about whether the cases routed to judges are of the same character as those routed to juries.[21] Because of this gap, the evidence does not show that judges would make the same decision as juries in particular cases. For now, the degree of similarity or difference between judge and jury decisions in this domain must remain an open question.

Even if judges and juries do produce similar decisions, our basic claims here would not be much affected. We have provided experimental evidence that in this domain judges are somewhat better than jurors at overcoming certain biases. But we have also emphasized that judges, like jurors, are human and therefore subject to the same cognitive problems as everyone else. Much more fundamentally, we have urged not that punitive damages decisions should be simply reallocated from juries to judges, but that some of the problems that we have discussed might be reduced if judges were explicitly required to make comparisons to other relevant cases, in the course of reviewing jury decisions. It is far from clear that judges would make the appropriate comparisons without being required to do so.

A. Damages Schedules: From Juries to Administrators

Now let us turn to the more dramatic alternative: dispensing with the jury entirely. Consider, for example, a schedule of fines and penalties, overseen by administrative officials of the sort that now impose the civil penalties imposed by the Environmental Protection Agency, the Federal Aviation Administration, the Internal Revenue Service, the Occupational Safety and Health Administration, and many more. In its ideal form, the damages schedule would be developed after extensive discus-

21. Indeed, the authors themselves note several probable differences between jury and bench trials in the frequency of types of cases (e.g., tort trials, medical malpractice, contract cases) and in the severity of harm to the plaintiff. There are also large differences between counties in the relative frequencies of jury and bench trials for different types of cases, which suggests the existence of still other differences in routing decisions as well.

sion within the democratic process, discussion informed by specialists in the topics at hand.

As compared with the current approach, such a system would have many advantages. It would simplify matters, thus reducing the costs of litigation and decision. It would dramatically increase predictability. It should increase fairness, by ensuring that similarly situated people will be treated similarly. To the extent that officials seek to pursue optimal deterrence, a system of civil fines could be designed with that goal in mind.

There are many analogies for this proposal. These include both reform proposals in closely related domains and real-world precedents, in which ad hoc determinations have been replaced with a system designed to produce more in the way of coherence and rationality. Consider the following examples:

- The system of workers' compensation was created partly because of the randomness, and high litigation costs, produced by case-by-case jury judgments about, for example, the value of a lost limb.[22] In its current form, workers' compensation attempts to deal with problems of valuation by placing a fixed-dollar value on various injuries through a predetermined schedule produced by a legislature or administrative agency.
- In a related but more recent shift, the process of case-by-case judgment with respect to sentencing has been replaced by the more standardized sentencing guidelines. A central goal of the guidelines is to discipline the process of "mapping" complex normative judgments onto a relatively less-bounded scale of criminal punishments. The fact that judges, rather than juries, have traditionally made decisions about appropriate sentences raises a question about why a similar course is not followed for punitive damages.[23] The basic point is that in both of these cases, a process of bureaucratic rationalization has replaced one of relatively ad hoc judgments; it is easy to imagine a similar development with punitive damages.

22. See Fishback and Kantor, *supra* note 1.

23. There are, of course, differences between the two settings. The distinctive stigma associated with criminal punishment may make it seem especially important to insulate judgments from the kinds of passion and zeal that might operate in a jury. That stigma may also make a degree of specialized experience, and even guidelines, especially important. And juries do, of course, have some control over sentencing through choices about criminal liability, especially when there are different theories of liability.

• A useful model can be found in the "grid" used for social security disability determinations, which uses age, educational attainment, and residual functional capacity to produce standardized judgments about disability.[24] Administrative law judges are asked to make case-specific judgments, which become part of an assessment governed by the rulelike grid. It is helpful to ask, as a thought experiment, why juries, rather than grid-governed administrative law judges, are not asked to make disability determinations. Surely the answer is that jury determinations would suffer from a range of problems, including insufficient specialization and expertise, inevitable arbitrariness and unpredictability, and confusion stemming from the use of an unfamiliar scale.

• Discussion of pain-and-suffering awards has included many suggestions designed substantially to reduce the jury's role in the interest of more consistent and more expert judgments.[25]

• In the context of damages to natural resources, it has been suggested that contingent valuation should be replaced by a schedule of damages based on categories of harm.[26] In this way, an antecedent set of administrative or legislative judgments would form the backdrop for judgments by a trustee, thus making it unnecessary to ask what may be hopelessly uninformative questions of individuals about their willingness to pay.

• One of the most important developments of twentieth-century law has been the general rise of civil penalties, imposed by administrative agencies and displacing traditional jury judgments. Those who harm the environment or injure wildlife or expose workers to risks are subject to a system of damages through which agencies attempt to ensure a measure of sense and rationality.

Of course, none of these reforms is directly analogous to the domain of punitive damages. Compensatory awards, as in the cases of workers' compensation and pain and suffering, might well be easier to handle administratively—above all, because no punitive element is supposed to be

24. Jerry L. Mashaw, *Bureaucratic Justice: Managing Social Security Disability Claims* (1983).

25. See Baldus et al., *supra* note 12, at 1125–31; Bovbjerg et al., *supra* note 12, at 923.

26. See Richard B. Stewart, "Damages to Natural Resources," in *Analyzing Superfund: Economics, Science, and Law* 219, 241–44 (Richard L. Revesz and Richard B. Stewart eds., 1995).

involved. But if jury determinations are unpredictable, and if jurors are subject to various cognitive biases, it is worthwhile to consider the possibility of penalizing wrongdoers not through jury judgments but through civil fines. To those who think that this is an unacceptably undemocratic measure, the best response might involve the workers' compensation system. For all its problems, no one seriously urges that we should return to a system in which juries grasp at numbers to provide appropriate compensation. In fact, the workers' compensation system commanded an extraordinary consensus from those frustrated by the unreliable use of jury awards. Might not something similar make sense here? To those who urge a negative answer, the best response might involve the system of civil fines administered by the Environmental Protection Agency and the Occupational Safety and Health Administration. Do many people think that this system of fines should be replaced by ad hoc jury judgments?

To be sure, we have not said nearly enough to justify the abolition of punitive damages awards from juries. Radical changes of this kind inevitably call for a comparison of the likely performance of different governmental institutions. It is sensible to fear that administrative substitutes for the jury would be subject to problems of their own—perhaps because of their own biases, and perhaps because of the pressures likely to be imposed by well-organized private groups. Such changes might also be challenged on the ground that the populist elements of jury assessment should be retained, in order to ensure that public outrage plays a significant role in the legal system—perhaps because of its legitimating effect, providing people with a kind of assurance that the public has been directly consulted. If so, the more modest reforms are better. What we have sought to do here is to undertake the first step toward the necessary evaluation: providing a better understanding of what produces unpredictability and error in punitive awards.

IV. Mixed Approaches, Caps, and Multipliers

It is possible to imagine mixed approaches. We offer a brief discussion, not to urge final judgments, but to bring the various possibilities in contact with our findings and with the reforms that we have emphasized thus far.

If unpredictability is the major problem, a jury might be provided with a preselected set of "exemplar cases," accompanied by the damages actually or reasonably awarded in these cases. The jury's job might be to assess damages by comparing the case at hand to the preselected cases. This approach would not take the whole subject of dollar awards away from the jury. More modestly, it would attempt to root punitive awards in a set of judgments that could reasonably be compared with the case at hand. The damages in the exemplar cases might be based on actual past judgments, on judgments of mock juries, or on judgments of experts in the particular area. Similar approaches might attempt to supply a kind of modulus. Juries might, for example, be given average dollar awards for the type of injury at issue, or intervals (showing where a certain percentage of awards for similar injuries fell), or both average dollar awards and intervals. Doubtless a degree of experimentation would help show which approach works best.

Currently, both the federal government and the states are discussing more conventional reforms, which would impose caps or require punitive damages to be within some multiple of compensatory damages. It is clear that caps would reduce the problems associated with unjustifiably high awards, and for that reason they might seem a sensible response to some of the problems that we have identified. So too with multipliers, which have an additional advantage of simplicity. But our findings do not provide unambiguous support for caps and multipliers. To be sure, both reforms might do some good if the problem is that isolated juries come up with arbitrary or unpredictable outcomes. But there is evidence that a cap can even increase unjustified arbitrariness in awards: If the jury is aware of the cap, it might serve as an anchor for some jury judgments, thus producing more variability than there would otherwise be.[27] Perhaps the best that can be said about a cap is that with little administrative cost, it will eliminate the most egregiously large judgments. But this virtue comes with a vice: If the cap is too low, it will prevent large judgments that are entirely justified. In any case a cap does not respond to many of the problems that we have identified, including anchoring, hindsight bias, scaling issues, and difficulties in following judicial instructions.

A damages multiplier might be a bit better, in the sense that it would also reduce the complexity of the decision while allowing more flexibil-

---

27. See Michael J. Saks et al., "Reducing Variability in Civil Jury Awards," 21 *Law & Hum. Behav.* 243 (1997) (finding that caps are likely to increase variability in the context of noneconomic compensatory losses). See also Verlin B. Hinsz and Kristin E. Indahl, "Assimilation to Anchors for Damage Awards in a Mock Civil Trial," 25 *J. Applied Soc. Psychol.* 991 (1995) (finding anchoring effect from caps).

ity than a cap by permitting very high awards when the compensatory damages are especially serious. But any multiplier would have crudeness of its own. No theory of punitive damages justifies a multiplier approach.

For those sympathetic to the economic approach to risk management, there is an additional issue. If the problem is that juries are not now made to think in terms of optimal deterrence, both of these approaches seem extremely crude. There is no reason to think that either of these reforms would ensure that punitive awards are tailored to compensate for the likelihood that injured parties will not bring suit. If optimal deterrence is the goal, the best solution would be to abandon the jury and to delegate power to an institution willing and able to think well about optimal deterrence.

Of the less-ambitious reforms, a shift from jury to judicial determinations of punitive damages, or to more in the way of judicial supervision of awards, appears to be the most promising. The most important problem is that judges too are likely to have some of the shortcomings discussed here—including difficulties in mapping normative judgments onto dollar amounts. Some evidence supports the view that judges and juries do not much differ in punitive damages judgments.[28] Even if the judicial role is strengthened, there are likely to be continuing problems of erratic judgments or use of anchors that introduce arbitrariness of their own (see chapter 11). Judicially assessed punitive awards might well replicate some of the problems with judicially determined sentences.

Thus any movement from jury to judicial control of punitive damages awards might well be accompanied by some effort to discipline the process of scaling. As we have suggested, various reform combinations and alternatives might be imagined, including dollar awards that are chosen after exposure to comparison cases. Some judges have suggested that puntive awards should be assessed through careful comparisons to other awards in analogous cases.[29] This is a practice on which many courts should build.

28. See Theodore Eisenberg et al., "Juries, Judges, and Punitive Damages: An Empirical Study," Social Science Research Network (December 12, 2000) at http://papers.ssrn.com; Jennifer K. Robbennolt, "Punitive Damage Decision Making: The Decisions of Citizens and Trial Court Judges," Social Science Research Network (December 11, 2000) at http://papers.ssrn.com (*Law & Hum. Behav.* forthcoming 2001).

29. Compare Judge Weinstein's fascinating discussion of the use of comparison cases in the context of pain and suffering in *Geres v. Digital Equipment,* 980 F. Supp. 640, 657–60 (E.D. N.Y. 1997).

V. General Conclusions

Our empirical findings do not point directly to social reforms. But they do provide some support for a modest and incremental step, building on current practice: ensuring, in every jurisdiction, a serious oversight role for judges, calling not for individual judicial judgments about individual cases, but for judicial comparisons among various similar cases, so as to promote predictability, to respond to clear mistakes, and to ensure against dramatic outlier awards.

If our findings are correct, perhaps the ideal system of punitive damages awards would not involve juries or even judges, but specialists in the subject matter at hand, who would be able to create clear guidelines for punitive awards. These guidelines would be laid down in advance and based on a clear understanding of different forms of wrongdoing and of the social consequences of different awards. Dramatic though it might sound, a system of this kind can find support in the civil fines now imposed by many regulatory agencies. The practical question is whether it is possible to design that ideal system. The findings in this book do not resolve that question. But they do suggest that the current approach is very far from ideal. In imposing civil punishments for misconduct, a well-functioning legal system should be able to do much better.

Appendix

Judge's Instructions

Taken from *Jardel Company, Inc., et al. v. K. Hughes* (Supreme Court of Delaware, 1987).

The judge has given you the following instructions that you are required by law to use in deciding whether or not to award punitive damages.

The purposes of punitive damages are to punish a defendant and to deter a defendant and others from committing similar acts in the future.

Plaintiff has the burden of proving that punitive damages should be awarded by a preponderance of the evidence. You may award punitive damages only if you find that the defendant's conduct

(1) was malicious; or
(2) manifested reckless or callous disregard for the rights of others.

Conduct is malicious if it is accompanied by ill will, or spite, or if it is for the purpose of injuring another.

In order for conduct to be in reckless or callous disregard of the rights of others, four factors must be present. First, a defendant must be subjectively conscious of a particular grave danger or risk of harm, and the danger or risk must be a foreseeable and probable effect of the conduct. Second, the particular danger or risk of which the defendant was subjectively conscious must in fact have eventuated. Third, a defendant must have disregarded the risk in deciding how to act. Fourth, a defendant's conduct in ignoring the danger or risk must have involved a gross deviation from the level of care which an ordinary person would use, having due regard to all the circumstances.

Reckless conduct is not the same as negligence. Negligence is the failure to use such care as a reasonable, prudent, and careful person would use under similar circumstances. Reckless conduct differs from negligence in that it requires a conscious choice of action, either with knowledge of serious danger to others or with knowledge of facts which would disclose the danger to any reasonable person.

To "establish by a preponderance of the evidence" means to prove that something is more likely so than not so. In other words, a preponderance of the evidence in the case means such evidence, when considered and compared with that opposed to it, has more convincing force, and produces in your minds belief that what is sought to be proved is more likely true than not true.

In your decisions on issues of fact, a corporation is entitled to the same fair trial at your hands as a private individual. All persons, including corporations, partnerships, and other organizations, stand equal before the law, and are to be dealt with by the judge and jury as equals in a court of justice.

The verdict must represent the considered judgment of each juror. In order to return a verdict, it is necessary that each juror agree thereto. Your verdict must be unanimous.

Upon retiring to the jury room, you will select one of your number to act as your presiding juror. The presiding juror will preside over your deliberations.

Glossary

ad damnum Refers to the section of a petition containing claims for damages, usually in terms of dollars.

additur Amount added to a jury's financial award by the trial judge or appellate court.

analysis of variance Statistical method used to analyze empirical studies to determine if experimental manipulations have a causal effect on measures of outcomes or behavior. The name of the method comes from the underlying strategy of the analysis whereby variance in an individual measure is separated into effects attributable to causal variables (usually experimental manipulations) and to unsystematic error or noise. Thus, the test of whether a manipulated treatment had an effect on the measure is to compare the variance due to the effect to the unsystematic error variance. If this ratio, called an F-ratio (after R. A. Fisher, the inventor of the method of the analysis), is large, the effect is deemed statistically significant or reliable. (N.B., the underlying statistical model for analysis of variance is the same as for regression analysis, *see* regression analysis and multiple regression, below.)

anchor Starting point or reference amount used in reasoning to a quantity or other magnitude. Likely to play a major determining role in the assessment of degrees of confidence, causality, responsibility, or a dollar-award amount.

anchor-and-adjust strategy Heuristic whereby a juror assesses a magnitude, for example, a dollar award, by starting from a salient anchor amount, and then adjusting from it by factoring in additional considerations.

bench trial Trial in which a judge, rather than a jury, serves as the decision maker.

benefit-cost analysis *See* cost-benefit analysis.

bifurcated procedure A trial in two parts. The first part establishes liability and compensatory damages. A second phase decides punitive damages.

bounded numerical scale Range of numbers, defined at each end by an anchor and an upper limit.

cap Defined upper limit or ceiling; for example, a total dollar amount that cannot be exceeded by a jury in assessing a punitive damages award.

category scale Range that is defined and bounded by verbal descriptions.

choice shift Tendency of group discussion to produce a group decision that is shifted away from the mode, mean, or median of the initial, individual group members' positions. A typical finding is that the group shift moves to a more extreme position away from the midpoint of the scale on which the decision is expressed (*see* group polarization).

closing argument Final statement by the attorney for one litigant of a lawsuit. Usually summarizes the evidence and that litigant's position.

cognitive engineering The design of intellectual tasks to capitalize on an effective match of human capabilities to the demands of the tasks.

compensatory damages Dollar amount awarded to the plaintiff to compensate for physical, emotional, or financial losses attributable to the defendant's acts.

contingent valuation Survey method used to estimate the value of a good, such as an environmental good, that is difficult to value because it does not have a market. Respondents are typically asked how much they would be willing to pay for preservation or restoration of the environmental feature that has been harmed.

correlation coefficient A single number expressing the strength of the linear relationship between two sets of paired numbers. The correlation coefficient, abbreviated r, ranges from $+1.00$, representing a perfect direct linear relationship, to -1.00, representing a perfect indirect relationship, with 0.00 indicating the absence of any linear relationship.

cost-benefit analysis Systematic evaluation to determine if a project or action is likely to yield a global benefit or loss. The traditional evaluation requires the estimation of all potential costs and benefits of the action on quantitative scales and then the numerical calculation of a comprehensive summary utility or net value.

damages schedule Predetermined list of fines and penalties to be imposed for specific damages.

defendant In a lawsuit, the party that is accused of harming the plaintiff.

deliberation-shift analysis An empirical examination of the relationship between the postdeliberation verdict of a jury and the predeliberation judgments of the individual jurors.

deliberation-shift measure (DSM) A statistic summarizing the difference between the observed and the predicted rank of a jury verdict, as a percentage of the maximum possible shift in the same direction.

ex ante Before the event.

ex post After the event.

exemplar cases Previously decided cases offered to suggest standards for use by jurors.

group polarization The tendency of deliberating groups to reach more extreme conclusions than the median initial position (*see* choice shift).

hindsight bias The tendency to believe, after an event has occurred, that the outcome should or could have been anticipated.

hung jury A jury that is unable to reach a unanimous decision.

jury instructions Information about procedures and the applicable law, given by the judge to the jury before they begin deliberation.

Learned Hand formula A method for determining if a defendant is negligent and hence liable for having taken insufficient precaution before an accident.

The formula says the defendant is liable if the cost of taking the necessary precautions was less than the cost of the harm multiplied by the event's probability of occurrence. Named for Judge Learned Hand, who served on the U.S. Court of Appeals.

liability Legal responsibility.

magnitude scale Unbounded scale with a meaningful zero point. Examples are brightness of light, loudness of sound, heaviness of weight, or, in legal contexts, a dollar scale for damages.

malicious Having intent to harm.

mean A measure of the central value in a set of numbers: the arithmetic average of a group of numbers.

median A measure of the central value in a set of numbers: the middle value of a group of numbers; the point that divides a set of numbers into two equal halves.

mock jury Group of individuals performing as a jury in a simulated trial setting.

mode A measure of the typical value in a set of numbers; the most common or frequent number in the set.

modulus A standard or norm; for example, the unit of measurement on a scale.

multiple regression analysis *See* regression analysis.

negligence Failure to use such care as a reasonable, prudent, and careful person would use under similar circumstances.

noise In a scientific experiment, unwanted error that tends to obscure the true values of measured variables.

opening statement Statement by attorney to the jury before the presentation of actual evidence. Usually describes the facts of the case and the evidence to be presented and suggests the jury verdict desired by the attorney.

optimal deterrence The theoretical level of penalty that discourages undesirable behavior while not discouraging desirable behavior.

outlier An observation data point that deviates from most of the rest of the data in a sample or experimental treatment condition. More formally, an outlier is an observation that is distinctive or inconsistent with a model of the process that is assumed to generate the data.

plaintiff The party that files a lawsuit claiming compensation for harm.

Polinsky-Shavell instructions Instructions to jurors on how to set punitive damages awards so as to achieve optimal deterrence (developed by A. Mitchell Polinsky and Steven Shavell). Jurors are directed to calculate total damages by multiplying the compensatory damages award by the reciprocal of the probability of the injurer being found liable when he is truly liable.

post hoc Afterward.

products liability Liability of manufacturers for damages suffered because of defects in their product.

punitive damages Financial damages that are levied with the purpose of punishing a defendant and deterring that defendant and others from repeating the act.

recklessness As defined in typical juror instructions on punitive damages: Behavior in callous disregard of the rights of others. Four factors must be present for behavior to be classed as reckless. First, a defendant must be conscious of a particular risk or danger, and the danger or harm must be a foreseeable and probable effect of the behavior. Second, the particular risk or danger must in fact have eventuated. Third, the defendant must have disregarded the risk in deciding how to act. Fourth, the defendant's behavior in ignoring the danger or risk must have involved a gross deviation from the level of care that an ordinary person would use.

regression analysis In statistics, an analysis of the degree to which variations in one or more independent, predictor variables affect a dependent, criterion variable. The basic strategy of the analysis is to propose an algebraic model that relates the predictor variables to the criterion variable and then to estimate parameter values for the equation in a manner that provides a best fit, with reference to minimizing the sum of the squared errors of prediction (the differences between the criterion value predicted by the best-fitting equation and the actual observed criterion values). This criterion for goodness of fit is responsible for the alternate label for the method, "least squares regression analysis."

remittitur Reduction by the trial judge or an appellate court in the amount of a jury's award.

rhetorical asymmetry Advantage to one side during group deliberation in ease of producing persuasive arguments; rhetorical asymmetry tends to produce a preponderance of verdicts in a direction favoring the side with the advantage.

risk analysis Assessment of the probabilities and magnitudes of social, health, economic, and other consequences of specific actions. The procedure involves identifying hazards, estimating their potential magnitudes, and investigating means and costs for reducing the hazards.

root-mean-squared error (RMSE) Conventional measure of accuracy of estimation, which is analogous to the standard deviation of a data distribution.

schedule of damages *See* damages schedule.

sentencing guidelines Rules given to judges for setting punishment for specific crimes committed under specified conditions.

severity shift Tendency of jury deliberation to increase dollar awards over the median of individual predeliberation juror judgments. The dollar amount awarded by a jury is typically higher than the median judgment of the same jury's individual members before deliberation.

significance test A statistical procedure that is frequently used to assess the reliability or importance of a measure of an effect or a relationship in the data from an experiment or other empirical study (e.g., the effect in an analysis of variance, the correlational relationship between two variables). The result of a significance test is usually expressed as a *p*-value, which is the probability that the observed effect is not equal to zero or a null result (assuming a model in which the null result is true). The method is generally used in the behavioral sciences as a standard to determine if an empirical result is worthy of acceptance or consideration, although the exclusive reliance on significance tests for this purpose is highly controversial.

simulated jury *See* synthetic jury.

simulation Artificial creation of a situation that is analogous to a real situation, often for the purpose of conducting a controlled experiment or estimating a statistical value.

Spearman rank correlation An index of agreement between rankings that is determined by first converting each column to ranks and then computing the Pearson product moment correlation between the two sets of ranks.

standard deviation Measure of the dispersion or variability of data around its mean. The standard deviation is the square root of the variance of a distribution of numbers.

sui generis Unique.

synthetic jury Jury verdict created without deliberation by mathematically combining decisions of a sample of six or twelve individuals randomly drawn from the total pool of jurors. Same as "simulated jury."

taboo trade-off An equivalence that is viewed by society as inappropriate, for example, a monetary amount defined as appropriate to spend for averting a statistical human death.

unbounded scale Numerical scale having no limit at either one or both ends.

uncertainty Incomplete information or inability to predict the outcomes of a situation or process.

value of life The amount, determined by various methods, that is appropriate to spend per statistical death averted; often used in cost-benefit calculations.

variance In statistics, a measure of the dispersion or variability of a set of numbers around its mean value. The variance is calculated as the sum of the squared deviations of each number in the set from the mean value, divided by the number of values in the set.

voir dire Pretrial examination used to determine the suitability of individuals to serve on a jury.

wantonness Maliciousness, gratuitous cruelty.

wealth-redistribution hypothesis Idea that some decision makers (e.g., juries) are motivated to redistribute wealth from one party or account to other parties.

willful On purpose, deliberate.

willingness to pay Estimate by a person of the amount they would be willing to spend for a particular good or service, or to alter some hypothetical condition, for example, a defined environmental harm.

zero-risk mentality Expectation that the risk or harm or loss in a given situation can be reduced to zero.

Bibliography

Anderson, Michelle C., and Robert J. MacCoun. "Goal Conflict in Juror Assessments of Compensatory and Punitive Damages." 23(3) *Law and Human Behavior* 313–30 (1999).

Anderson, Norman H. *Foundations of Information Integration Theory.* New York: Academic Press, 1981.

Arkes, Hal R., and Cindy A. Schipani. "Medical Malpractice v. the Business Judgment Rule: Differences in Hindsight Bias." 73(3) *Oregon Law Review* 587–638 (1994).

Aronson, Peter, David E. Rovella, and Bob Van Voris. "Jurors: A Biased, Independent Lot; An NLJ-DecisionQuest Poll Finds Potential Jurors Will Ignore a Judge and Don't Like Big Business." 21(10) *National Law Journal* A1 (November 2, 1998).

Babcock, Linda, and Greg Pogarsky. "Damage Caps and Settlement: A Behavioral Approach." 28(2) *Journal of Legal Studies* 341–70 (1999).

Bailis, Daniel S., and Robert J. MacCoun. "Estimating Liability Risks with the Media as Your Guide: A Content Analysis of Media Coverage of Tort Litigation." 20(4) *Law and Human Behavior* 419–29 (1996).

Baldus, David, John C. MacQueen, and George Woodworth. "Improving Judicial Oversight of Jury Damages Assessments: A Proposal for the Comparative Additur/Remittur Review of Awards for Nonpecuniary Harms and Punitive Damages." 80(5) *Iowa Law Review* 1109–267 (1995).

Baron, Jonathan, R. Gowda, and Howard Kunreuther. "Attitudes toward Managing Hazardous Waste—What Should Be Cleaned Up and Who Should Pay for It?" 13(2) *Risk Analysis* 183–92 (1993).

Baron, Jonathan, and Ilana Ritov. "Intuitions about Penalties and Compensation in the Context of Tort Law." 7(1) *Journal of Risk and Uncertainty* 17–33 (1993).

Bentham, Jeremy. "Principles of Penal Law." In *The Works of Jeremy Bentham,* ed. John Bowring. Vol. 1, 365. New York: Russell & Russell, 1962.

Biddle, Frederic M. "GM Verdict Cut $3.8 Billion in Suit over Explosion." *Wall Street Journal* B5 (August 27, 1999).

Bodenhausen, Galen V. "Second-Guessing the Jury: Stereotypic and Hindsight Biases in Perceptions of Court Cases." 20(3) *Journal of Applied Social Psychology* 1112–21 (1990).

Bovbjerg, Randall R., Frank A. Sloan, and James F. Blumstein. "Valuing Life and Limb in Tort: Scheduling 'Pain and Suffering.'" 83(4) *Northwestern University Law Review* 908–76 (1989).

Breyer, Stephen G. *Breaking the Vicious Circle: Toward Effective Risk Regulation.* Cambridge: Harvard University Press, 1993.

Brown, Roger William. *Social Psychology.* New York: Free Press; 2nd ed. London: Collier Macmillan, 1986.

Calabresi, Guido, and Philip Bobbitt. *Tragic Choices.* New York: Norton, 1978.

California Jury Instructions, Civil; Book of Approved Jury Instructions, ed. Paul G. Breckenridge. 8th ed. St. Paul, Minn.: West Publishing, 1994.

Cather, Corinne, Edith Greene, and Robert Durham. "Plaintiff Injury and Defendant Reprehensibility: Implications for Compensatory and Punitive Damage Awards." 20(2) *Law and Human Behavior* 189–205 (1996).

Chapman, Gretchen B., and Brian H. Bornstein. "The More You Ask for, the More You Get: Anchoring in Personal Injury Verdicts." 10(6) *Applied Cognitive Psychology* 519–40 (1996).

Cooter, Robert D. "Economic Analysis of Punitive Damages." 56(1) *Southern California Law Review* 79–101 (1982).

———. "Punitive Damages for Deterrence: When and How Much?" 40(3) *Alabama Law Review* 1143–96 (1989).

Cooter, Robert D., and Daniel L. Rubinfeld. "Economic Analysis of Legal Disputes and Their Resolution." 27(3) *Journal of Economic Literature* 1067–97 (1989).

Craswell, Richard. "Deterrence and Damages: The Multiplier Principle and Its Alternatives." 97(7) *Michigan Law Review* 2185–238 (1999).

Daniels, Stephen, and Joanne Martin. "Myth and Reality in Punitive Damages." 75(1) *Minnesota Law Review* 1–64 (1990).

Davis, James H. "Group Decision and Social Interaction—A Theory of Social Decision Schemes." 80(2) *Psychological Review* 97–125 (1973).

"Developments in the Law—The Paths of Civil Litigation." 113(7) *Harvard Law Review* 1752–875 (2000)

Diamond, Shari S., and Jonathan D. Casper. "Blindfolding the Jury to Verdict Consequences: Damages, Experts, and the Civil Jury." 26(3) *Law & Society Review* 513–63 (1992).

Dobbs, Dan B. "Ending Punishment in 'Punitive' Damages: Deterrence-Measured Remedies." 40(3) *Alabama Law Review* 831–917 (1989).

Douglas, Mary. *Risk and Blame: Essays in Cultural Theory.* London: Routledge, 1992.

Dowie, Mark. "Pinto Madness: *Mother Jones* Has Obtained Secret Documents Showing that for Seven Years the Ford Motor Company Sold Cars in Which It Knew Hundreds of People Would Needlessly Burn to Death." 2 *Mother Jones* 18–24 (September–October 1977).

Dreyfus, Mark, and W. Kip Viscusi. "Rates of Time Preference and Consumer Valuations of Automobile Safety and Fuel Efficiency." 38(1) *Journal of Law and Economics* 79–105 (1995).

Eades, Ronald W. *Jury Instructions on Damages in Tort Actions.* 4th ed. Charlottesville, Va.: Lexis Law Publishers, 1998.

Eades, Ronald W., and Graham Douthwaite. *Jury Instructions on Damages in Tort Actions.* 3rd ed. Charlottesville, Va.: Michie and Company, 1993.

Economic Abstract of Alabama 2000, ed. Deborah Hamilton. Tuscaloosa: University of Alabama Center for Business and Economic Research, 2000.

Eisenberg, Theodore, John Goerdt, Brian Ostrom, David Rottman, and Martin T. Wells. "The Predictability of Punitive Damages." 26(2) *Journal of Legal Studies* 623–61 (1997).

Eisenberg, Theodore, Neil LaFountain, Brian Ostrom, David Rottman, and Martin Wells. "Juries, Judges, and Punitive Damages: An Empirical Study." Social Science Research Network (December 12, 2000) at http://papers.ssrn.com.

Ellsworth, Phoebe C., and Samuel R. Gross. "Hardening of the Attitudes: Americans' Views on the Death Penalty." 50(2) *Journal of Social Issues* 19–52 (1994).

Feigenson, Neal. *Legal Blame: How Jurors Think and Talk about Accidents.* Washington, D.C.: American Psychological Association Books, 2000.

Feigenson, Neal, Jaihyun Park, and Peter Salovey. "Effect of Blameworthiness and Outcome Severity on Attributions of Responsibility and Damage Awards in Comparative Negligence Cases." 21 *Law and Human Behavior* 597–617 (1997).

Fincham, Frank D., and Joseph M. Jaspars. "Attribution of Responsibility: From Man the Scientist to Man as Lawyer." 13 *Advances in Experimental Social Psychology* 81–138 (1980).

Finkel, Norman J. *Commonsense Justice: Jurors' Notions of the Law.* Cambridge: Harvard University Press, 1995.

Fischhoff, Baruch. "Hindsight ≠ Foresight: The Effect of Outcome Knowledge on Judgment under Uncertainty." 1(3) *Journal of Experimental Psychology: Human Perception and Performance* 288–99 (1975).

Fischhoff, Baruch, Sarah Lichtenstein, Paul Slovic, Stephen L. Derby, and Ralph L. Keeney. *Acceptable Risk.* New York: Cambridge University Press, 1981.

Fishback, Price V., and Shawn E. Kantor. *A Prelude to the Welfare State: The Origins of Workers' Compensation.* Chicago: University of Chicago Press, 2000.

Galanter, Marc. "Real World Torts: An Antidote to Anecdote." 55(4) *Maryland Law Review* 1093–160 (1996).

Garber, Steven. "Punitive Damages and Deterrence of Efficiency—Promoting Analysis: A Problem without a Solution?" 52(6) *Stanford Law Review* 1809–20 (2000).

Garber, Steven, and Anthony G. Bower. "Newspaper Coverage of Automotive Product Liability Verdicts." 33(1) *Law and Human Behavior* 93–122 (1999).

Ghiaridi, James D., and John J. Kircher. *Punitive Damages: Law and Practice.* Deerfield, Ill.: Clark, Boardman and Callaghan, 1995.

Gigerenzer, Gerd, and Ulrich Hoffrage. "How to Improve Bayesian Reasoning without Instruction—Frequency Formats." 102(4) *Psychological Review* 684–704 (1995).

Glassner, Barry. *The Culture of Fear: Why Americans Are Afraid of the Wrong Things.* New York: Basic Books, 1999.

"GM Vows to Appeal California Judge's Order Cutting Record Punitive Award to $1.2 Billion." 27(35) *Bureau of National Affairs Product Safety & Liability Reporter* 866 (September 3, 1999).

Grether, David M., and Charles R. Plott. "Economic Theory of Choice and the Preference Reversal Phenomenon." 69(4) *American Economic Review* 623–38 (1979).

Gross, Samuel R., and Kent D. Syverud. "Getting to No: A Study of Settlement

Negotiations and the Selection of Cases for Trial." 90(2) *Michigan Law Review* 319–93 (1991).

Hamilton, James T., and W. Kip Viscusi. *Calculating Risks? The Spatial and Political Dimensions of Hazardous Waste Policy.* Vol. 21, Regulation of Economic Activity Series. Cambridge: MIT Press, 1999.

Hammond, Kenneth R. *Human Judgment and Social Policy: Irreducible Uncertainty, Inevitable Error, Unavoidable Injustice.* New York: Oxford University Press, 1996.

Hans, Valerie P. *Business on Trial: The Civil Jury and Corporate Responsibility.* New Haven: Yale University Press, 2000.

Hastie, Reid. "The Role of 'Stories' in Civil Jury Judgments." 32(2) *University of Michigan Journal of Law Reform* 227–39 (1999).

Hastie, Reid, David A. Schkade, and John W. Payne. "Reply to Vidmar." 23 *Law and Hum. Behav.* 715–18 (1999).

Hastie, Reid, and W. Kip Viscusi. "Juries, Hindsight, and Punitive Damages: A Reply to Lempert," under review (2001).

Hawkins, Scott A., and Reid Hastie. "Hindsight: Biased Judgments of Past Events after the Outcomes Are Known." 107(3) *Psychological Bulletin* 311–27 (1990).

Hayes, Arthur S. "Bronx Cheer: Inner-City Jurors Tend to Rebuff Prosecutors and to Back Plaintiffs." 219(58) *Wall Street Journal* A1, A6 (March 24, 1992).

Himelstein, Linda. "Jackpots from Alabama Juries: A String of Mammoth Awards Has Insurers Starting to Flee." *Business Week* 83 (March 24, 1992).

Hinsz, Verlin B., and Kristin E. Indahl. "Assimilation to Anchors for Damage Awards in a Mock Civil Trial." 25(11) *Journal of Applied Social Psychology* 991–1026 (1995).

Hsee, Christopher K., George F. Loewenstein, Sally Blount, and Max H. Bazerman. "Preference Reversals between Joint and Separate Evaluations of Options: A Review and Theoretical Analysis." 125(5) *Psychological Bulletin* 576–90 (1999).

Jaynes, Gregory. "Where the Torts Blossom: While Washington Debates Rules about Litigation, Down in Alabama, the Lawsuits Grow Thick and Wild; Excessive Lawsuits and Damage Awards in Barbour County, Alabama." 145 *Time* 38–40 (March 20, 1995).

Jolls, Christine, Cass R. Sunstein, and Richard Thaler. "A Behavioral Approach to Law and Economics." 50(5) *Stanford Law Review* 1471–550 (1998).

"Jury Orders G.M. Corp. to Pay $4.9 Billion." *Boulder (Colorado) Daily Camera* 1A, 5A (July 10, 1999).

Kahneman, Daniel, Ilana Ritov, and David A. Schkade. "Economic Preferences or Attitude Expressions? An Analysis of Dollar Responses to Public Issues." 19(1–3) *Journal of Risk and Uncertainty* 203–36 (1999).

Kahneman, Daniel, David A. Schkade, Ilana Ritov, and Cass R. Sunstein. "Predictably Incoherent Judgments: Comparing Cases from Different Categories." Unpublished Manuscript. Department of Management, University of Texas, Austin, 2000.

Kahneman, Daniel, David A. Schkade, and Cass R. Sunstein. "Shared Outrage and Erratic Awards: The Psychology of Punitive Awards." 16(1) *Journal of Risk and Uncertainty* 49–86 (1998).

Kahneman, Daniel, Paul Slovic, and Amos Tversky, eds. *Judgment under Uncertainty: Heuristics and Biases.* New York: Cambridge University Press, 1982.

Kahneman, Daniel, and Amos Tversky. "Prospect Theory: An Analysis of Decision under Risk." 47(2) *Econometrica* 263–91 (1979).

Kalven, Harry, Jr. "The Jury, the Law, and the Personal Injury Damage Award." 19 *Ohio State Law Journal* 158 (1958).

———. "The Dignity of the Civil Jury." 50 *Virginia Law Review* 1055 (1964).

Kalven, Harry, Jr., and Hans Zeisel, with Thomas Callahan and Philip Ennis. *The American Jury.* Boston: Little, Brown, 1966.

Kamin, Kim A., and Jeffrey J. Rachlinski. "Ex Post ≠ Ex Ante: Determining Liability in Hindsight." 19(1) *Law and Human Behavior* 89–104 (1995).

Karlovac, Marylie, and John M. Darley. "Attribution of Responsibility for Accidents—A Negligence Law Analogy." 6(4) *Social Cognition* 287–318 (1988).

Karpoff, Jonathan M., and John R. Lott Jr. "On the Determinants and Importance of Punitive Damage Awards." 42(1) *Journal of Law and Economics* 527–73 (1999).

Keeton, W. Page, and William Lloyd Prosser. *Prosser and Keeton on the Law of Torts.* 5th ed. St. Paul, Minn.: West Publishing, 1984.

Kelman, Mark, David E. Fallas, and Hilary Folger. "Decomposing Hindsight Bias." 16(3) *Journal of Risk and Uncertainty* 251–69 (1998).

Kelman, Mark, Yuval Rottenstreich, and Amos Tversky. "Context-Dependence in Legal Decision Making." 25(2) *Journal of Legal Studies* 287–318 (1996).

Kerr, Norbert L., Robert J. MacCoun, and Geoffrey P. Kramer. "Bias in Judgment: Comparing Individuals and Groups." 103(4) *Psychological Review* 687–719 (1996).

Koenig, Thomas, and Michael Rustad. "The Quiet Revolution Revisited: An Empirical Study of the Impact of State Tort Reform of Punitive Damages in Products Liability." 16(2) *Justice System Journal* 21–44 (1993).

Kunreuther, Howard. *Disaster Insurance Protection: Public Policy Lessons.* New York: Wiley, 1978.

LaBine, Susan J., and Gary LaBine. "Determinations of Negligence and the Hindsight Bias." 20(5) *Law and Human Behavior* 501–16 (1996).

Landes, William M., and Richard A. Posner. *The Economic Structure of Tort Law.* Cambridge: Harvard University Press, 1987.

Lempert, Richard O. "Juries, Hindsight, and Punitive Damage Awards: Failures of a Social Science Case for Change (Response to Reid Hastie and W. Kip Viscusi, 40(3) *Arizona Law Review* 901–21 [1998])." 48(4) *DePaul Law Review* 867–94 (1999).

Lichtenstein, Sarah, Paul Slovic, Baruch Fischhoff, Mark Layman, and Barbara Combs. "Judged Frequency of Lethal Events." 4(6) *Journal of Experimental Psychology: Human Learning and Memory,* 551–78 (1978).

Luginbuhl, James. "Comprehension of Judge's Instructions in the Penalty Phase of a Capital Trial." 16 *Law and Human Behavior* 203 (1992).

MacCoun, Robert J. "Differential Treatment of Corporate Defendants by Juries: An Examination of the 'Deep Pockets' Hypothesis." 30(1) *Law & Society Review* 121–61 (1996).

———. "The Costs and Benefits of Letting Juries Punish Corporations: Comment on Viscusi (Response to W. Kip Viscusi, same issue, 547)." 52(6) *Stanford Law Review* 1821–28 (2000).

Mashaw, Jerry L. *Bureaucratic Justice: Managing Social Security Disability Claims.* New Haven: Yale University Press, 1983.

McGovern, Francis E. "Resolving Mature Mass Tort Litigation." 69(3) *Boston University Law Review* 659–94 (1989).

———. "The Alabama DDT Settlement Fund." 53(4) *Law and Contemporary Problems* 61–78 (1990).

Noll, Roger G., and James E. Krier. "Some Implications of Cognitive Psychology for Risk Regulation." 19(2) *Journal of Legal Studies* 747–79 (1990).

O'Neill, Ann W., Henry Weinstein, and Eric Malnic. "G.M. Ordered to Pay $4.9 Billion in Crash Verdict Liability: An L.A. Jury Awards Record Damages in Blaming Auto Maker for a Fire that Burned Six in a Chevy Malibu; Legal Experts Expect the Amount Will Not Withstand Appeal." *Los Angeles Times* A1 (July 10, 1999).

Payne, John W., James R. Bettman, and Mary F. Luce. "Behavioral Decision Research: An Overview." In *Measurement, Judgment, and Decision Making,* ed. Michael H. Birnbaum, 303–59. San Diego: Academic Press, 1998.

Payne, John W., James R. Bettman, and David A. Schkade. "Measuring Constructed Preferences: Towards a Building Code." 19(1–3) *Journal of Risk and Uncertainty* 243–70 (1999).

Pennington, Nancy, and Reid Hastie. "A Cognitive Theory of Juror Decision Making: The Story Model." 13(2–3) *Cardozo Law Review* 519–57 (1991).

———. "A Theory of Explanation-Based Decision Making." In *Decision Making in Action: Models and Methods,* eds. Gary A. Klein, J. Orasanu, R. Calderwood, and C. E. Zsambok, 188–204. Norwood, N.J.: Ablex, 1993.

Polinsky, A. Mitchell. *An Introduction to Law and Economics.* Boston: Little, Brown; 2nd ed., New York: Aspen, 1989.

———. "Are Punitive Damages Really Insignificant, Predictable, and Rational? (Response to Theodore Eisenberg, John Goerdt, Brian Ostrom, David Rattan, and Martin T. Wells, same issue, 623)." 26(2) *Journal of Legal Studies* 663–77 (1997).

Polinsky, A. Mitchell, and Steven Shavell. "Punitive Damages: An Economic Analysis." 111(4) *Harvard Law Review* 869–962 (1998).

Pollack, Andrew. "$4.9 Billion Jury Verdict in G.M. Fuel Tank Case: Penalty Highlights Cracks in Legal System." *New York Times* A7 (July 10, 1999).

———. "Paper Trail Haunts G.M. after It Loses Injury Suit: An Old Memo Hinted at the Price of Safety." *New York Times* A12 (July 12, 1999).

Posner, Richard A. *Economic Analysis of Law.* 3rd ed. New York: Aspen, 1986.

———. *Economic Analysis of Law.* 5th ed. New York: Aspen, 1998.

Priest, George L. "The Role of the Civil Jury in a System of Private Adjudication." *University of Chicago Legal Forum* 161 (1990).

———. "Punitive Damages Reform: The Case of Alabama." 56 *Louisiana Law Review* 825–40 (1996).

Priest, George L., and Benjamin Klein. "The Selection of Disputes for Litigation." 13(1) *Journal of Legal Studies* 1–55 (1984).

Rachlinski, Jeffrey J. "A Positive Psychological Theory of Judging in Hindsight." 65(2) *University of Chicago Law Review* 571–625 (1998).

Reifman, Alan, Spencer M. Gusick, and Phoebe C. Ellsworth. "Real Jurors' Understanding of the Law in Real Cases." 16(5) *Law and Human Behavior* 539–54 (1992).

Robbennolt, Jennifer K. "Punitive Damage Decision Making: The Decisions of Citizens and Trial Court Judges." Social Science Research Network (December 11, 2000) at http://papers.ssrn.com. (Forthcoming in *Law and Human Behavior,* in press; 2001).

Robbennolt, Jennifer K., and Christina A. Studebaker. "Anchoring in the Courtroom: The Effects of Caps on Punitive Damages." 23(3) *Law and Human Behavior* 353–73 (1999).

Robinson, Paul. H., and John M. Darley. *Justice, Liability, and Blame: Community Views and the Criminal Law.* Boulder, Colo.: Westview Press, 1995.

Roeca, Arthur F. "Damages." In *Toxic Torts: Litigation of Hazardous Substance Cases,* ed. Gary. Z. Nothstein, 494–524. Trial Practice Series. Colorado Springs: Shepard's; New York: McGraw-Hill, 1984.

Rubin, Paul H., John E. Calfee, and Mark F. Grady. "BMW v. Gore: Mitigating the Punitive Economics of Punitive Damages." In *Supreme Court Economic Review,* eds. Harold Demsetz, Ernest Gellhorn, and Nelson Lund, vol. 5, 179–216. Chicago: University of Chicago Press, 1997.

Rustad, Michael L. "Unraveling Punitive Damages: Current Data and Further Inquiry." 1 *Wisconsin Law Review* 15–69 (1998).

Saks, Michael J., Lisa A. Hollinger, Roselle L. Wissler, David Lee Evans, and Allen J. Hart. "Reducing Variability in Civil Jury Awards." 21(3) *Law and Human Behavior* 243–56 (1997).

Schwartz, Gary T. "The Myth of the Ford Pinto Case." 43(4) *Rutgers Law Review* 1013–68 (1991).

Sharkey, Lisa M. "Judge or Jury: Who Should Assess Punitive Damages?" 64(3) *University of Cincinnati Law Review* 1089–139 (1996).

Slovic, Paul. "Perception of Risk." 236(4799): *Science* 280–85 (1987).

———. "The Construction of Preference." 50(5) *American Psychologist* 364–71 (1995).

Stahlberg, Dagmar, Frank Eller, Anne Maass, and Dieter Frey. "We Knew It All Along: Hindsight Bias in Groups." 63(1) *Organizational Behavior and Human Decision Processes* 46–58 (1995).

Stevens, Stanley Smith. *Psychophysics: Introduction to Its Perceptual, Neural, and Social Prospects,* ed. Geraldine Stevens. New York: John Wiley and Sons, 1975; reprint, New Brunswick, N.J.: Transaction Books, 1986.

Stewart, Richard B. "Damages to Natural Resources." In *Analyzing Superfund: Economics, Science, and Law,* eds. Richard L. Revesz and Richard B. Stewart, 219, 241–44. Washington, D.C.: Resources for the Future, 1995.

Sunstein, Cass R. "Deliberative Trouble? Why Groups Go to Extremes." 110(1) *Yale Law Journal* 71–119 (2000).

Sunstein, Cass R., Daniel Kahneman, and David A. Schkade. "Assessing Punitive Damages (with Notes on Cognition and Valuation in Law)." 107(7) *Yale Law Journal* 2071–153 (1998).

Turner, John C., Penelope J. Oakes, S. Alexander Haslam, and Craig McGarty. "Self and Collective: Cognition and Social Context." 20 *Personality and Social Psychology Bulletin* 454–63 (1994).

Tversky, Amos, and Daniel Kahneman. "Judgment under Uncertainty: Heuristics and Biases." 185(4157) *Science* 1124–31 (1974).

———. "Extensional versus Intuitive Reasoning: The Conjunction Fallacy in Probability Judgment." 90(4) *Psychological Review* 293–315 (1983).

Tversky, Amos, Shmuel Sattath, and Paul Slovic. "Contingent Weighting in Judgment and Choice." 95(3) *Psychological Review* 371–84 (1988).

Tyler, Tom R., and Renee Weber. "Support for the Death Penalty: Instrumental Response to Crime, or Symbolic Attitude." 17(1) *Law & Society Review* 21–45 (1982).

U.S. Office of Management and Budget, *Regulatory Program of the United States Government, April 1, 1992–March 31, 1993.* Washington, D.C.: U.S. Office of Management and Budget, 1993.

Vidmar, N. "Juries Don't Make Legal Decisions! And Other Problems: A Critique of Hastie et al. on Punitive Damages." 23 *Law and Hum. Behav.* 705–14 (1999).

Viscusi, W. Kip. "Prospective Reference Theory: Towards an Explanation of the Paradoxes." 2(3) *Journal of Risk and Uncertainty* 235–63 (1989).

———. *Fatal Tradeoffs: Public and Private Responsibilities for Risk.* New York: Oxford University Press, 1992.

———. "The Value of Risks to Life and Health." 31(4) *Journal of Economic Literature* 1912–46 (1993).

———. *Rational Risk Policy.* Arne Ryde Memorial Lectures Series. Oxford: Oxford University Press, 1998.

———. "The Social Costs of Punitive Damages against Corporations in Environmental and Safety Torts." 87(2) *Georgetown Law Journal* 285–345 (1998).

———. "Why There Is No Defense of Punitive Damages. (Reply to Theodore Eisenberg and to David Luban, same issue, 347, 359)." 87(2) *Georgetown Law Journal* 381–95 (1998).

———. "Corporate Risk Analysis: A Reckless Act?" 52(3) *Stanford Law Review* 547–97 (2000).

———. "Jurors, Judges, and the Mistreatment of Risk by the Courts." 30(1) *Journal of Legal Studies* 107–42 (2001).

Wade, John W. "On the Nature of Strict Liability for Products." 44(5) *Mississippi Law Journal* 825–51 (1973).

Walster, Elaine. "'Second Guessing' Important Events." 20(3) *Human Relations* 239–49 (1967).

Wexler, David B., and Robert F. Schopp. "How and When to Correct for Juror Hindsight Bias in Mental Health Malpractice Litigation: Some Preliminary Observations." 7(4) *Behavioral Sciences and the Law* 485–504 (1989).

Wiener, Richard L., Kristen Habert, Gina Shkodriani, and Caryn Staebler. "The Social Psychology of Jury Nullification: Predicting When Jurors Disobey the Law." 21(17) *Journal of Applied Social Psychology* 1379–401 (1991).

Wiener, Richard L., Christine C. Pritchard, and Minda Weston. "Comprehensibility of Approved Jury Instructions in Capital Murder Cases." 80(4) *Journal of Applied Psychology* 455–67 (1995).

Wildavsky, Aaron B. *Searching for Safety.* New Brunswick, N.J.: Transaction Books, 1988.

————. *But Is It True? A Citizen's Guide to Environmental Health and Safety Issues.* Cambridge: Harvard University Press, 1995.

Wilson, Timothy D., and Nancy Brekke. "Mental Contamination and Mental Correction: Unwanted Influences on Judgments and Evaluations." 116(1) *Psychological Bulletin* 117–42 (1994).

Wilson, Timothy D., Christopher E. Houston, Kathryn M. Etling, and Nancy Brekke. "A New Look at Anchoring Effects: Basic Anchoring and Its Antecedents." 125(4) *Journal of Experimental Psychology: General* 387–402 (1996).

Contributors

CASS R. SUNSTEIN is Karl N. Llewellyn Distinguished Service Professor of Jurisprudence at the Law School and professor of political science at the University of Chicago. He is the author of *After the Rights Revolution: Reconceiving the Regulatory State* (1990), *The Partial Constitution* (1993), *Democracy and the Problem of Free Speech* (1993), *Legal Reasoning and Political Conflict* (1996), *Free Markets and Social Justice* (1997), *One Case at a Time* (1999), *Republic.com* (2001), *Designing Democracy* (2001), and *Risk and Reason* (2002) and coauthor of *Constitutional Law* (1995), *The Cost of Rights* (1999), and *Administrative Law and Regulatory Policy* (2002).

REID HASTIE is professor of behavioral science in the Graduate School of Business at the University of Chicago.

JOHN W. PAYNE is Joseph J. Ruvane Jr. Professor of Management, professor of psychology, and research professor of statistics and decision sciences at the Fuqua School of Business at Duke University.

GEORGE L. PRIEST is the John M. Olin Professor of Law and Economics at Yale Law School and is director of the Law School's Program in Civil Liability.

DAVID A. SCHKADE is Herbert D. Kelleher Regents Professor of Business at the University of Texas, Austin.

W. KIP VISCUSI is John F. Cogan Jr. Professor of Law and Economics at Harvard Law School. He is the author of over two hundred articles and seventeen books, including *Reforming Products Liability* (1991), *Fatal Tradeoffs* (1992), *Smoking: Making the Risky Decision* (1992), *Rational Risk Policy* (1998), and *Economics of Regulation and Antitrust* (2000).

Index

absolute judgments, 225–26
absolute-risks level, 126
accidents, probability of, 23*t*, 25*t*, 130–31
administrative management, 252–55
ambiguous cost-benefits results, 198–200
The American Jury (Kalven & Zeisel), 222–23
Ammerman v. Ford Motor Co., 3, 120
amounts awarded. *See* dollar awards
analyses of risks. *See* cost-benefits analyses
anchor-and-adjust strategy, 74, 216, 239–40
anchor-and-insufficient-adjustment process, 73–74
anchoring effects, 30, 32*f*, 64–74, 216–19, 239–40
  compensatory awards, 69, 245–47
  cost-benefits analyses, 129, 218, 232
  vs. deterrence approaches, 143, 217–18
  plaintiff requests, 22*t*, 24*t*, 26, 42, 62, 157, 164, 245, 248
  Polinsky-Shavell formula, 146, 149–50, 156–57, 164
  value of life, 125–26
Anderson et al. v. General Motors Corp., 1, 3, 112, 120, 217
Anderson v. Whittaker Corp., 80, 85
appeals process, 16 n. 17
attitudes, 7, 32–33
Avery et al. v. State Farm Insurance, 1
award-setting strategies, 213–14
awareness of grave danger, 96–98, 104–7

Babcock, L., 218
Baron, J., 134–35
base punitive damages amount, 165

behavioral decision-making processes, 236–38
benefit-cost test. *See* cost-benefits analyses
Bentham, J., 142–43
bias, 211, 232–33
  cognitive factors, 110–11
  common sense, 106, 222
  debiasing procedures, 107–8
  geographic, 22*t*, 26, 30, 64–74, 219
  See also hindsight bias; risk judgments
bifurcated procedure, 10–11
blame, 79, 87, 149, 166, 239
BMW of North America, Inc. v. Gore, 2–3, 16 n. 17, 243–44, 248
Bodenhausen, G. V., 97
Brekke, N., 107–8
Breyer, Supreme Court Justice Stephen, 183, 243–44, 248

caps, 218, 244, 256
Carlisle v. Whirlpool Financial National Bank et al., 1–3
Casper, J. D., 215
category scales, 41
causality, 63
choice shifts, 51
Chrysler Corporation, Jimenez v., 1
cigarettes. *See* tobacco cases
citizens' role, 105–6, 110–11
  hindsight bias, 97, 99, 101
civil fines, 245, 252–55, 258
class factors, 235
coding procedures, 85–86, 90–91
cognitive factors, 79, 92, 248
  anchor-and-adjust strategies, 216

behavioral decision-making, 236–38
bias, 110–11
comprehension of instructions, 90–91,
   145, 160–62, 221–24, 241
formulaic determination of dollar awards,
   145
optimal deterrence, 134
reasoning demands, 172–73, 227–33
Combs, B., 181
common sense, 79, 92–93, 106, 222
See also moral judgments
community sentiment, 40–41
company size, 34
comparative approach, 249–52
compensatory damage awards, 8–10, 20, 78,
   89–90, 217 n. 7
impact on punitive awards, 69, 245–47
probability of detection, 132
comprehension of instructions, 90–92, 145,
   160–62, 223–24
consensus, 21, 25, 31–32
consequences. *See* deterrence
constitutional questions, 243–44
consumer safety. *See* safety
context, 217 n. 7
corporate factors
motives, 114 n. 7
punishment, 133 n. 3
reckless conduct, 79–95
wealth, 40, 64
See also cost-benefits analyses; safety
cost-per-life-saved, 126
See also value of life
cost-benefits analyses, 15, 24t, 110, 112–31,
   174–75, 228–34
ambiguous results, 198–200
anchoring, 129, 218, 232
dollar awards, 110, 123–24, 128–29
hindsight bias, 25, 130
individual results, 115–26
judges' results, 190–207
mock jury results, 126–29
reasoning demands, 228
zero-risk mentality, 130, 183–85, 204, 206
criminal acts, 133 n. 4
cursory deliberation, 88–90

damage caps, 218, 244, 256
damages factor, 97, 102–3
damages schedules, 242–43, 245, 252–55

death, 129
See also value of life
debiasing procedures, 107–8
defendants, 12, 15
income level, 26, 32, 34, 40, 64
location effects, 30, 71, 219, 227
deliberation process, 43–61, 77, 79, 84–90,
   241
behavioral decision-making, 236–38
cost-benefits analyses, 126–29
dollar amounts, 26, 29–30
jury deliberation, 84–90
outrage, 224
polarization, 57–58
severity shift, 57–58
thoroughness, 88–92
unpredictability, 43–44, 215–16
deliberation-shift measure (DSM), 48t, 50–
   51, 51 n. 2
demographic findings
anchoring, 74
comprehension of instructions, 91, 160–62
defendants, 26, 32, 34
dollar ratings, 40, 53, 64
hindsight bias, 235
liability determinations, 84
moral evaluation/outrage, 31, 33, 35–36,
   36t
Polinsky-Shavell formula study, 150–51,
   160–62
punitive intent, 35–36, 36t, 54t, 224–25
risk judgments study, 174
detection. *See* probability of detection
deterrence, 24t, 26, 132–41, 219–21, 239–41,
   257
instructions, 142–70
optimal insurance, 178
plaintiff requests, 66–67, 70, 73–74
Polinsky-Shavell formula, 144–46, 165–66
See also optimal deterrence
Diamond, S. S., 215
disregard of risks, 96–98, 104–5
dollar awards, 26, 36–39, 212–21, 239–40
caps, 218, 244, 256
community sentiment, 40–41
context, 217 n. 7
cost-benefits analyses, 110, 123–24, 128–
   29, 230–31
defendant factors, 32, 40
deterrence, 132–41, 133 n. 3

formulaic determinations, 142
magnitude scaling, 41–42
moral judgments, 31–32
optimal deterrence, 134
Polinsky-Shavell formula, 144–46, 157,
  166
punitive intent, 34, 44, 70
See also anchoring effects; predictability
dollar ratings, 46, 48–49, 51–56
dollar scales, 41, 63
due process, 16n. 17, 243–44

Easterbrook, Judge Frank H., 131, 188
economic efficiency principle, 193, 197–98,
  235
economic theory of deterrence, 132–34, 141,
  235
education factors
  comprehension of instructions, 91
  moral evaluation/outrage, 31, 35–36
  Polinsky-Shavell formula, 162
  punitive intent, 35–36
efficient deterrence. *See* Polinsky-Shavell
  formula
Eisenberg, T., 245–47, 251–52
environmental damages, 254
ethnic factors. *See* racial/ethnic factors
everyday vs. legal concepts, 79, 92–93
See also moral judgments
evidentiary standards, 12n. 14
exemplar cases, 249–50, 255–57
experimental methods, 4–5, 14–21, 211
See also study designs and results

fact-finding processes, 229
Fallas, D. E., 106–7
Fischhoff, B., 181
Folger, H., 106–7
Ford Motor Co., Ammerman v., 3, 120
foreseeability. *See* predictability
formulaic determinations of awards. *See*
  Polinsky-Shavell formula study

gender factors
  moral evaluation/outrage, 31, 35–36
  Polinsky-Shavell formula, 161
  punitive intent, 35–36
General Motors Corp., Anderson et al. v., 1,
  3, 112, 120, 217
geographic factors, 64–74

defendants, 30, 71, 219
dollar awards, 26, 30, 53, 62, 221, 227
Goerdt, J., 245–47, 251
Gore, BMW of North America, Inc. v., 2–3,
  16n. 17, 243–44, 248
government agency analyses, 120
group process effects. *See* deliberation
  process

Hand, Learned, 123, 233
harm, 32f, 33–34, 39–40, 99
Harper v. Zapata Off-Shore Co., 80
hindsight bias, 15, 23–25, 211, 222, 226–27
  cost-benefits analyses, 130
  judges, 188–93, 235
  juries, 75–76, 96–108, 235, 239
Hinsz, V. B., 218
Hughes, Jardel Co., Inc. v., 80–81, 93–95,
  172, 259–60

illicit gain, 133n. 4
income factors
  comprehension of instructions, 91
  defendants, 26, 32, 34
  dollar awards, 40, 64
  liability, 84
  moral evaluation/outrage, 31, 35–36
  punitive intent, 35–36
Indahl, K. E., 218
individual ratings, 43–44, 45t, 46
  cost-benefits analyses, 115–26
  dollar awards, 33, 52–53, 61, 215
  instructions, 90
  outrage and punitive intent, 35–36, 224
  plaintiff requests, 67, 68t
  Polinsky-Shavell formula, 146–59
  probability of detection, 136–39
  risk judgments, 174–85
  zero vs. nonzero verdicts, 49–50, 215
instructions, 11–15, 20–21, 23t, 24t, 77–93,
  241, 248
  absolute vs. relative judgments, 226
  comprehension, 90–92, 145, 160–62, 222–
    27
  consensus, 25
  deterrence, 142–70, 219–21
  plaintiff requests, 62, 65–66
  Polinsky-Shavell instructions, 142–46
  probability of detection, 110, 133–34
  reckless conduct, 80–81

risk judgments, 172
sample, 259–60
insurance, 178
intentionality, 63, 75

Jardel Co., Inc. v. Hughes, 80–81, 93–95, 172, 259–60
Jimenez v. Chrysler Corporation, 1
judges, 1, 79, 110–11
  hindsight bias, 25*t,* 188–93
  vs. juries, 23*t,* 190–93, 197–207, 234–35
  review role, 242, 244, 248–55, 257
  risk judgments, 190–206
  See also instructions
judicial review, 242, 244, 248–55, 257
juries, 56–57, 79, 84–90, 241
  comprehension of instructions, 90–92, 145, 160–62, 222–27
  vs. judges, 23*t,* 79, 109–11, 190–93, 197–207, 234–35
  polarization, 57–58
  as risk managers, 109–11
  selection process, 6–7, 20
  size factors, 56 n. 6
  See also cognitive factors; deliberation process; demographic findings

Kalven, H., Jr., 4 n. 11, 222–23
Kamin, K. A., 97–98, 107
Kearse, Judge Amalya, 250
Kelman, M., 106–7

LaFountain, N., 251–52
law students, 139–40
Layman, M., 181
Learned Hand test for negligence, 123, 233
learning from experience, 107
legal criteria, 75–76, 221–27, 239, 241
  evidentiary standards, 12 n. 14
  fact-finding, 229
  judicial review, 248–55
  punitive intent, 77–93
  reckless conduct, 98–99, 221–22
  risk judgments, 172–73
  standards of proof, 80–81
legislative options, 244
Lempert, R. O., 235 n. 40
leniency shift, 51
levels of misconduct, 75–76

liability determinations, 8–11, 15, 20, 221–27, 248–49
  consensus, 25
  demographic factors, 84
  jury deliberation process, 84–90
  Polinsky-Shavell formula, 144, 165
Lichtenstein, S., 181
life. *See* value of life
local biases, 64–74
  defendants, 30, 71, 219
  dollar awards, 26, 30, 62, 219, 227

MacCoun, R. J., 130
magnitude scales, 41, 63
majority-decision model, 49–50
malicious intent, 15 n. 16, 63, 78, 221, 259
  hindsight bias, 105
  jury awards, 87–88
In re Marine Sulphur Queen (MSQ), 80
market forces, 121 n. 11
mean dollar awards, 59–60, 60 n. 9, 60 n. 10
media, 17–18, 156–57, 164
median dollar awards, 54–55, 61
memory for instructions, 90–92, 145, 160–62, 223–24
  See also cognitive factors
mock jury methods, 5, 17, 43–46, 82, 224
models
  decision-making processes, 17
  majority-decision rule, 49–50
  outrage, 32*f,* 39–40
  situation, 222
modulus, 29–30, 40–42, 213–14, 216, 240
moral judgments, 211, 222–23, 225, 239–40
  deterrence, 140
  dollar amounts, 26
  juries, 21–22, 25, 31, 61
  vs. legal criteria, 75–76, 92–93
  See also outrage
mortality risks, 180–84, 200–4, 234–35
  See also value of life
multiplier approach, 133 n. 4, 256–57

narrative process, 86
negligent conduct, 25, 259
  cost-benefits analyses, 123
  hindsight, 98, 107
  vs. reckless conduct, 75, 78, 81, 90, 98, 107
  risk judgments, 171–73, 193, 198, 233
nonzero verdicts, 49–50

"one-case or one-day" limit, 6
optimal deterrence, 15, 24*t*, 109–10, 132–42,
    257
  enforcement, 149
  Polinsky-Shavell formula, 162–63, 220–21
  See also deterrence
ordinary level of care, 96–98, 104–5
Ostrom, B., 245–47, 251–52
outrage, 15, 26, 31–36, 239–40
  cost-benefits analyses, 129
  harm, 33–34, 39–40
  punitive intent, 224–25
  See also moral judgments
overdeterrence, 109–10

pain-and-suffering awards, 10, 254
participant-role factors, 96–108
perceptions of risks, 180–84, 200–4, 234–
    35
Petition of Kinsman Transit Co., 97–98
plaintiffs
  award requests, 22*t*, 24*t*, 26, 62–74, 157,
    164, 218–19, 248
  local bias, 22*t*, 26, 30, 64–74, 219
Pogarsky, G., 218
Polinsky, A. M., 133–34, 133 n. 3, 134 n. 4,
    138, 142–70, 220
Polinsky-Shavell formula study, 142–64,
    220–21, 241
  exhibits, 164–70
potential damage, 180
predictability, 22*t*, 63, 78, 99, 211–12, 245–55
  dollar awards, 30, 36–39, 61
  dollar ratings, 53–56
  hindsight bias, 96–98, 104–5
  judges, 189–93
  juries, 37, 86–90, 100–8
  outrage, 26
  recklessness, 221–22
  See also unpredictability
preponderance of evidence standard, 12 n. 14
probability estimates. *See* risk judgments
probability of accidents, 23*t*, 25*t*, 130–31,
    228
probability of detection, 110, 165, 241
  optimal deterrence, 132–41
  Polinsky-Shavell formula, 144, 152–54,
    163, 220–21
probability of punishment, 24*t*
products liability cases, 112–31

punishment, 24*t*, 60 n. 8, 77–93, 133 n. 3, 134–
    35
  anchoring, 74
  economic theory, 132–34, 141
  levels of misconduct, 75–76
  optimal deterrence, 132–41
  Polinsky-Shavell formula, 166
  See also deterrence
punishment ratings, 46, 48–49
  deliberation-shift measure (DSM), 48*t*,
    50–51, 51
punitive intent, 31–36, 224–26, 240
  cost-benefit analyses, 123–24
  dollar awards, 34, 44, 63, 70, 212
  harm effect, 33–34, 39–40
  mock juries, 127–28

Rachlinski, J. J., 97–98, 107, 227
racial/ethnic factors
  comprehension of instructions, 91
  determining liability, 84
  moral evaluation/outrage, 31, 35–36
  Polinsky-Shavell formula, 161–62
  punitive intent, 35–36
reasoning demands, 172–73, 227–33
reckless conduct, 25, 32*f*, 65, 78–90, 221–27,
    259
  definition, 81, 98–99
  hindsight bias, 75–76, 96–99, 107
  perceptions of risks, 180–84
  risk judgments, 171–85
reform options, 242–58
relative judgments, 225–26
reliability, 18–19, 40–41, 216–17
research methods, 4–5, 14–21, 211
  See also study designs and results
retribution, 109–10, 240–41
rhetorical asymmetry, 44, 58–59, 61
risk judgments, 109–11, 227–35, 239–41
  judges, 193–206
  jurors, 171–85
risks analyses. *See* cost-benefits analyses
Ritov, I., 134–35, 135 n. 7
Robbennolt, J. K., 218, 234
Rottman, D., 245–47, 251–52

safety, 113, 125, 129, 134–35, 135 n. 7, 193,
    204, 206
  See also value of life
scaling, 33

within a modulus, 29–30, 40–42, 213–14,
    216, 240
    using examples, 249–50, 255–57
severity shift, 43–44, 51–53, 57–61, 215–16,
    241
shared outrage, 33
Shavell, S., 133–34, 133n. 3, 134n. 4, 138,
    142–70, 220
situation model, 222
Slovic, P., 181
social consequences. *See* optimal deterrence
social factors, 77, 79
    behavioral decision-making, 236–38
    jury deliberation, 84–90
    outrage, 32–33
    severity shift, 57–58
    See also deliberation process
standards, legal. *See* legal criteria
State Farm Insurance, Avery et al. v., 1
statistical analyses
    comprehension of instructions, 90–91
    cost-benefits analyses, 118*t,* 119–26, 195–
        206
    deliberation-shift measure (DSM), 48*t,*
        50–51, 51n. 2
    dollar awards, 55–57, 60
    hindsight bias, 103–6
    judges' cost-benefits analyses, 195–206
    judges' hindsight bias, 189–93
    jury size, 56n. 6
    jury verdicts, 86–90
    mean vs. median dollar verdicts, 60,
        60n. 9
    optimal deterrence, 140–41
    Polinsky-Shavell formula, 151–60
    predicted dollar amounts, 55–57, 56n. 4,
        56n. 5
    probability of detection, 137–39, 137n. 9
    risk judgments, 176–77, 179–84
    thoroughness of deliberation, 88–90
    See also cost-benefits analyses
stealthy behavior, 152–54
Stevens, Supreme Court Justice John Paul,
    78
Studebaker, C. A., 218
study designs and results
    cost-benefits analyses, 115–29
    deliberation process, 43–46
    dollar awards, 36–40
    geographic origin of plaintiff, 64–74

harm and consequences, 39–40
hindsight bias, 96–108, 188–93
instructions, 79–86, 90–91, 145
    judges' hindsight bias, 188–93
    judges' risk judgments, 193–206
    legal criteria for punishment, 77–93
    optimal deterrence, 132–41, 146–64
    outrage, 34–35
    perceptions of risks, 181–84
    plaintiff requests, 64–74
    Polinsky-Shavell formula, 146–64
    probability of detection, 132–41
    punitive intent, 35–36
    reckless conduct assessments, 77–93
    rhetorical asymmetry, 58–59
    risk judgments, 174–85, 193–206
synthetic juries, 159–60
    See also mock jury methods

taboo trade-offs, 130
temporal perspectives. *See* hindsight bias
thoroughness of deliberation, 88–92
tobacco cases, 1, 112n. 2, 113n. 6
trial options, 234
trial process, 6–14

unanimity quorum requirement, 80–81
unbounded magnitude scales, 63
unified procedure, 10–11
unpredictability, 31–42, 239, 245
    deliberation process, 43–44, 215–16
    dollar awards, 56–57, 212–13, 215
U.S. Constitution, 16n. 17, 243–44
U.S. Office of Management and Budget,
    120
U.S. Supreme Court, 16n. 17
    Ammerman v. Ford Motor Co., 3
    BMW of North America v. Gore, 243–44
    comparative approach, 250–51
    defendant identity, 64

value of life, 114–21, 123, 126, 218
    anchoring, 125, 129–30, 230–31
    judges, 204–6, 234
    juries, 183–84, 234
    mortality risks, 180–84, 200–4
    risk judgments, 232–33
variability of verdict size, 2–4, 18–19, 26, 29
    See also unpredictability
victim identity, 32*f*

wealth redistribution, 64, 70, 73, 227
Wells, M. T., 245–47, 251–52
*Whirlpool Financial National Bank et al.,
Carlisle v.,* 1–3
Whittaker Corp., Anderson v., 80, 85
Wilson, T. D., 107–8
worst-case scenarios, 180, 185, 200, 228

Zapata Off-Shore Co., Harper v., 80
Zeisel, H., 222–23
zero punishment ratings, 49–50
zero-risk mentality, 130, 183–85, 204, 206,
228–30, 233–34